Microsoft®

OUTLOOK™ 97

Step by Step

Other titles in the *Step by Step* series:

Step by Step books are also available for the Microsoft Office 95 programs.

* These books are approved courseware for Certified Microsoft Office User (CMOU) exams. For more details about the CMOU program, see page xvii.

Microsoft®

OUTLOOK™ 97

Step by Step

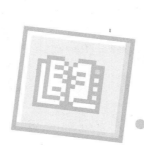

Microsoft Press

PUBLISHED BY
Microsoft Press
A Division of Microsoft Corporation
One Microsoft Way
Redmond, Washington 98052-6399

Copyright © 1997 by Catapult, Inc.

Library of Congress Cataloging-in-Publication Data
Microsoft Outlook 97 step by step / Catapult, Inc.
        p.   cm.
    Includes index.
    ISBN 1-57231-382-X
    1. Microsoft Outlook.   2. Time management--Computer programs.
3. Personal information management--Computer programs.
I. Catapult, Inc.
HD69.T54M53   1997
005.369--dc20   96-38984
                                                         CIP

Printed and bound in the United States of America.

2 3 4 5 6 7 8 9   Rand–T   2 1 0 9 8 7

Distributed to the book trade in Canada by Macmillan of Canada, a division of Canada
Publishing Corporation.

A CIP catalogue record for this book is available from the British Library.

Microsoft Press books are available through booksellers and distributors worldwide. For further
information about international editions, contact your local Microsoft Corporation office. Or
contact Microsoft Press International directly at fax (206) 936-7329.

FoxPro, Microsoft, Microsoft Press, MS, MS-DOS, PowerPoint, Windows, and Windows NT
are registered trademarks and Outlook and MSN are trademarks of Microsoft Corporation. Other product and company names mentioned herein may be the trademarks of
their respective owners.

Companies, names, and/or data used in screens and sample output are fictitious unless
otherwise noted.

For Catapult, Inc.   **For Microsoft Press**
Managing Editor: Diana Stiles   **Acquisitions Editor:** Casey D. Doyle
Writer: Kim Douglas   **Project Editor:** Laura Sackerman
Project Editor: Armelle O'Neal
Technical Editor: Karen Deinhard
Production/Layout: Jeanne Hunt, Editor;
    Anne Kim
Indexer: Julie Kawabata

Catapult, Inc. & Microsoft Press

Microsoft Outlook 97 Step by Step has been created by the professional trainers and writers at Catapult, Inc., to the exacting standards you've come to expect from Microsoft Press. Together, we are pleased to present this self-paced training guide, which you can use individually or as part of a class.

Catapult, Inc., is a software training company with years of experience in PC and Macintosh instruction. Catapult's exclusive Performance-Based Training system is available in Catapult training centers across North America and at customer sites. Based on the principles of adult learning, Performance-Based Training ensures that students leave the classroom with confidence and the ability to apply skills to real-world scenarios. *Microsoft Outlook 97 Step by Step* incorporates Catapult's training expertise to ensure that you'll receive the maximum return on your training time. You'll focus on the skills that can increase your productivity the most while working at your own pace and convenience.

Microsoft Press is the book publishing division of Microsoft Corporation. The leading publisher of information about Microsoft products and services, Microsoft Press is dedicated to providing the highest quality computer books and multimedia training and reference tools that make using Microsoft software easier, more enjoyable, and more productive.

Table of Contents

Table of Contents

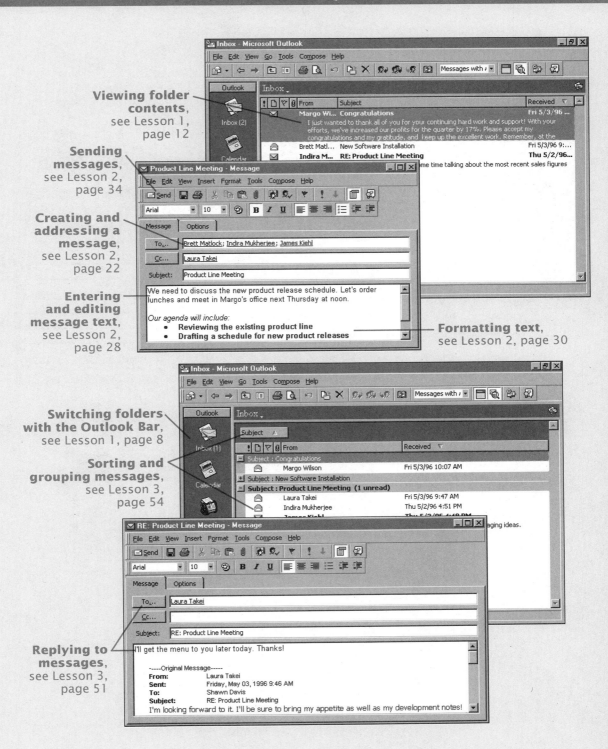

Viewing folder contents,
see Lesson 1,
page 12

Sending messages,
see Lesson 2,
page 34

Creating and addressing a message,
see Lesson 2,
page 22

Entering and editing message text,
see Lesson 2,
page 28

Formatting text,
see Lesson 2, page 30

Switching folders with the Outlook Bar,
see Lesson 1, page 8

Sorting and grouping messages,
see Lesson 3,
page 54

Replying to messages,
see Lesson 3,
page 51

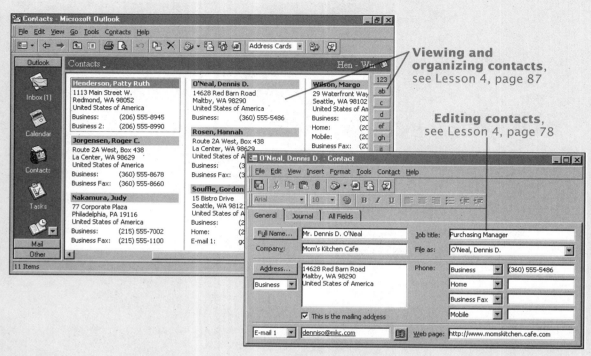

Viewing and organizing contacts, see Lesson 4, page 87

Editing contacts, see Lesson 4, page 78

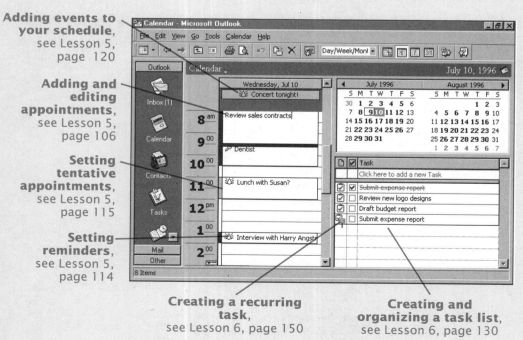

Adding events to your schedule, see Lesson 5, page 120

Adding and editing appointments, see Lesson 5, page 106

Setting tentative appointments, see Lesson 5, page 115

Setting reminders, see Lesson 5, page 114

Creating a recurring task, see Lesson 6, page 150

Creating and organizing a task list, see Lesson 6, page 130

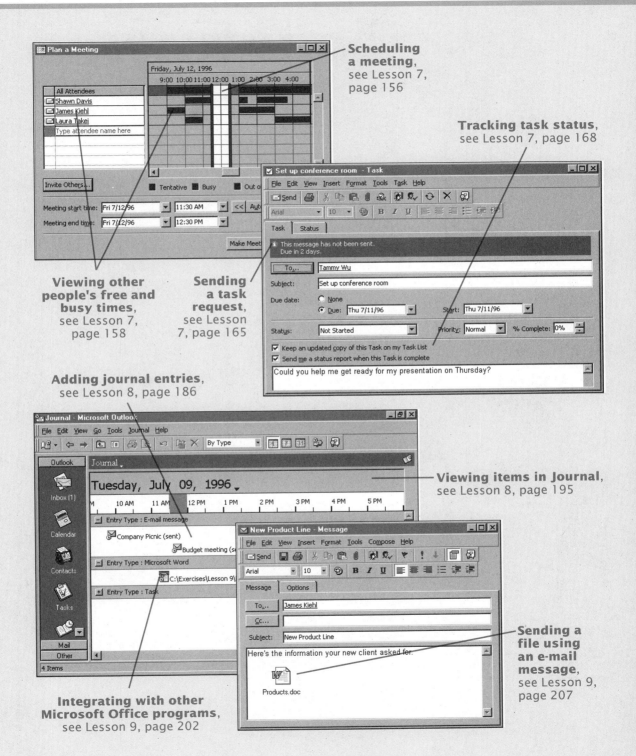

Scheduling a meeting, see Lesson 7, page 156

Tracking task status, see Lesson 7, page 168

Viewing other people's free and busy times, see Lesson 7, page 158

Sending a task request, see Lesson 7, page 165

Adding journal entries, see Lesson 8, page 186

Viewing items in Journal, see Lesson 8, page 195

Sending a file using an e-mail message, see Lesson 9, page 207

Integrating with other Microsoft Office programs, see Lesson 9, page 202

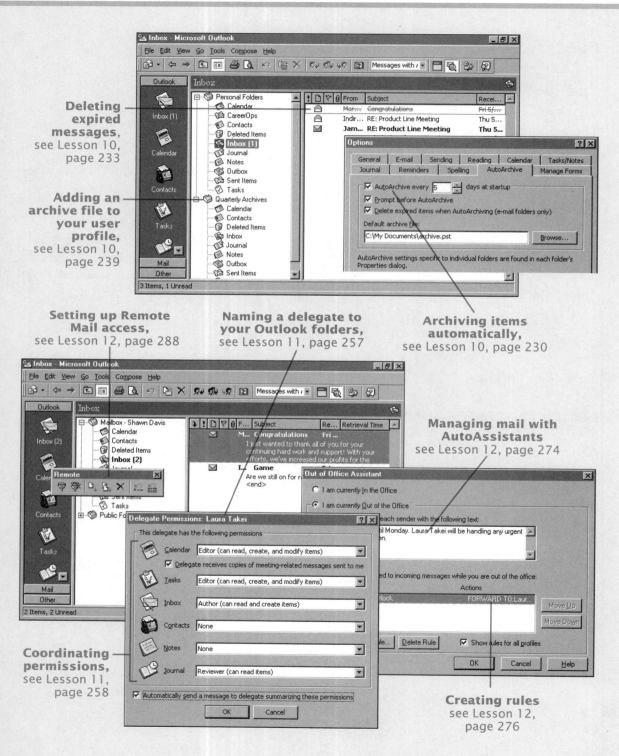

Deleting expired messages, see Lesson 10, page 233

Adding an archive file to your user profile, see Lesson 10, page 239

Setting up Remote Mail access, see Lesson 12, page 288

Naming a delegate to your Outlook folders, see Lesson 11, page 257

Archiving items automatically, see Lesson 10, page 230

Managing mail with AutoAssistants see Lesson 12, page 274

Coordinating permissions, see Lesson 11, page 258

Creating rules see Lesson 12, page 276

Finding Your Best Starting Point

Microsoft Outlook is a powerful personal information management program that you can use to efficiently communicate with others, schedule appointments and tasks, record information about your personal and business contacts, and organize your files. With *Microsoft Outlook 97 Step by Step*, you'll quickly and easily learn how to use Outlook to get your work done.

 IMPORTANT This book is designed for use with Microsoft Outlook 97 for the Windows 95 and Windows NT version 4.0 operating systems. To find out what software you're running, you can check the product package or you can start the program, click the Help menu at the top of the screen, and then click About Microsoft Outlook. If your product is not compatible with this book, a Step by Step book for your program is probably available. Many of the Step by Step titles are listed on the second page of this book. If the book you want isn't listed, please visit our World Wide Web site at http://www.microsoft.com/mspress/ or call 1-800-MSPRESS for more information.

Finding Your Best Starting Point in This Book

This book is designed for beginning users of personal information management, electronic messaging, and scheduling software, as well as readers who have had experience with these types of programs and are switching to Outlook. Use the following table to find your best starting point in this book.

If you are	Follow these steps
New... to computers to graphical (as opposed to text-only) computer programs to Windows 95 or Windows NT	**1** Install the practice files as described in "Installing and Using the Practice Files." **2** Become acquainted with the Windows 95 or Windows NT operating system and how to use the online Help system by working through Appendix A, "If You Are New to Windows 95 or Windows NT and Outlook." **3** Learn basic skills for using Outlook by working through Lesson 1. Then, you can work through Lessons 2 through 10 in any order. To work through Lessons 11 and 12, you must be using Outlook with a Microsoft Exchange Server.
Switching... from Lotus Notes from Lotus Organizer	**1** Install the practice files as described in "Installing and Using the Practice Files." **2** Learn basic skills for using Outlook by working through Lesson 1. Then, you can work through Lessons 2 through 10 in any order. To work through Lessons 11 and 12, you must be using Outlook with a Microsoft Exchange Server.
Upgrading... from Microsoft Mail from Microsoft Exchange from Microsoft Schedule+	**1** Learn about the features of Outlook that are covered in this book by reading through the following section, "Outlook Features." **2** Install the practice files as described in "Installing and Using the Practice Files." **3** Complete the lessons that cover the topics you need. You can use the table of contents and the *Quick*Look Guide to locate information about general topics. You can use the index to find information about a specific topic or feature.
Referencing... this book after working through the lessons	**1** Use the index to locate information about specific topics, and use the table of contents and the *Quick*Look Guide to locate information about general topics. **2** Read the Lesson Summary at the end of each lesson for a brief review of the major tasks in the lesson. The Lesson Summary topics are listed in the same order as they are presented in the lesson.

Certified Microsoft Office User Program

The Certified Microsoft Office User (CMOU) program is designed for business professionals and students who use Microsoft Office 97 products in their daily work. The program enables participants to showcase their skill level to potential employers. It benefits accountants, administrators, executive assistants, program managers, sales representatives, students, and many others. To receive certified user credentials for a software program, candidates must pass a hands-on exam in which they use the program to complete real-world tasks.

The CMOU program offers two levels of certification: Proficient and Expert. The following table indicates the levels available for each Microsoft Office 97 program. (You can find out more about the certification levels by visiting the CMOU program World Wide Web site at: http://www.microsoft.com/office/train_cert/)

Software	Proficient level	Expert level
Microsoft Word 97	✔	✔
Microsoft Excel 97	✔	✔
Microsoft Access 97		✔
Microsoft PowerPoint 97		✔
Microsoft Outlook 97		✔
Microsoft FrontPage 97		✔

Microsoft Press offers the following books in the *Step by Step* series as approved courseware for the CMOU exams:

Proficient level:
Microsoft Word 97 Step by Step, by Catapult, Inc. ISBN: 1-57231-313-7
Microsoft Excel 97 Step by Step, by Catapult, Inc. ISBN: 1-57231-314-5

Expert level:
Microsoft Word 97 Step by Step, Advanced Topics by Catapult, Inc.
   ISBN: 1-57231-563-6
Microsoft Excel 97 Step by Step, Advanced Topics by Catapult, Inc.
   ISBN: 1-57231-564-4
Microsoft Access 97 Step by Step, by Catapult, Inc. ISBN: 1-57231-316-1
Microsoft PowerPoint 97 Step by Step, by Perspection, Inc. ISBN: 1-57231-315-3
Microsoft Outlook 97 Step by Step, by Catapult, Inc. ISBN: 1-57231-382-X
Microsoft FrontPage 97 Step by Step, by Catapult, Inc. ISBN: 1-57231-336-6

Candidates may take exams at any participating Sylvan Test Center, participating corporations, or participating employment agencies. Exams have a suggested retail price of $50 each.

To become a candidate for certification or for more information about the certification process, please visit the CMOU program World Wide Web site at:

http://www.microsoft.com/office/train_cert/

or call 1-800-933-4493 in the United States.

Outlook Features

The following table lists the major features of Outlook that are covered in this book. The table shows the lesson in which you can learn how to use each feature. You can also use the index to find specific information about a feature or a task you want to do.

To learn how to	See
Create, format, and send messages	Lesson 2
Read, respond to, and organize messages	Lesson 3
Create, edit, organize, and communicate with contacts	Lesson 4
Schedule appointments and events	Lesson 5
Create and maintain a task list	Lesson 6
Schedule meetings and assign tasks to others	Lesson 7
Create and maintain a record of all your activities in Journal	Lesson 8
Integrate Outlook with other Microsoft Office 97 programs	Lesson 9
Keep your Outlook files up to date by archiving and exporting items	Lesson 10
Share folder access with other users on your network	Lesson 11
Work with Outlook while away from your office	Lesson 12
Create and modify Outlook forms	Appendix C

Corrections, Comments, and Help

Every effort has been made to ensure the accuracy of this book and the contents of the practice files disk. Microsoft Press provides corrections and additional content for its books through the World Wide Web at:

> http://www.microsoft.com/mspress/support/

If you have comments, questions, or ideas regarding this book or the practice files disk, please send them to us.

Send e-mail to:

> mspinput@microsoft.com

Or send postal mail to:

> Microsoft Press
> Attn: Step by Step Series Editor
> One Microsoft Way
> Redmond, WA 98052-6399

Please note that support for the Outlook software product itself is not offered through the above addresses. For help using Outlook, you can call Outlook AnswerPoint at (206) 635-7031 on weekdays between 6 a.m. and 6 p.m., Pacific time.

Visit Our World Wide Web Site

We invite you to visit the Microsoft Press World Wide Web site. You can visit us at the following location:

http://www.microsoft.com/mspress/

You'll find descriptions for all of our books, information about ordering titles, notice of special features and events, additional content for Microsoft Press books, and much more.

You can also find out the latest in software developments and news from Microsoft Corporation by visiting the following World Wide Web site:

http://www.microsoft.com/

We look forward to your visit on the Web!

Installing and Using the Practice Files

The disk inside the back cover of this book contains practice files that you'll use as you perform the exercises in the book. For example, when you're learning how to read and organize your e-mail, you'll move several of the practice files—in this case, sample e-mail messages—into your Inbox, and then open, read, and respond to them. By using the practice files, you won't waste time creating the samples used in the lessons—instead, you can concentrate on learning how to use Microsoft Outlook. With the files and the step-by-step instructions in the lessons, you'll also learn by doing, which is an easy and effective way to acquire and remember new skills.

 IMPORTANT Before you break the seal on the practice disk package, be sure that this book matches your version of the software. This book is designed for use with Microsoft Outlook 97 for the Windows 95 and Windows NT version 4.0 operating systems. To find out what software you're running, you can check the product package or start the program, and then on the Help menu at the top of the screen, click About Microsoft Outlook. If your program is not compatible with this book, a Step by Step book matching your product is probably available. For a complete list of our books, please visit our World Wide Web site at http://www.microsoft.com/mspress/ or call 1-800-MSPRESS for more information.

Install the practice files on your computer

Follow these steps to install the practice files on your computer's hard disk so that you can use them with the exercises in this book.

> **NOTE** If you are new to Windows 95 or Windows NT, you might want to work through Appendix A, "If You Are New to Windows 95 or Windows NT and Outlook," before installing the practice files.

1 If your computer isn't on, turn it on now.

2 If you're using Windows NT, press CTRL+ALT+DEL to display a dialog box asking for your username and password. If you are using Windows 95, you will see this dialog box if your computer is connected to a network.

Close

In Windows 95, you will also be prompted for a username and password if your computer is configured for user profiles.

3 Type your username and password in the appropriate boxes, and then click OK. If you see the Welcome dialog box, click the Close button.

4 Remove the disk from the package inside the back cover of this book.

5 Insert the disk in drive A or drive B of your computer.

6 On the taskbar at the bottom of your screen, click the Start button.

The Start menu appears.

7 On the Start menu, click Run.

The Run dialog box appears.

8 In the Open box, type **a:setup** (or **b:setup** if the disk is in drive B). Don't add spaces as you type.

9 Click OK, and then follow the instructions on the screen.

The setup program window appears with recommended options preselected for you. For best results in using the practice files with this book, accept these preselected settings.

10 When the files have been installed, remove the disk from your drive and replace it in the package inside the back cover of the book.

A folder called Outlook SBS Practice has been created on your hard disk, and the practice files have been put in that folder.

Microsoft
Press
Welcome

Camcorder
Files On The
Internet

> **NOTE** In addition to installing the practice files, the Setup program has created two shortcuts on your Desktop. If your computer is set up to connect to the Internet, you can double-click the Microsoft Press Welcome shortcut to visit the Microsoft Press Web site. You can also connect to this Web site directly at http://www.microsoft.com/mspress/
>
> You can double-click the Camcorder Files On The Internet shortcut to connect to the *Microsoft Outlook 97 Step by Step* Camcorder files Web page. This page contains audiovisual demonstrations of how to do a number of tasks in Outlook, which you can copy to your computer for viewing. You can connect to this Web site directly at http://www.microsoft.com/mspress/products/1043/

Using the Practice Files

Each lesson in this book explains when and how to use any practice files for that lesson. When it's time to use a practice file, the book will list instructions for how to open the file. The lessons are built around scenarios that simulate a real work environment, so you can easily apply the skills you learn to your own work. For the scenarios in this book, imagine that you're the Operations Coordinator for the Margo Tea Company, a small but growing company that creates and distributes quality teas to clients nationwide. As Operations Coordinator, you are responsible for coordinating schedules and task assignments among your co-workers. In this book, you'll learn how to use Outlook to manage your own communications and scheduling tasks, and then apply those skills in a networked environment.

The screen illustrations in this book might look different than what you see on your computer, depending on how your computer has been set up. To help make your screen match the illustrations in this book, please follow the instructions in Appendix B, "Matching the Exercises."

For those of you who like to know all the details, here's a list of the files included on the practice disk:

Filename	Description
Lesson 3	
Congratulations.msg	Sample incoming message to open and read in your Inbox.
New Software Installation.msg	Sample incoming message to open and read in your Inbox.
Product Line Meeting.msg	Sample incoming message to open and read in your Inbox.
RE: Product Line Meeting (2).msg	Sample incoming message to open and read in your Inbox.
RE: Product Line Meeting (3).msg	Sample incoming message to open and read in your Inbox.
RE: Product Line Meeting.msg	Sample incoming message to open and read in your Inbox.
Lesson 4	
Contacts.csv	Text file containing sample contact entries that you import into your Outlook contact list.

Filename	Description
Review & Practice 1	
Game.msg	Sample incoming message to open and read in your Inbox.
RE: Catering References (2).msg	Sample incoming message to open and read in your Inbox.
RE: Catering References (3).msg	Sample incoming message to open and read in your Inbox.
RE: Catering References .msg	Sample incoming message to open and read in your Inbox.
Lesson 7	
Plane Reservations.msg	Sample message that you use to create a task in your Tasks folder.
Lesson 9	
History.doc	Microsoft Word document you view and route to multiple users from Outlook.
Margo.bmp	Microsoft Paint graphic file of the Margo Tea Company logo you embed in an e-mail message.
Products.doc	Microsoft Word document you view and send to another user from Outlook.
Routed Margo Tea Company_Company History.msg	Sample e-mail message with an attached Microsoft Word document containing revisions from **several** routing recipients.
Lesson 10	
Congratulations.msg	Sample incoming message you move to an archive file to save Outlook folder space.
Game.msg	Sample incoming message you move to an archive file to save Outlook folder space.
New Contract!.msg	Sample incoming message you move to an archive file to save Outlook folder space.
New Software Installation.msg	Sample incoming message you move to an archive file to save Outlook folder space.
Plane Reservations.msg	Sample incoming message you move to an archive file to save Outlook folder space.

Filename	Description
Review & Practice 3	
Budget.xls	Microsoft Excel spreadsheet you view and route to multiple users from Outlook.
Lesson 11	
Congratulations.msg	Sample incoming message for your delegate to view in your Inbox.
Lesson 12	
Congratulations.msg	Sample incoming message for you to download to your offsite Inbox.
Game.msg	Sample incoming message for you to download to your offsite Inbox.
New Contract!.msg	Sample incoming message for you to download to your offsite Inbox.
New Software Installation.msg	Sample incoming message for you to download to your offsite Inbox.
Wgpo0000	Sample workgroup postoffice containing fictitious names.
Glossary.htm	Definitions of the important terms used in this book.

Creating a Profile

Before you can start using Outlook, you must have a user profile. Your profile contains information about customized options that you can use while you are working in Outlook, including your password and a list of the available information services. Your default profile will probably be set up for you by your system administrator.

Before you begin, it is strongly recommended that you perform the following steps to create an additional profile for a fictional person, Shawn Davis. Creating this profile will give you a clean environment in which you can practice performing tasks. In addition, what you see on your screen will more closely match the illustrations in this book as you work through the lessons.

Modify Outlook startup settings

Microsoft
Outlook

1 Double-click the Microsoft Outlook shortcut icon on the Desktop.

Outlook starts.

2 On the Tools menu, click Options.

The Options dialog box apears.

3   Be sure that the General tab is selected.

4   In the Startup Settings area, click the Prompt For A Profile To Be Used option button, and then click OK.

   The next time you start Outlook, you will be prompted for a user profile.

5   On the File menu, click Exit And Log Off.

Create a practice profile

1   Double-click the Microsoft Outlook shortcut icon on the Desktop.

   The Choose Profile dialog box appears.

2   Click New.

   The Inbox Setup wizard starts.

3   Verify that the Use The Following Information Services option button is selected, and then verify that only the Microsoft Mail and the Microsoft Exchange Server check boxes are selected. Click Next.

   The Microsoft Mail and Microsoft Exchange Server should be the only information services selected for the purposes of this book. If any other check boxes are selected, click them to clear them.

IMPORTANT   If you do not have access to an Exchange Server, clear the Microsoft Exchange Server check box. An Exchange Server is required to complete Lessons 11 and 12.

4   In the Profile Name box, type **Shawn Davis** and then click Next.

If you are not sure what the name of your server is, ask your system administrator.

5   Type the name of your Exchange Server and verify your mailbox name. Click Next.

IMPORTANT   If you are setting up a practice profile on your offsite computer to prepare for Lesson 12, "Working When Away From the Office," be sure to click Yes when you are asked if you travel with this computer. If you are not going to work on Lesson 12, click No.

6   Click the Yes option button under Do You Travel With This Computer?

7   Click Browse.

   The Browse For Postoffice dialog box appears.

8   Double-click your hard disk, double-click the Outlook SBS Practice folder, and then click the Wgpo0000 folder. Click Next.

   This is the path to the practice postoffice you installed on your hard disk as part of the practice files.

9 Select the name Shawn Davis from the list of names, and then click Next.

10 Type **password** in the Password box, and then click Next.

Create a practice personal address book and personal folder file

In this exercise, you create a practice personal address book associated with the Shawn Davis profile so that entries you add to the practice personal address book are not mixed up with your real personal address book. You also create a practice personal folder file, or set of Outlook folders, for the same reason.

1 In the path box, select the text "mailbox.pab," type **shawnd.pab** and then click Next.

2 Verify that the Do Not Add Inbox To StartUp Group option button is selected, and then click Next.

3 Click Finish. Click Cancel to close the Choose Profile dialog box.

You will use the Shawn Davis profile to start Outlook in Lesson 1.

 NOTE If you plan to complete Lesson 12, "Working When Away From the Office," you should also set up the Shawn Davis Offline practice profile on your offsite computer. For more help, see Lesson 12.

Uninstalling the Practice Files

Use the following steps to delete the practice files added to your hard drive by the Step by Step Setup program.

1 Click Start, point to Settings, and then click Control Panel.

2 Double-click the Add/Remove Programs icon.

3 Select Microsoft Outlook 97 Step by Step from the list, and then click Add/Remove.

A confirmation message appears.

4 Click Yes.

The practice files are uninstalled.

5 Click OK to close the Add/Remove Programs Properties dialog box.

6 Close the Control Panel window.

Need Help with the Practice Files?

Every effort has been made to ensure the accuracy of this book and the contents of the practice files disk. If you do run into a problem, Microsoft Press provides corrections for its books through the World Wide Web at:

http://www.microsoft.com/mspress/support/

We also invite you to visit our main Web page at:

http://www.microsoft.com/mspress/

You'll find descriptions for all of our books, information about ordering titles, notices of special features and events, additional content for Microsoft Press books, and much more.

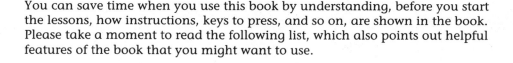

Conventions and Features in This Book

You can save time when you use this book by understanding, before you start the lessons, how instructions, keys to press, and so on, are shown in the book. Please take a moment to read the following list, which also points out helpful features of the book that you might want to use.

 NOTE If you are unfamiliar with Windows 95, Windows NT, or mouse terminology, see Appendix A, "If You Are New to Windows 95 or Windows NT and Outlook."

Conventions

- Hands-on exercises for you to follow are given in numbered lists of steps (1, 2, and so on). An arrowhead bullet (▶) indicates an exercise that has only one step.
- Text that you are to type appears in **bold**.
- A plus sign (+) between two key names means that you must press those keys at the same time. For example, "Press ALT+TAB" means that you hold down the ALT key while you press TAB.

The following icons identify the different types of supplementary material:

Note labeled	Alerts you to
Note	Additional information for a step.
Tip	Suggested additional methods for a step or helpful hints.
Important	Essential information that you should check before continuing with the lesson.
Troubleshooting	Possible error messages or computer difficulties, and solutions.
Demonstration	Skills that are demonstrated in audio-visual files on the Microsoft Press Web site.

Other Features of This Book

- You can get a quick reminder of how to perform the tasks you learned by reading the Lesson Summary at the end of each lesson.

- You can quickly determine what online Help topics are available for additional information by referring to the Help topics listed at the end of each lesson. To learn more about online Help, see Appendix A.

- You can practice the major skills presented in the lessons by working through the Review & Practice section at the end of each part. These sections offer challenges that reinforce what you have learned and demonstrate new ways you can apply your newly acquired skills.

- If you have Web browser software and access to the World Wide Web, you can view audiovisual demonstrations of how to perform some of the more complicated tasks in Outlook by downloading supplementary files from the Web. Double-click the Camcorder Files On The Internet shortcut that was created on your Desktop when you installed the practice files for this book, or connect directly to htttp:/www.microsoft.com/mspress/products/1043. The Web page that opens contains full instructions for copying and viewing the demonstration files.

Part 1

Communicating with Others

Exploring the Microsoft Outlook Environment

Estimated time

25 min.

In this lesson you will learn how to:

- Explore the different Outlook folders.
- Create new Outlook items.
- View the contents of folders.

In today's business world, keeping track of all the information that crosses your desk can almost be a full-time job. In a typical work environment, you might have different types of vital information stored in many different places. For example, you might keep track of your schedule in a desk calendar or a daily planner. You might use electronic mail, or *e-mail*, to communicate with your co-workers and colleagues, in addition to keeping their phone numbers and addresses in an address book. You probably store important documents on your computer's hard disk, or print and keep paper copies in file cabinets in your office. And, if you are like many people, you have a few sticky notes or lists posted around your desk to remind you of other things you need to do, like pick up groceries or call a client.

Microsoft Outlook is a desktop information manager that you can use to organize, find, and view all of the above information. With Outlook, you can schedule appointments for yourself or coordinate meetings with a group. You can send messages and documents to other users to share information, or view and arrange your own e-mail messages and other files without leaving the program. You can maintain a daily task list to keep track of all the things you need to accomplish. You can even create notes and reminders for yourself, right on the Desktop. All of these functions are fully integrated with one another, and with Microsoft Office 97 so that you can manage each day's workload using a single program.

Setting the Scene

As you work through the exercises in this book, imagine that you are the Operations Coordinator for the Margo Tea Company, a rapidly growing organization that specializes in the sales and distribution of quality teas from around the world. In addition to maintaining your own schedule, e-mail messages, task list, and personal contacts, you are responsible for organizing meetings between employees and assigning tasks to your co-workers when appropriate. In this lesson, you'll take your first steps toward using Outlook to do your daily work—you'll familiarize yourself with the work environment and learn how to explore the different information areas within the program.

Starting Microsoft Outlook

When you start Outlook, the Information viewer is the first area you see. This is the main window you use to view and work with all types of information in Outlook. By default, the Information viewer shows the contents of the Inbox folder when you first start Outlook. The Inbox folder contains messages that are sent to you from other users.

To begin working through this lesson, you start Outlook by choosing the Shawn Davis profile. A user profile contains information about customized options that you can use while you are working in Outlook, including your password and a list of the available information services. You can also use your own profile for these exercises, but it is recommended that you use the Shawn Davis profile so that the exercises and illustrations in the book will match what you see on your screen. When you start Outlook using a new user profile, a "Welcome to Microsoft Outlook!" message from Microsoft appears in the Inbox automatically.

 IMPORTANT If you don't have an Outlook SBS Practice folder or a profile for Outlook, refer to "Installing and Using the Practice Files," earlier in this book. You can also ask your system administrator for further help.

Start Outlook

1   On your Desktop, double-click the Microsoft Outlook shortcut icon.

Outlook starts. The Choose Profile dialog box appears.

2   Click the down arrow, and then click Shawn Davis.

For the purposes of this book, you'll use the Shawn Davis profile.

3   Click OK.

To learn more about the Office Assistant, refer to the "An Introduction to the Office Assistant" section later in this lesson.

The Information viewer appears, and the Inbox folder opens. The Office Assistant appears in the lower-right corner of your screen, and the Welcome To Microsoft Outlook! Help balloon appears.

4   Click to clear the Show These Choices At Startup check box, and then click OK.

The Help balloon closes, and a message appears asking if you want to use Word as your e-mail editor.

5   Click No.

Maximize

6   Click the Maximize button on the Microsoft Outlook window.

A "Welcome to Microsoft Outlook!" message from Microsoft appears in the Inbox. Your screen should look similar to the following illustration.

You can also double-click the title bar to maximize the window.

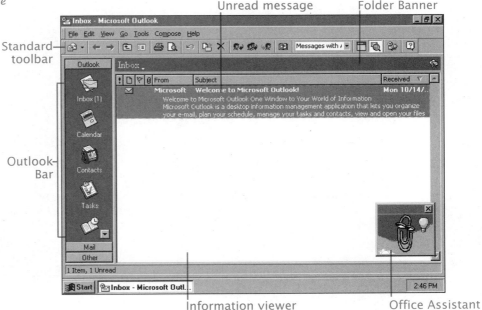

IMPORTANT   For the purposes of this book, the Office Assistant will not appear in the illustrations. If you want to hide the Office Assistant temporarily to match the illustrations, use the right mouse button to click the Office Assistant, and then click Hide Assistant. If the Office Assistant is in your way but you want to leave it on to help guide you, simply drag it to another area on the screen.

An Introduction to the Office Assistant

While you are working with Microsoft Office 97, an animated character called the *Office Assistant* pops up on your screen to help you work productively. The Office Assistant offers help messages as you work. You can ask the Office Assistant questions by typing your question, and then clicking Search. The Office Assistant then shows you the answer to your question.

You can close any Office Assistant tip or message by pressing ESC.

You will sometimes see a light bulb next to the Office Assistant—clicking the light bulb displays a tip about the action you are currently performing. You can view more tips by clicking Tips in the Office Assistant balloon when the Office Assistant appears. In addition, the Office Assistant is tailored to how your work—after you master a particular skill, the Office Assistant stops offering tips.

Clippit, an Office Assistant, in action

The Office Assistant appears in the following situations:

- When you click the Office Assistant button on the Standard toolbar.

Office Assistant

- When you choose Microsoft Outlook Help on the Help menu or when you press F1.

- When you use certain features. For example, you might see the Office Assistant when you are importing or exporting files with the Import And Export wizard.

The Office Assistant is a shared application—any settings that you change will affect the Office Assistant in other Office 97 programs. You can customize the Office Assistant in two ways. You can:

Determining when you want to see the Office Assistant

You can use the right mouse button to click the Office Assistant, and then click Options to open the Office Assistant dialog box. You can then define when you want the Office Assistant to appear and what kind of help you want it to offer.

Changing your Office Assistant character

You can use the right mouse button to click the Office Assistant, and then click Options to open the Office Assistant dialog box. Click the Gallery tab to select another Office Assistant character.

Navigating in Outlook

To work efficiently in Outlook, you first need to find the information you want. *Items*, or units of information, such as messages, appointments, or tasks, can be stored in many different folders within Outlook. You must be able to locate and open the correct folders to display the items you need.

When you install Outlook on your computer, an *information store*, or container for a series of folders, is created on your hard disk automatically. This information store, Personal Folders, contains the built-in folders for your personal use in Outlook. Folders in Outlook are arranged in three *groups*: Outlook, Mail, and Other. Each of these groups contains several built-in folders that are either created automatically when you install Outlook, or are included as part of the Windows 95 or Windows NT operating system.

The Outlook group contains folders that are specific to Outlook's personal information management functions, including folders for your schedule and a list of important contacts. The Mail group contains those folders that are specific to e-mail functions, including folders where you can read your mail or store copies of messages you have sent to others. The Other group provides access to the other folders and documents you work with, whether they are stored on your computer's hard drive or on an office network. Some folders appear in more than one group. For example, the Inbox and Deleted Items folders can be accessed from the Outlook group or from the Mail group. The following table describes the built-in folders for each group.

Group	Folder	Description
Outlook	Inbox	Stores the e-mail messages that you receive.
	Calendar	Displays an appointment book where you can keep track of your schedule.
	Contacts	Stores the names, phone numbers, and addresses of the people with whom you correspond and work.
	Tasks	Displays a to-do list of your personal and business tasks.
	Journal	Displays a history of your recorded activities in a timeline format.
	Notes	Stores general information, such as ideas, grocery lists, or directions, in one location.
	Deleted Items	Temporarily stores the items that you delete until you permanently delete them or quit Outlook.
Mail	Inbox	Stores the e-mail messages that you receive.
	Sent Items	Stores copies of the e-mail messages that you send.

Group	Folder	Description
	Outbox	Holds e-mail messages that you send until they are delivered to recipients.
	Deleted Items	Temporarily stores the e-mail messages that you delete until you permanently delete them or quit Outlook.
Other	My Computer	Provides access to other drives, folders, and files on your computer.
	My Documents	Stores documents created using other Microsoft Office 97 programs, such as Microsoft Excel or Microsoft Word.
	Favorites	Stores shortcuts to important Internet addresses.

Switching Folders Using the Outlook Bar

The Outlook Bar is the thick vertical bar that appears to the left of the Information viewer. Icons for the available folders in Outlook appear on the Outlook Bar; each icon acts as a shortcut to the designated folder. The folder icons are also arranged in their respective groups, separated by shortcut bars labeled with the name of each folder group. You can switch between groups by clicking the appropriate shortcut bar. The following illustration shows the default folder selection when you start Outlook.

Open different folders

In this exercise, you use the Outlook Bar to switch between folders to familiarize yourself with the different Outlook groups.

1   Be sure that the Inbox folder is currently open.

"Inbox" should appear in the Folder Banner, and a "Welcome to Microsoft Outlook!" message from Microsoft should appear in the Information viewer.

Calendar

2   On the Outlook Bar, click the Calendar icon.

Calendar appears, and the current date appears in the Folder Banner. Your screen should look similar to this illustration.

The current date on your screen might be different from the date in the illustrations in this book, depending on when you start the exercises.

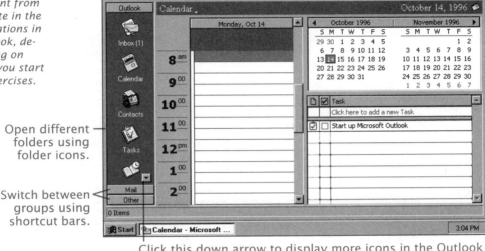

Open different folders using folder icons.

Switch between groups using shortcut bars.

Click this down arrow to display more icons in the Outlook group.

3 On the Outlook Bar, click the down arrow above the Mail shortcut bar.

The list of icons scrolls upward to display more icons in the Outlook group.

If you did not maximize the Inbox window, click the down arrow several times to see the Journal icon.

4 On the Outlook Bar, click the Journal icon.

Journal appears in the Information viewer. The current date appears above the timeline, and the current hour is selected in the timeline display. Your screen should look similar to this illustration.

Journal

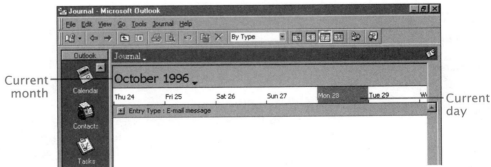

Current month

Current day

Switch folder groups

In this exercise, you use the shortcut bars to display the different groups of folder icons on the Outlook Bar.

1   On the Outlook Bar, click the Other shortcut bar.

Icons for the folders in the Other group appear on the Outlook Bar. Journal still appears in the Information viewer because you have not selected another folder yet.

My Computer

You might notice a similarity between the My Computer folder contents and Windows Explorer.

2   On the Outlook Bar, click the My Computer icon.

The available drives for your computer appear in the Information viewer. Your screen should look similar to the following illustration.

You may have more available drives, depending on your network configuration.

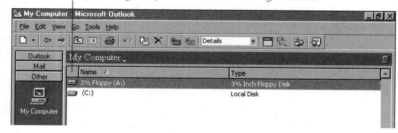

3   On the Outlook Bar, click the Mail shortcut bar.

Icons for the folders in the Mail group appear on the Outlook Bar. My Computer still appears in the Information viewer.

4   On the Outlook Bar, click the Deleted Items icon.

The Deleted Items contents appear in the Information viewer. You can open the Deleted Items folder from either the Mail group or the Outlook group.

Deleted Items

The Deleted Items folder should be empty, unless you have deleted items recently.

5   Click the Outlook shortcut bar.

Icons for the folders in the Outlook group appear on the Outlook Bar.

6   Click the Inbox icon.

The contents of the Inbox folder appear in the Information viewer. You can open the Inbox folder from either the Mail group or the Outlook group. The number of unread messages in a folder appears in parentheses next to the Inbox.

Creating Notes to Store Information

You can easily create new items of any kind in Outlook. In fact, you do not even need to be in the appropriate folder before you create a particular kind of item; you can add a contact or a note from Calendar, or start a new message while viewing your contact list.

New Appointment

 NOTE The New button appears on the toolbar in each Outlook folder, but the picture on the button, its full name, and the item it creates change depending on which folder is open. For example, in Calendar, the New button is called the New Appointment button and it creates a new appointment for your schedule.

In the following exercises, you'll practice the basic skills necessary to create new items by creating an electronic note, one of the many item types in Outlook. You will learn more about creating other types of items, such as appointments, in subsequent lessons. You'll also learn about the different ways to view various types of items in your Outlook folders.

You have probably used sticky notes or scrap paper to jot down those pieces of information that don't really belong anywhere else—the confirmation number for an airline reservation, perhaps, or a reminder to yourself to pick up your dry cleaning in the afternoon. If you accumulate a lot of these notes, however, you might find it difficult to locate a particular one; you might misplace or even lose notes if they are scattered around your work area. With Outlook, you can create electronic versions of these notes and store them in your Notes folder so that they are always in one secure, convenient location. You can also keep important notes open on your Desktop as you work, just as you might post a sticky note on the edge of your monitor to remind you throughout the day of something important.

Create an electronic note

In this exercise, you create a note to remind yourself that it is your turn to bring refreshments to the weekly team meeting.

Notes

New Note

1 On the Outlook Bar, click the Notes icon.

   The Notes folder opens, and a sample note appears in the Information viewer. The New button displays a picture of a note.

2 On the Standard toolbar, click the New Note button.

   A blank note appears.

3 Type **Bring bagels for tomorrow's meeting!**

   The text is immediately saved—changes to a note are saved automatically. Your screen should look similar to the following illustration.

11

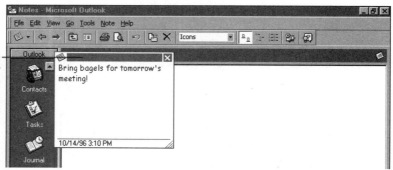

You can move a note to any location on your screen by dragging the title bar.

Close

4 Click the Close button on the note.

The note closes and a note icon appears in the Information viewer.

> **TIP** You can change the color of your notes to suit your taste or to help color-code notes on particular topics. On the Tools menu, click Options. On the Tasks/Notes tab under Note Defaults, click the Color down arrow, and then select a color from the list. To change the size or the font of your notes, click the appropriate down arrows in the Note Defaults area and make your changes. You can also use the right mouse button to click individual notes, point to Color on the shortcut menu, and then click a color name.

Viewing Folder Contents

Just as you can switch between folders to display different types of items, you can apply different *views* to the items in those folders so that the information appears in a way that is most useful to you. Each folder in Outlook comes with a different set of standard views depending on the type of items contained in the folder. For example, you can display your scheduled appointments in a daily, weekly, or monthly format in Calendar. In your Inbox, you can display messages organized by the name of the person who sent them, or in a timeline according to when they were received. You can easily select a different view for a folder by choosing a menu command or by clicking a drop-down arrow on the Standard toolbar. You can also create your own custom folder views by modifying the existing views or by designing your own unique view.

You will learn more about AutoPreview in Lesson 3.

The first time you start Outlook, the Inbox folder opens by default, and the Messages With AutoPreview view is applied to the contents of the folder. AutoPreview allows you to see the first three lines of new messages so that you can quickly scan your messages and decide which ones need your attention first. After you have read a message, the AutoPreview text for that message is no longer shown in the Information viewer. In the following exercises, you will experiment with the standard views in different folders, so you can see a variety of ways to display your information.

Change the Inbox folder view

In this exercise, you apply standard views to the contents of the Inbox folder to display your messages by sender, and then by the received time.

Inbox

You can also point to Current View on the View menu, and then select a view name.

1 On the Outlook Bar, click the Inbox icon. Be sure that the current view is Messages With AutoPreview.

The name of the current view appears in the Current View box on the Standard toolbar.

2 On the Standard toolbar, click the Current View down arrow.

A list of the available views appears.

3 Click By Sender.

The By Sender view is applied to your Inbox. Your screen should look similar to the following illustration.

Sender category

Click the plus sign button to expand a category.

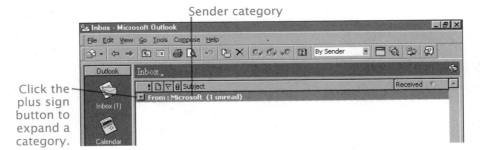

4 Click the plus sign button next to the "From: Microsoft" category.

The category expands to show the "Welcome to Microsoft Outlook!" message from Microsoft. If you receive any other messages from Microsoft, they will appear under the "From: Microsoft" heading.

The Standard toolbar buttons change to reflect the current view.

5 On the Standard toolbar, click the Current View down arrow.

The list of available views appears.

6 Click Message Timeline.

The Message Timeline view is applied to your Inbox. The "Welcome to Microsoft Outlook!" message from Microsoft appears in the timeline when it was received. In this case, the message was received when you created the Shawn Davis profile. Your screen should look similar to the following illustration.

7 On the Standard toolbar, click the Current View down arrow, and then select Messages With AutoPreview.

The default view is reapplied to your Inbox.

Change the Calendar folder view

The default view for Calendar is Day/Week/Month, and when you first open Calendar, your schedule appears in a single-day format. A weekly format and a monthly format are available as subsets of the Day/Week/Month view, and can be applied by clicking the appropriate toolbar button. In this exercise, you apply standard views to the Calendar folder to display your schedule in weekly and monthly formats.

Calendar

1 On the Outlook Bar, click the Calendar icon.

The contents of the Calendar folder appear in single-day format.

2 On the Standard toolbar, click the Week button.

The current week appears in Calendar, and the current date is selected. Your screen should look similar to the following illustration.

Week

You will learn more about adding items to Calendar in Lesson 5.

The current week and date are also selected in the Date Navigator

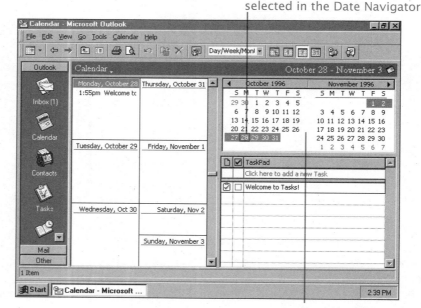

Date Navigator

Month

3 On the Standard toolbar, click the Month button.

The current month appears in Calendar, and the current date is selected. Your screen should look similar to the following illustration.

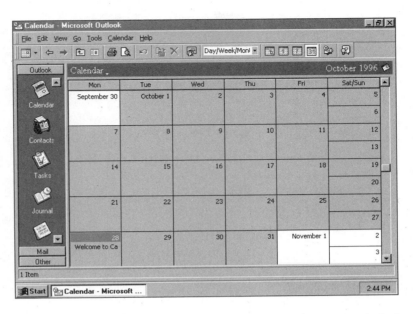

Day

4   On the Standard toolbar, click the Day button. Be sure to click the Day button and not the Go To Today button. The Day button has the number 1 on it.

Calendar returns to single-day view, and the current date appears.

Adding Folders to the Outlook Bar

As you have seen, it is very easy to move between all your important folders with the Outlook Bar and shortcut bars. By using My Computer in the Other group, you can view the contents of any folder on your computer or on the network. If there are particular folders that you use frequently, you can create shortcuts directly to those folders, and add new shortcut icons and even new groups to the Outlook Bar.

Create a new group on the Outlook Bar

In this exercise, you add a folder group for current projects to the Outlook Bar.

1   Use the right mouse button to click the Other shortcut bar on the Outlook Bar.

2   Click Add New Group.

A new shortcut bar, New Group, appears below the Other shortcut bar.

3   Type **Current Projects**, and then press ENTER.

The highlighted text is replaced as you type, and the new name appears on the shortcut bar.

4   On the Outlook Bar, click the Current Projects shortcut bar.

There are no folders in the Current Projects group yet.

Create a new folder

You have just been asked to give a presentation on time management to this month's management conference. In this exercise, you create a folder on your hard disk to store your notes and documents for the upcoming conference.

1   In the Outlook Bar, click the Other shortcut bar.

The folders in the Other group appear.

2   On the Outlook Bar, click the My Computer icon.

The available drives for your computer appear in the Information viewer.

3   In the Information viewer, double-click Drive C.

The contents of Drive C appear.

4   On the File menu, point to New, and then click Folder.

The Create New Folder dialog box appears.

5   In the Name box, type **Conference**, and then click OK.

The new folder is added as a subfolder of Drive C. Your screen should look similar to the following illustration.

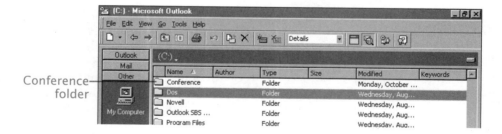

Conference—
folder

Add a folder shortcut to the Outlook Bar

In this exercise, you add the Conference folder to the Current Projects group on the Outlook Bar so that you can find it immediately.

1   In the Information viewer, click the Conference folder.

2   On the Outlook Bar, click the Current Projects shortcut bar.

3   Drag the Conference folder onto the Outlook Bar, below the Current Projects group heading.

An icon for the Conference folder appears in the Current Projects group. Your screen should look similar to the following illustration.

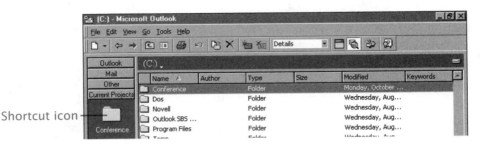

Shortcut icon

Remove a group from the Outlook Bar

After you have finished working with a group of folders, you can remove those folder shortcuts from the Outlook Bar. In this exercise, you remove the Current Projects group and the folder shortcut it contains.

> **IMPORTANT** Removing folder shortcuts from the Outlook Bar will not delete the folders themselves from your hard disk. Deleted folder groups from the Outlook Bar are not sent to the Deleted Items folder.

You can also use the right mouse button to remove individual shortcut icons from a group.

1 Use the right mouse button to click the Current Projects shortcut bar.

A shortcut menu appears.

2 Click Remove Group.

You are prompted to remove the group.

3 Click Yes.

The group, and the folder shortcut it contains, are removed from the Outlook Bar.

Finish the lesson

Delete

1 To continue to the next lesson, click the Conference folder, and then click the Delete button.

2 On the Outlook Bar, click the Inbox icon.

3 If you are finished using Outlook for now, on the File menu, click Exit And Log Off.

> **IMPORTANT** If you use the Exit command, you are logged off the server computer, but not other messaging applications, such as Microsoft Mail. By using the Exit And Log Off command, you are logged off all messaging applications.

Lesson Summary

To	Do this	Button
Start Outlook	On the Desktop, double-click the Microsoft Outlook shortcut icon. Select a profile, and then click OK.	
Open folders	On the Outlook Bar, click the folder icon you want.	
Switch between folder groups	In the Outlook Bar, click the shortcut bar for the group you want.	
Create an electronic note	In the Notes folder, click the New Note button, and then type the text of your note.	
Change the folder view	On the Standard toolbar, click the Current View down arrow, and then select a view.	
Display a single day, a week, or a month in Calendar	Click the Day, Week, or Month button.	
Delete an item	Select the item. On the Standard toolbar, click the Delete button.	
Create a new group on the Outlook Bar	Use the right mouse button to click the Other shortcut bar on the Outlook Bar. Click Add New Group. Type a name for the new group, and then press ENTER.	
Add a folder to the Outlook Bar	In the Information viewer, select the folder you want to add. Drag the folder onto the Outlook Bar where you want it to appear.	
Remove a group from the Outlook Bar	Use the right mouse button to click the group shortcut bar, and then click Remove Group. Click Yes.	
Quit Outlook	On the File menu, click Exit And Log Off.	

For online information about	On the Help menu, click Contents And Index, click the Index tab, and then type
Navigating in Outlook	**Navigation**
Viewing folder contents	**Opening, folders** *or* **Folders, viewing**
Creating new items	**Creating**
Changing folder views	**Views, changing**
Modifying the Outlook Bar	**Shortcuts, creating**

Creating and Sending Messages

Estimated time
30 min.

In this lesson you will learn how to:

- Create and address new messages.
- Enter and edit message content.
- Format text.
- Send messages.

With Microsoft Outlook, it's easy to communicate information quickly to others in your organization. For example, if you want to give a co-worker a memo, you could print the memo, and then leave it on her desk. If your co-worker is in another building or a branch office, you could fax or mail the memo to her. However, if you use Outlook, you can send the memo using electronic mail, or *e-mail*, or as a fax, without leaving your computer. You can also receive e-mail messages and faxes from your co-workers directly on your computer, in your Inbox.

Sending your messages using electronic mail is a particularly efficient way to communicate. You can use e-mail for anything you might use the postal service or telephone for, such as sending reports, new hire announcements, or correspondence regarding a project. If you need to send copies of your message to other people, you can easily add more recipients to your message or forward it to others. After a message is sent, the recipient gets it within seconds or minutes, depending on how fast it is processed. Sending e-mail over a network of computers allows you to communicate exclusively online, saving both time and paper.

Not only can you exchange e-mail messages with others in your organization, but you can also send messages to and receive messages from people all over the world by using the *Internet*. The Internet is a vast system of linked computers, a worldwide "network of networks," that connects educational institutions, research organizations, businesses, government entities, and millions of private individuals. E-mail is the most commonly used service of the Internet. Anyone with a computer and a modem or a network connection can use the Internet through an Internet access provider or Internet service provider, such as The Microsoft Network. Internet access providers supply the link between the Internet user and the Internet supercomputers.

Start Outlook

In this exercise, you start Outlook using the Shawn Davis profile.

 IMPORTANT If you don't have an Outlook SBS Practice folder or a profile for Outlook, refer to "Installing and Using the Practice Files," earlier in this book. You can also ask your system administrator for further help.

If the Office Assistant appears, you can hide it. To learn more about the Office Assistant, see Lesson 1.

1 On the Desktop, double-click the Microsoft Outlook shortcut icon.

Outlook starts. The Choose Profile dialog box appears.

2 Click the down arrow, and then click Shawn Davis.

For the purposes of this book, you'll use the Shawn Davis profile.

3 Click OK.

The Information viewer appears, with the Inbox folder open.

4 On the Outlook Bar, click the Mail shortcut bar.

You will only be working with the Mail group in this lesson.

Creating Messages

When you create a new message using Outlook, a blank form called the Mail Form appears. This form serves as a template to help you compose your message and identify the recipients.

Start a message

In this exercise, you create an e-mail message.

1 Be sure that the Inbox folder is open and that the messages appear in Messages With AutoPreview view.

New Mail Message

2 On the Standard toolbar, click the New Mail Message button.

A blank message appears. Your screen should look similar to the following illustration.

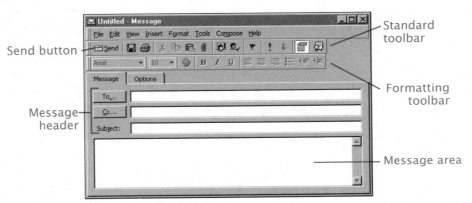

Addressing Messages

Before you start writing the text of your message, you address it by entering recipient names in the To area located at the top of the *message header*. This is similar to a paper memo where the recipients are identified at the top of the first page. In Outlook, you identify recipients using the *Address Book*, the central location where the names of all the users to whom you can send messages are stored. The Address Book can include more than one address list.

The *global address list* contains a directory of all users in your company or organization. A company's global address list might include the names of all employees in a single building, as well as the names of all employees at several out-of-state branch offices. Every user in your company has access to the global address list, but depending on how your mailbox is configured, your global address list might look different from other users'. The system administrator creates and maintains the global address list for your organization on the server so that all users' computers are linked together.

In addition to your global address list, your Address Book contains a *personal address book*. If you send messages to someone who isn't listed on the global address list for your organization, such as a client who works for another company, you can add that name and e-mail address to your personal address book. Because only you have access to your personal address book, you are responsible for adding entries and maintaining it.

You will learn more about the Contacts folder in Lesson 4.

Finally, your Address Book contains an Outlook Address Book which lists e-mail addresses for your business and personal contacts from the Contacts folder. Any time you enter an e-mail address for a contact, the Outlook Address Book is automatically updated to include that information.

For the purposes of this book, you have also created a *postoffice address list* by installing the practice files. The postoffice address list is typically created by the system administrator, and contains the names and e-mail addresses of a particular group of users; usually, these names are a subset of the names in an organization's global address list. In this case, the names are fictitious names of the employees of the Margo Tea Company. In the following exercises, you will address messages using these fictitious names rather than sending messages to your real co-workers.

Address a message using the postoffice address list

As the Operations Coordinator at the Margo Tea Company, you need to arrange a meeting with members of the Sales and Production departments to discuss this year's line of gourmet teas. You decide to notify employees of the meeting via e-mail using Outlook. In this exercise, you insert the names of the appropriate employees in your message header using the Address Book.

If your computer is only connected to the practice workgroup postoffice, you won't see a global address list.

1 In the message header, click the To button.

The Select Names dialog box appears containing names from your Address Book. The global address list for your organization appears by default. Therefore, your Select Names dialog box will look different from the following illustration.

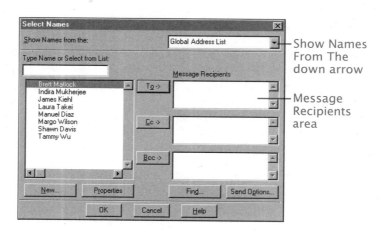

2 Click the Show Names From The down arrow, and then select Postoffice Address List.

The names of the Margo Tea Company employees appear.

3 In the list, click Laura Takei, and then click the To button.

Laura Takei appears in the To box in the Message Recipients area to the right of the list.

4 Click OK.

Your message appears again with Laura Takei's name in the To box in the message header. Your message should look similar to the following illustration.

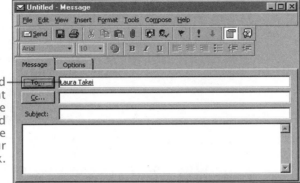

Underlined recipient names have been checked against the names in your Address Book.

Check Names

> **NOTE** When you address a message, you can also simply type a recipient name, or part of a recipient name, into the To box on the message form. Before you send the message, the names you type are checked against the Address Book names automatically and exact matches are underlined in the To box. If more than one match is found, a red wavy line appears under the name. Click the wavy-underlined name to see a list of possible matches. You can also check names manually by clicking the Check Names button on the Standard toolbar.

Send a copy to another recipient

You're addressing your message to those recipients you want to attend the meeting. If there are other people that you want to inform about the meeting, you can send them a copy. For the purposes of this exercise, you address a copy of the message to yourself, using your profile name, Shawn Davis. Normally, you would not send yourself a copy of a message because a copy of every message you send is automatically stored in the Sent Items folder.

The abbreviation "Cc" stands for "carbon copy" or "courtesy copy."

1 Click the Cc button.

The Select Names dialog box appears.

2 Click the Show Names From The down arrow, and then select the Postoffice Address List.

The names of the Margo Tea Company employees appear.

3 Click Shawn Davis, and then click the Cc button.

Shawn Davis appears in the Cc box, in the Message Recipients area.

4 Click OK.

Your message appears again, with Shawn Davis in the Cc box.

NOTE You can also send a blind copy of a message. A blind copy (Bcc) is similar to a copy, except that only the blind copy recipient and the sender are aware that the message included the blind copy recipient. To view the Bcc box in the message header, on the View menu, click Bcc Box.

Add names to your personal address book

In this exercise, you add several names from the postoffice address list to your personal address book, because you communicate with those people frequently and you want to be able to find their e-mail addresses more quickly.

Address Book

1 On the Standard toolbar, click the Address Book button.

The Select Names dialog box appears.

2 Click the Show Names From The down arrow, and then select Postoffice Address List.

The names of Margo Tea Company employees appear.

3 Use the right mouse button to click James Kiehl.

A shortcut menu appears.

4 Click Add To Personal Address Book.

James Kiehl is added to your personal address book. Although you do not see the results immediately, you will check your personal address book in the next exercise.

5 Click Indira Mukherjee, hold down CTRL, and then click Tammy Wu.

When the desired names do not directly follow one another in the list, you hold down CTRL to select them.

To select a name, you can also click Properties, and then click Personal Address Book in the Add To area.

6 Use the right mouse button to click one of the selected names.

A shortcut menu appears.

7 Click Add To Personal Address Book.

Indira Mukherjee and Tammy Wu are added to your personal address book.

Address a message using your personal address book

In this exercise, you add a name from your personal address book as a message recipient.

1 Click the Show Names From The down arrow, and then select Personal Address Book.

The names you added to your personal address book—Indira Mukherjee, James Kiehl, and Tammy Wu—appear.

2 Select Indira Mukherjee, and then click To.

Indira Mukherjee appears in the To box under Message Recipients.

3 Click OK.

Indira Mukherjee appears in the To box.

You can also double-click a name to add it to the To box.

Add an Internet address to your personal address book

Entries in your personal address book can include recipients who use another e-mail or messaging system outside your company. A common way to send e-mail to someone outside your company is by using the Internet.

In this exercise, you add the Internet address for Debbie Abdul, the Account Executive in charge of the Margo Tea Company advertising campaign, to your personal address book.

1 On the Standard toolbar, click the Address Book button.

The Select Names dialog box appears.

2 Click New.

The New Entry dialog box appears.

3 Under Select The Entry Type, click Other Address.

4 In the Put This Entry area, be sure that the "In The Personal Address Book" option button is selected.

You do not need to open your personal address book to add names to it.

5 Click OK.

The New Other Address Properties dialog box appears.

You can also use an alias, such as "Debbie at work," for a Display Name.

6 In the Display Name box, type **Debbie Abdul**, and then press TAB.

This is the way the name will appear in your personal address book.

7 In the E-mail Address box, type **dabdul@fitch_mather.com**, and then press TAB.

The fictional e-mail address for Debbie Abdul is added to your personal address book.

8 In the E-mail Type box, type **Internet**

This specifies the type of e-mail address you are adding. Your dialog box should look similar to the following illustration.

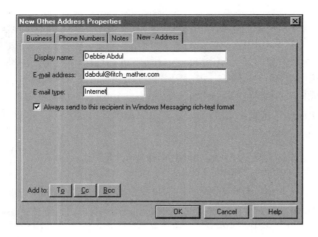

9 Click OK.

The new address is added to your personal address book, and Debbie Abdul appears in the To box in your message header.

Entering and Editing Message Content

You can also type your message subject and text before you identify the message recipients.

Now that you have identified the recipients of your message, you can finish the message by entering a subject, and then typing the message itself in the blank area located at the bottom of the Mail Form. The message area expands as you type, so your messages can be brief or lengthy. Adding a message subject helps recipients identify the message topic, since the subject appears in the message header in recipients' Inboxes.

You can enter and edit text in your message just as you would using a word processor. In Outlook, you can use the BACKSPACE key or the DELETE key to delete text, and move or copy text by dragging and dropping. You can also reverse an action by using the Undo command on the Edit menu.

Enter and edit the message text

In this exercise, you type the subject of your message, and then add the main content of the message. You'll start off by inviting everyone to the meeting to discuss this year's product line, and then you'll make changes to the text.

1 Click in the Subject box, and then type **Product Line Meeting**

2 Press TAB to move the insertion point to the message area, and then type **We need to discuss the new porduct release schedule. Let's order boxed lunches and meet in her office Tuesday at noon.**

Be sure you type the word "product" incorrectly as "porduct" so you can spell-check it later.

You can also drag to select text.

3   Double-click the word "boxed" to select it, and then press the DELETE key.

4   Double-click the word "her," and then type **Margo's**

5   Click in front of the word "Tuesday," type **next**, and then press the SPACEBAR.

Your message should look similar to the following illustration.

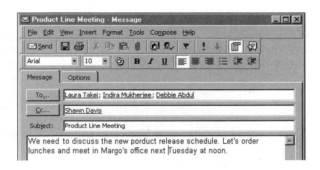

Checking the Spelling of Messages

You can use the spell checker in Outlook to identify and correct spelling errors in your messages before you send them. It is a good idea to check the spelling of all your outgoing messages, whether or not you think you made any mistakes. When you start the spell checker, your message is checked from the beginning of the message, no matter where the insertion point is placed. If you don't want to check the spelling for the entire message, you can select part of it, even a single word. The text in the Subject box is also checked for spelling, but recipient names are ignored.

If the spelling of a word isn't recognized when you check your message, you can correct the word contained in your message by selecting the correctly spelled word from a list of suggestions. If the spelling of a word is correct as is, but the spell checker does not recognize it, you can either add the word to the dictionary, or ignore the word and continue the spell check. In addition to misspelled words, duplicated words are recognized, and the second word can be deleted using the spell checker. The buttons used in the Spelling dialog box are described in the following table.

Use this button	To
Ignore	Ignore only that occurrence of the word.
Ignore All	Ignore all instances of the word in the message.
Change	Change only that occurrence of the word.
Change All	Change all instances of the word in the message.
Add	Add the word to the dictionary for future reference.

Use this button	To
Suggest	Display a list of proposed spellings or words.
Options	Set options for spell checks.
Undo Last	Reverse the last spell-check change.
Cancel	Cancel the spell check.

Spell check your message

In this exercise, you check your message for spelling, especially since you deliberately made a spelling error in the previous exercise.

1   On the Tools menu, click Spelling.

The spell checker starts. The Spelling dialog box appears and the word "porduct" is not recognized by the dictionary. A suggested word appears in the Suggestions box.

2   Be sure that the word "product" is selected in the Suggestions box, and then click Change.

The word is corrected in your message, and the next unrecognized word, "Margo's," appears in the Change To box.

3   Click Ignore.

The word "Margo's" is a valid name. A message appears indicating that the spell check is complete.

4   Click OK.

TIP   To have all messages automatically checked for spelling before they are sent, click Options on the Tools menu in the Outlook window, click the Spelling tab, and then select the Always Check Spelling Before Sending check box.

Formatting Text

In Outlook, you can format the text in your messages to help emphasize your ideas and create interest. For example, you can choose from a series of *fonts* to create a different look, or you can format text as bold, italic, or underlined. These text characteristics, or attributes, are also known as *rich text format*. When you create a message in rich text format, the text attributes can be recognized by different programs so that you can send formatted messages even to users who might not have Outlook. You can also add bullets to highlight and separate the main points of your message, or change the color of the text.

To format text, you first select the text you want to format, and then apply the formatting. If you do not select any text before you format, the formatting you define will be applied to any text that you type after the insertion point. Only the text in the message area can be formatted.

You can use the buttons on the Formatting toolbar to change text attributes, such as bold, italic, underline, and text color. Or you can use the Font command on the Format menu to change the appearance of the text. You can also change text formatting and paragraph formatting. Paragraph formatting includes alignment, indentation, and bullets.

Add text

At the Margo Tea Company, you want all of your messages to be interesting and effective. You decide to experiment with text and paragraph formatting in your message about the upcoming product line meeting. In this exercise, you add some information about the meeting agenda to your message. You will format this text in the next two exercises.

1   Press CTRL+END to move the insertion point to the end of your message text, and then press ENTER twice.

    The insertion point moves to a new line.

2   Type the following text, pressing ENTER after each line.

    Our agenda will include:

    Reviewing the existing product line

    Drafting a schedule for new product releases

    Approving a new label design

Format text

In this exercise, you use buttons on the Formatting toolbar to change the appearance of the text you just typed.

Italic

1   Triple-click the line "Our agenda will include" to select it.

2   On the Formatting toolbar, click the Italic button.

    The text is italicized.

3   Select the text "Reviewing the existing product line" through "Approving a new label design."

Bold

4   On the Formatting toolbar, click the Bold button.

    The text is formatted as bold.

Font Color

5 On the Formatting toolbar, click the Font Color button.

A color palette appears.

6 Click Green, the fifth color in the top row.

The text is formatted with the color green.

 NOTE You must have a color printer to print text in color. If you use a black and white printer to print colored text, the text will appear in shades of gray.

Format the paragraph

In this exercise, you use buttons on the Formatting toolbar to format several lines of text.

Bullets

Increase Indent

1 Be sure that the text "Reviewing the existing product line" through "Approving a new label design" is selected.

2 On the Formatting toolbar, click the Bullets button.

Bullets are added in front of each new paragraph of text.

3 On the Formatting toolbar, click the Increase Indent button.

The text is indented to the right.

4 Click anywhere in the text.

The selection is cleared. Your message should look similar to the following illustration.

TIP You can automatically sign all of your e-mail messages with a particular phrase or selection of text. To do this, create a message, and then add and format the text you want to use as an AutoSignature. For example, your AutoSignature text could be "Shawn Davis, Operations Coordinator." Select the AutoSignature text. On the Tools menu, click AutoSignature. Click Yes to save the selected text as your AutoSignature. The text will now appear at the end of each outgoing message you send. To remove an AutoSignature, you can delete it from an individual message before sending it.

Creating a Reusable Message Template

Using Microsoft Word 97 as your e-mail editor, you can edit your Outlook messages and modify their appearance. For example, suppose you want to send a weekly message to the members of your project team, containing a table that lists this week's meeting agenda items. You can create an original message template or modify an existing Outlook message template and save the changes with a new name.

To select an existing template to modify, verify that the contents of your Inbox appear in the Information viewer. On the Compose menu, click Choose Template. A list of all the available Outlook templates appears in the Choose Template dialog box. (You can also access the list of templates from the Calendar menu in Calendar, the Contacts menu in Contacts, the Tasks menu in Tasks, and so on. The Choose Template command appears on each of these menus.) Select a template from the list and click OK to open it.

To enable WordMail tools, click Options on the Tools menu. Select the Use Microsoft Word As The E-mail Editor checkbox. After you have opened a template, use the message tools and WordMail tools to modify the template to suit your needs. For example, you can use Word 97 to create a table in the message area, and use the regular message formatting tools to change its appearance. When you have finished designing your template, you can save it with the rest of the Outlook templates.

To save an original template, on the File menu, click Save As. Save the template in the Program Files/Microsoft Office/WinWord/Wordmail folder. Type a name for the new template, such as "Meeting Agenda," in the File Name box. Finally, be sure to click the Save As Type down arrow and select Outlook Template (*.oft). Your original template will be stored with the rest of the Outlook templates. You can use an original template at any time by clicking the Choose Template command on the Compose menu, and then double-clicking the template you want to use.

Sending Messages

Now that you have addressed and composed a message, you are ready to send it. When you send a message, it is moved to your Outbox folder, where it is temporarily stored, usually for a few seconds, until it's delivered to the recipient or recipients. Message recipients do not need to be present to receive a message; the message is delivered to and stored in his or her Inbox until he or she logs on to Outlook and opens the message. If your e-mail message cannot be delivered because of a network problem or an incorrect address, you will receive a notification message from the server. Before you send your e-mail message, you can select several options that will affect its delivery.

Tracking Sent Messages

If you want to make sure that your message was successfully sent, or if you want to know when the message was opened by the recipient, you can select a *tracking* option. Depending on the tracking option you assign, a notification is sent to you when the recipient receives a message, when the recipient opens the message, or both. A notification message informing you that a message has been delivered is also called a *Delivery Receipt*. A notification message indicating that a message has been read by the recipient is called a *Read Receipt*. Assigning tracking options to your messages is similar to using registered mail. Tracking can be useful if your message is time-sensitive.

 IMPORTANT Any options you select on the Options tab in a message apply only to that message.

You can check the tracking results for a message you have sent by reading the receipts from your system administrator, or by opening the copy of the message in your Sent Items folder. The Tracking tab records the message status for each recipient.

 NOTE You can also conduct a vote with a message; the voting results are maintained on the Tracking tab. You can learn about setting voting options on an outgoing message in the "Conducting a Vote with a Message" section in Lesson 3, "Reading, Processing, and Organizing Messages."

Set tracking options for a message

In this exercise, you set the tracking options for your message to make sure all the recipients successfully receive and read it. Since you are sending your message to fictional users in this exercise, you will receive an Undeliverable Receipt from the system administrator.

1   Click the Options tab, and then maximize the message.

Your message should look similar to the following illustration.

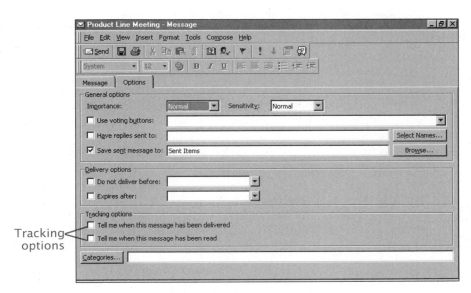

Tracking
options

2   In the Tracking Options area, select the Tell Me When This Message Has Been Delivered check box.

You will be notified when the recipients receive this message.

3   In the Tracking Options area, select the Tell Me When This Message Has Been Read check box.

You will be notified when the recipients open this message.

4   Restore the size of the message window.

TIP   If you want to set tracking options for all outgoing messages, on the Tools menu in the Outlook window, click Options. On the Sending tab, select the Tell Me When All Messages Have Been Delivered check box and/or the Tell Me When All Messages Have Been Read check box, and then click OK. You can also process receipts automatically so that tracking information is recorded on the Tracking tab and receipts are deleted after they have been processed. To do this, on the Tools menu, click Options. Click the E-mail tab, and then select the options you want in the Settings For Automatic Processing Of Mail area.

Assigning Priority to Messages

You can also assign a priority to a message so that the recipient can determine its importance before opening it. By default, messages are sent with a normal priority, but you can mark them with a low or a high priority, depending on their importance. For example, you want the recipients of your message regarding the product line meeting to know that it requires immediate attention, so you assign it a high priority.

After you send a message, recipients are able to identify the priority level by looking at the message header in their Information viewers. Messages with a high priority level are indicated with a red exclamation point next to the message header, while messages with a low priority have a blue downward-pointing arrow. Normal priority messages do not have a symbol next to the message header. The priority symbols are listed in the following table.

Symbol	Priority level
! ✉	High priority
↓ ✉	Low priority

Assign high priority to a message

In this exercise, you assign high priority to your message because you want to emphasize the importance of the upcoming product line meeting.

*Importance:
High*

➤ On the Standard toolbar, click the "Importance: High" button.

The message is assigned a high priority and the text in the Importance box on the Options tab changes to High.

TIP If you are sending a message that requires further action—for example, a message that the recipient must respond to—you can also attach a message flag to draw attention to the message. On the Standard toolbar in the Mail Form, click the Message Flag button, and then select a flag message. You will learn more about message flags in Lesson 3, "Reading and Organizing Messages."

Message Flag

Send your message

Now that you have set all the delivery options for your message, you are ready to send it.

➤ On the Standard toolbar, click the Send button.

After a moment, your message is sent and a copy is created in the Sent Items folder. Because you addressed a carbon copy to yourself, a new message also appears in your Inbox.

TROUBLESHOOTING You should receive several receipts from your system administrator, including a Delivery Receipt indicating that your message was received by the recipients in your workgroup, and an Undeliverable Receipt for the fictitious Internet address. If you receive a message stating that you have no transport provider, click OK; this means that your network has not been set up for Internet messaging.

Recalling a Message

Occasionally, you might want to retrieve a message you've sent. For example, suppose you have sent someone a message containing incorrect information or addressed a message to the wrong person. With Outlook, you can recall messages you have sent as long as the recipient has not yet opened the message. If a recipient has already opened your message, it cannot be retrieved.

When you recall messages, you can choose to simply delete your unread message from the recipient's Inbox or replace the original message with a different one. Either way, the recipient of the original message is notified that it was recalled.

Replace a message

You just remembered that you will be out of the office all day on Tuesday to attend a seminar, and therefore won't be able to hold the product line meeting. In this exercise, you recall your original message and request a meeting on a different date.

Sent Items

1 On the Outlook Bar, click the Sent Items icon.

The contents of the Sent Items folder are displayed in the Information viewer.

2 Double-click the Product Line Meeting message in the Information viewer.

A copy of your sent message appears.

3 On the Tools menu, click Recall This Message.

A message appears, prompting you to delete or replace the existing message from the recipients' Inboxes.

4 Click the Delete Unread Copies And Replace With A New Message option button, and then click OK.

Your original Product Line Meeting message appears.

5 In the message, double-click the word "Tuesday," and then type **Thursday**

6 On the Standard toolbar, click the Send button.

The replacement message is sent. On the copy of the message in your Sent Items folder, a note appears in the Comment area above the message header, reminding you that you attempted to recall the message. Your screen should look similar to the following illustration.

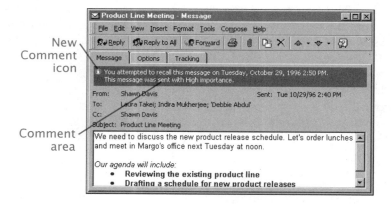

7 Click the Close button on the message window.

Copies of both the original message and the replacement message are displayed in your Sent Items folder.

IMPORTANT If you choose to replace a recalled message, you must specifically send the replacement message. If you do not resend a replacement message, the original is simply deleted from the recipients' Inboxes.

View the replacement message

Since you did not open the carbon copy of the message you sent to yourself, the replacement message is delivered to your Inbox in place of the original. In this exercise, you use AutoPreview to make sure that the corrected replacement message is in your Inbox.

1   On the Outlook Bar, click the Inbox icon.

The contents of your Inbox appear.

2   Be sure that Messages With AutoPreview is the current view.

The name of the current view appears in the Current View box on the Standard toolbar. Your screen should look similar to the following illustration.

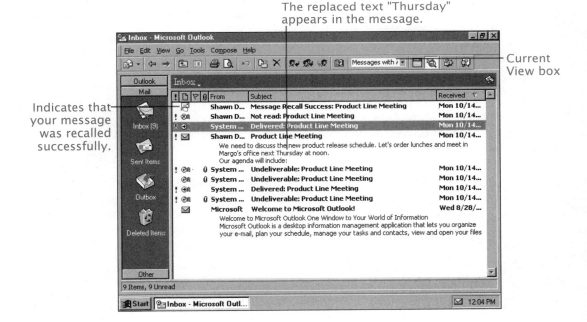

The replaced text "Thursday" appears in the message.

Current View box

Indicates that your message was recalled successfully.

Finish the lesson

Follow these steps to delete the practice messages you used in this lesson, so that you have a clean Inbox folder to work with in the next lesson. You will learn more about deleting items in Lesson 3, "Reading and Organizing Messages."

1   Be sure the contents of the Inbox are displayed.

2 On the Edit menu, click Select All.

The contents of your Inbox are selected.

3 On the Standard toolbar, click the Delete button.

The messages are deleted.

Delete

4 To continue to the next lesson, on the Outlook Bar, click the Inbox icon.

5 If you are finished using Outlook for now, on the Files menu, click Exit And Log Off.

Lesson Summary

To	Do this	Button
Start a message	In the Inbox folder, click the New Mail Message button.	
Address a message	Click To, and then select an address list. Select recipient names, and then click To.	
Send a carbon copy	Click Cc, select recipient names, and then click Cc.	
Add names to your personal address book from another address list	In the Address Book, use the right mouse button to click a name. Click Add To Personal Address Book.	
Add an Internet address to your personal address book	In the Address Book, click New, click Other Address, and then click OK. Type a Display Name, an E-mail Address, and an E-mail Type.	
Enter and edit message text	In the message area, type your text. To edit, place the insertion point where you want to edit, and then use BACKSPACE to delete text or type new text.	

To	Do this	Button
Spell check a message	On the Tools menu, click Spelling, and then accept or reject the changes.	
Format text	Select the text you want to format. On the Formatting toolbar, click the appropriate buttons for the formatting effects you want to apply.	
Track sent messages	On the Options tab, select the options you want in the Tracking Options area.	
Assign a high or low priority to a message	On the Standard toolbar, click the "Importance: High" button or the "Importance: Low" button.	
Recall a message	On the Outlook Bar, click the Sent Items icon. Open the message you want to recall.	
Delete or replace a message	On the Tools menu, click Recall This Message. Delete or replace the message.	

For online information about	On the Help menu, click Contents And Index, click the Index tab, and then type
Creating and sending messages	**Sending mail**
Using the Address Book	**Addresses, e-mail**
Adding Internet addresses	**Internet**
Tracking messages	**Tracking**
Assigning priorities	**Prioritizing messages**
Sending messages	**Sending mail**

41

Reading and Organizing Messages

Estimated time
35 min.

In this lesson you will learn how to:

- Locate and read messages.
- Reply to and forward messages.
- Organize messages.
- Create and manage folders.

You probably have already received messages from other people, or at least are aware that messages have been sent to you. Now, you need to be able to locate them, and then read them. In addition to reading your messages, you need to find out what you can do with them after you read them. For example, you can reply to or forward messages to share information with others. You can also store messages about a specific project in a separate folder or delete messages that you no longer need.

At the Margo Tea Company, you have received several messages concerning the new product line meeting. In this lesson, you'll learn how to quickly respond to your messages so that you can be prepared for the upcoming discussion. You'll also organize the messages in your Inbox so that you can quickly file and later find the information that you need.

Start Outlook

1 On the Desktop, double-click the Microsoft Outlook shortcut icon.

Outlook starts. The Choose Profile dialog box appears.

2 Click the down arrow, and then click Shawn Davis.

For the purposes of this book, you'll use the Shawn Davis profile.

3 Click OK.

The Information viewer appears, with the Inbox folder open.

4 On the Outlook Bar, click the Mail shortcut bar.

You will only be working with the Mail group in this lesson.

Set up your Inbox for this lesson

For the purposes of this lesson, and to be able to complete the following exercises, you must drag messages from the Outlook SBS Practice folder into the Inbox to simulate receiving mail. Normally, messages you receive appear automatically in the Inbox.

 IMPORTANT   To complete this lesson, you must move practice messages from the exercise disk into your Outlook Inbox. If you have not yet set up the practice files, work through the "Installing and Using the Practice Files" section earlier in this book.

1 Click the Start button, point to Programs, and then click Windows Explorer or Windows NT Explorer.

2 In the left side of the window, titled All Folders, click drive C.

3 In the right side of the window, titled Contents Of, double-click the Outlook SBS Practice folder.

The contents of the practice folder appear.

4 Double-click the Lesson 3 folder.

The messages used in this lesson appear.

5 Click an open area in the taskbar with the right mouse button, and then click Tile Horizontally.

The Exploring–Lesson 3 and Inbox–Microsoft Outlook windows are tiled horizontally, or arranged one on top of the other. Your screen should look similar to the following illustration.

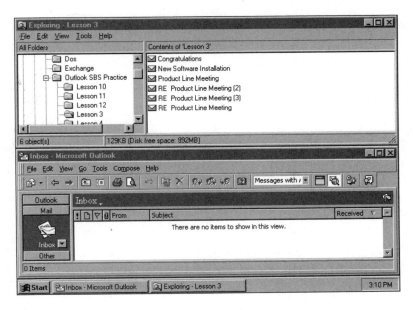

6 In the Exploring–Lesson 3 window, on the Edit menu, click Select All.

7 Drag the selected files to the Information viewer area, in the Inbox–Microsoft Outlook window.

The practice files are copied, and you are ready to start the lesson.

8 Click the Close button on the Exploring–Lesson 3 window.

9 Click the Maximize button on the Inbox window.

Locating and Reading Messages

After you start Outlook, you can start working with your messages in the Information viewer. You can easily identify and manage your incoming messages because they are automatically placed in the Inbox folder.

You can readily distinguish between messages in the folder contents list by reading the message header. The message header identifies the sender, the subject, and when the message was sent. Messages that have not been opened appear in bold type, while messages that have been opened are in regular type. In addition, the number of unread messages in a folder appears next to the folder name in parentheses, in both the Outlook bar and in the Folder List.

 TIP When you receive incoming messages, a message icon appears on the taskbar. If Outlook is not the active window, you can quickly open your Inbox by double-clicking the message icon.

45

Explore your mailbox folders

In this exercise, you open your built-in folders to view where different messages are stored. You can review the message you sent about the Product Line Meeting and find out if any messages are located in any other folders in your Inbox.

1   On the Outlook Bar, click the Deleted Items icon.

If you have deleted any messages recently, they will appear in the Deleted Items folder.

2   On the Outlook Bar, click the Outbox icon.

The Information viewer should show no messages stored in the Outbox because you have not sent any messages recently.

3   On the Outlook Bar, click the Sent Items icon.

Any messages you have sent appear.

4   On the Outlook Bar, click the Inbox icon.

The practice items in your Inbox appear in the Information viewer.

Open a message

In this exercise, you open the Product Line Meeting message so you can read it.

1   In the Information viewer, double-click the Product Line Meeting message from Shawn Davis.

A copy of the message you sent in Lesson 2 opens. In the header, you can see the name of the sender, the date and time it was sent, and the message recipients' names. Your message should look similar to the following illustration.

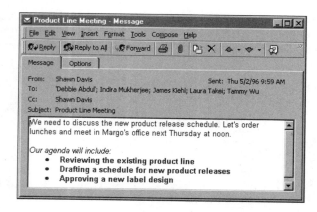

You can also click Close on the File menu.

2 On the Product Line Meeting–Message window, click the Close button. The message closes.

Browsing Through Messages Using AutoPreview

By default, the messages in your Inbox appear in Messages With AutoPreview view. With AutoPreview, the first three lines of text are displayed for all new, unopened messages. You can preview the message contents at a glance and decide which of your new messages you should open and read first. If a message is short enough, you do not even need to open it to read the entire message. After you open a message, the message header no longer appears in bold type, and the first three lines of text are no longer displayed.

 TIP If you want AutoPreview text to appear for both unread and read messages, on the View menu, click Format View. In the AutoPreview area, click the Preview All Items option button, and then click OK. To turn off AutoPreview, click the No AutoPreview option button.

You will learn more about messaging options, such as attaching a file to a message, in Lesson 9.

As you look in the Information viewer, you can also see that icons appear to the left of messages. Different kinds of messages have different icons associated with them to help you identify them. For example, an icon for an e-mail message with an attachment looks like an envelope with a paper clip, while a Delivery Receipt icon looks like a postage meter stamp with a green arrow. These icons can also help you determine which messages need your immediate attention. Some of the different icons used to identify messages in the Information viewer are listed in the following table.

Icon	Description
✉	Standard e-mail with normal priority
❗✉	E-mail with high priority
↓✉	E-mail with low priority
✉ 📎	E-mail with an attached file
	Postmark for Delivery Receipt
	Postmark for Undeliverable Receipt
	Postmark for read messages
	Postmark for unread messages
	E-mail message that you have replied to
	E-mail message that you have forwarded
	E-mail message with comment or note in the message header

In the Information viewer, columns divide the message header by priority, item type, message flag, attachment, sender, subject, received date, and size. By default, messages are sorted by date, with the most recent message at the top of the list. You will learn how to sort your messages differently later in this lesson.

NOTE Your Inbox might have more or fewer messages than in the illustrations in this lesson. If your messages appear in a different order, click the Received column button in the Information viewer until your Inbox messages are sorted by date.

Most of your unread messages are responses to the Product Line Meeting message that you sent. Because you have not read these messages, they are in bold type, and the first three lines of text are displayed below each message header. You can now review and read your new messages. When you open a message, it appears as a Mail Form, which is very similar to the Mail Form you use to compose and send messages.

Read an entire message

With AutoPreview, the first three lines of Laura Takei's response to your Product Line Meeting message are visible, but the message continues past the range of AutoPreview. In this exercise, you open Laura's message so you can read it in its entirety. When you open a message that is a reply or a forward, the original message text is appended to the bottom of the message by default.

You can also click Open on the File menu.

1   Double-click the "RE: Product Line Meeting" message from Laura Takei.

The message opens. The complete message text appears.

2   Scroll downward, as necessary, to read the entire message.

Following Laura Takei's reply is the text of your original message.

Browse through messages

Instead of opening and closing each message individually, you can quickly browse through them by opening a message, and then clicking the Next Item or Previous Item buttons on the Standard toolbar. In this exercise, you browse through your messages, including the replies to your Product Line Meeting message.

Previous Item

1   On the Standard toolbar, click the Previous Item button until the message from Brett Matlock appears.

The title of the message is New Software Installation. Your message should look like the following illustration.

2   Click the Previous Item button again.

The previous message, a Congratulations message from Margo Wilson, appears.

Next Item

3 On the Standard toolbar, click the Next Item button three times, until the message from Indira Mukherjee, responding to the Product Line Meeting message, appears.

4 Click the Next Item button again.

A reply from James Kiehl appears.

5 On the message window, click the Close button.

The messages you have opened and read no longer appear in bold type, and no longer show any message text in AutoPreview.

Flagging Messages for Action

Suppose you need to follow up on an issue that was brought to your attention by a particular message, such as reviewing an attached report or placing a conference call to the sender. You do not have to follow up on the message immediately, but you don't want to forget to do it later, either. With Outlook, you can *flag* a message in your Inbox with a reminder to follow up on the issue at another time. If you want, you can add a specific due date to the message flag. You can also attach flags to the messages that you send to others to alert them that an action item is included in your message, and needs their close attention. When a recipient receives a message with a flag, a note about the purpose of the flag appears in the comment area above the message header.

You can choose from a predetermined list of message flags, such as "Call" or "No Response Necessary." If the existing flags in Outlook do not meet your needs, you can also create your own. If a message contains a flag, a red flag icon appears in the message flag column in the Inbox. Once you have followed up on a message, you can mark its flag as completed; a gray flag icon appears in the message flag column to indicate a completed follow-up.

Flag a message

In this exercise, you flag the message from Brett Matlock because you want to remind yourself to call him and ask about Outlook training for all employees.

1 Double-click the New Software Installation message from Brett Matlock.

The message opens.

2 Maximize the message.

You must maximize the message to see the entire Standard toolbar on the Mail Form.

3 On the Standard toolbar, click the Message Flag button.

The Flag Message dialog box appears.

Message Flag

4 Click the Flag down arrow.

A list of message flags appears.

5 Select Call.

6 Click the By down arrow.

A drop-down calendar appears; the current date is selected.

7 Click Today.

The current date appears in the By box.

8 Click OK.

A note about the message flag appears in the comment area above the message header. Your message should look similar to the following illustration.

Comment area—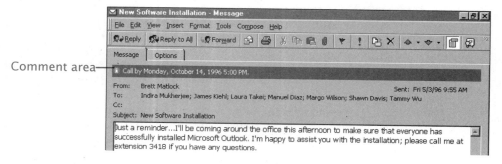

9 Click the Close button on the message window.

A red message flag appears in the message flag column. Your screen should look similar to the following illustration.

Message flag—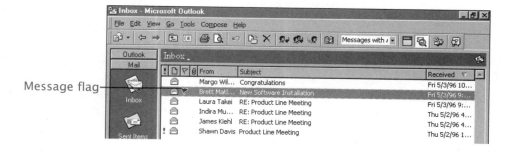

 NOTE If you have maximized a message, all your messages will appear maximized from that moment on. Similarly, if you restore a message, all messages will appear restored until you choose differently.

Flag a message as completed

Suppose you just called Brett and asked him your question. In this exercise, you mark the message with a completed flag to remind yourself that you have taken care of the issue.

Message Flag

If you want to remove the message flag, click Clear Flag.

1 Double-click the message from Brett Matlock.

2 Click the Message Flag button.

The Flag Message dialog box appears.

3 Select the Completed check box, and then click OK.

A note is added to the comment area, including the time and date that the message was flagged as completed.

4 Click the Close button on the message window.

A gray flag appears in the message flag column.

Responding to Messages

Suppose you want to respond to a message you have received or pass message information along to somebody else. You could create a new message, add the recipient and the subject, and then try to recall the details of the original message that you want to discuss. A much faster way to respond, however, is to select or open a message, and then use a toolbar button to direct the message back to the sender or to a new recipient. Your reply is added above the original message text. In the Mail Form, the names of the message response buttons appear directly on the buttons in the Standard toolbar.

Replying to Messages

When you *reply* to a message, you can either respond only to the person who sent the original message or include all the carbon copy recipients listed in the original message. For example, if your team lead sends a message inviting everyone on the team to a lunch meeting, you can inform the lead and your fellow team members that you cannot attend, all in a single message. Reply messages are identified by the letters "RE" in the subject area.

Reply to a recipient

In this exercise, you reply to Laura Takei's message regarding the lunch orders for the Product Line Meeting.

1 Click the "RE: Product Line Meeting" message from Laura Takei.

You do not need to open a message to reply to it.

Reply

2 On the Standard toolbar, click the Reply button.

A Mail Form appears. The To and Subject boxes are automatically filled in, with the subject preceded by "RE:" Notice that Laura's message appears below the message area where you will type your text.

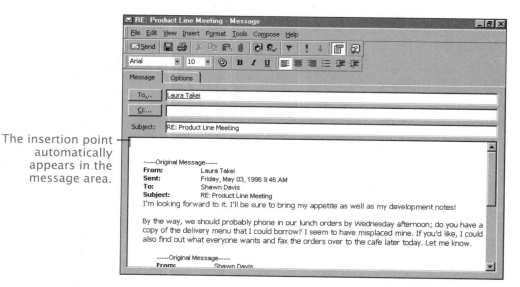

The insertion point automatically appears in the message area.

3 Type **Thanks for your help! Drop by my desk and I'll give you copies of the menu and the order form.**

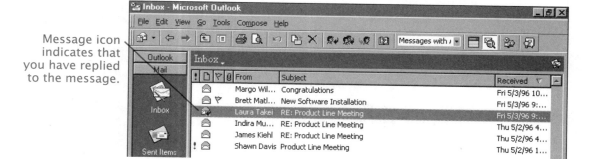

Send

4 On the Standard toolbar, click the Send button.

Your reply is sent to Laura Takei. The message icon in the Information viewer changes to indicate that you have replied to the message.

Message icon indicates that you have replied to the message.

5 Double-click the "RE: Product Line Meeting" message from Laura Takei.

The message opens, and a note appears in the comment area, recording the date and time of your reply.

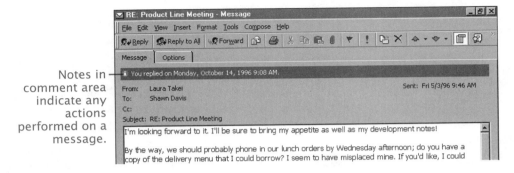

Notes in comment area indicate any actions performed on a message.

6   Click the Close button on the message window.

Reply to All

> **NOTE**   If you want to reply to all the original recipients of a message, click the Reply To All button on the Standard toolbar.

Forwarding Messages

Sometimes you receive messages that you think another person should also see. Or, you might not be the best person to reply to a message. When this happens, you can *forward* a copy of the message to a new recipient, rather than retype the message or show a printout of the message to the person who needs to see it. You can forward a message to several people, or add Cc and Bcc recipients, just as you can when you create a message. Keep in mind that just as you can forward messages that you receive from other people, others can forward your messages to whomever they want; therefore you should exercise caution when forwarding confidential information.

Forwarded messages are similar to replies in that the original message is appended at the end of the message. If you want to precede the message with text, you can type your own message before the appended text. For example, you can type background information on a forwarded message so that the recipient can handle the message without asking you why you are forwarding it. Forwarded messages are identified by the letters "FW" in the subject area.

Forward a message

In this exercise, you forward the message about recent sales figures from Indira Mukherjee to Margo Wilson, since Margo has the most current profit information.

1   Double-click the "RE: Product Line Meeting" message from Indira Mukherjee.

2   On the Standard toolbar, click the Forward button.

A Mail Form appears with the Subject box filled in.

Check Names

You can also press CTRL+K to check names.

3 In the To box, type **margo**

4 On the Standard toolbar, click the Check Names button.

The name Margo Wilson appears automatically after it is checked against the Address Book.

5 Click in the message area, and type **Since you have the most current profit reports, could you get them to Indira for her meeting presentation? Thanks!**

6 On the Standard toolbar, click the Send button.

Indira's message is forwarded to Margo Wilson. A note is added to the comment area on the original message, with the date and time the message was forwarded.

7 Click the Close button on the original message window from Indira Mukherjee.

The message icon in the Information viewer changes to indicate that you have forwarded the message. Your screen should look similar to the following illustration.

Message icon indicates the message has been forwarded.

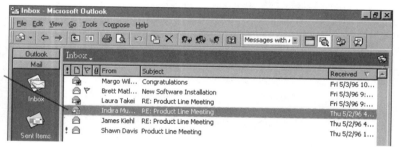

Organizing Messages

Although you can let your messages accumulate in your Inbox, you'll find that organizing your messages will allow you to find them more quickly later. You can organize your mail folders in several ways depending on your preferences and work habits. For example, you can create folders for different types of messages, and then move your messages into the appropriate folders. In addition, you can delete messages or save them on your hard disk.

Sorting Messages

When your Inbox contains several messages, you can organize the messages by arranging them according to specific criteria, or *sorting* them. The information in the message header is used to sort messages by column, such as sender, subject, and received date. Other columns in the message header show the message type, and whether or not there is a priority or attached file associated with the message.

Depending on the type of information in the column, messages can be sorted in ascending or descending order. An ascending sort lists data from A to Z, from the lowest to the highest number, or from the earliest to the latest date. A descending sort lists data from Z to A, from the highest to the lowest number, or from the latest to the earliest date. By default, messages in your Inbox are sorted by date, in descending order so that the most recent message appears at the top of the list. A down arrow in a Received column heading indicates that messages are sorted in descending order while an up arrow indicates an ascending sort. The following illustration shows the default sort for a typical Inbox.

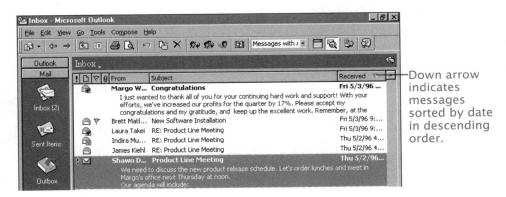

Down arrow indicates messages sorted by date in descending order.

To quickly change how your messages are sorted, you can click a column heading. For example, if you click the Received column heading, the messages are sorted in ascending order to show the oldest message at the top of the list. You can have different sort orders for different folders.

Sort messages

In this exercise, you experiment with sorting to find a good way to organize the different types of messages contained in your Inbox.

By default, the From column is sorted by first name, and then by last name.

1 In the Information viewer, click the From column heading.

The messages in your Inbox are sorted in ascending order by sender. Your screen should look similar to the following illustration.

2 Click the From column heading again.

The messages are sorted in descending order by sender.

Up arrow
indicates an
ascending sort
for this column.

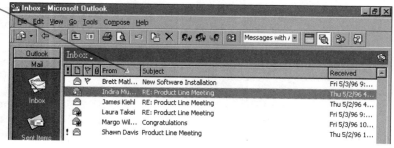

The letters "RE"
and "FW" are
not taken into
account when
you sort.

3   Click the Subject column heading.

The messages are sorted in ascending order by subject.

4   Click the Subject column heading again.

The messages are sorted in descending order by subject.

 TIP   You can modify the way usernames are listed in your personal address book. For example, if the From column is sorted based on first names, you can change the properties to sort by last names. To do this, on the Tools menu, click Services, select Personal Address Book, click Properties, and then click the Last Name option button. However, you cannot modify the way usernames appear in the global address list; the sort order is set by your system administrator.

Grouping Messages

For a demon-
stration of how
to group mes-
sages, double-
click the Cam-
corder Files On
The Internet
shortcut on your
Desktop or con-
nect to the
Internet address
listed on p. xxx.

You can sort messages, one category at a time, by clicking the different column headings in the Information viewer. However, if you want to sort messages using more than one category at a time, you can group them into well-defined categories. You can group messages by up to five criteria at once. For example, you can group messages to sort by sender, then by subject, and then by date. By grouping messages, you set the level of detail that you want to use to display your messages in any folder.

Grouped messages are organized in an outline form using the grouping categories you select, with the first sort farthest to the left in the Information viewer. A plus sign (+) indicates that a category is collapsed and any information below it is hidden. A minus sign (-) indicates that the category is expanded. If there are any unread messages in a category, the number of unread messages appears in parentheses next to the category heading.

Group messages

As the Operations Coordinator, you want to organize your Inbox so that you can easily find information about your different projects. In this exercise, you group your messages.

Group By Box

You can also group messages by clicking Group By on the View menu, and then selecting the grouping and sorting criteria you want to apply.

1 On the Standard toolbar, click the Group By Box button.

The Group By box appears below the Folder Banner in the Information viewer. Your screen should look similar to the following illustration.

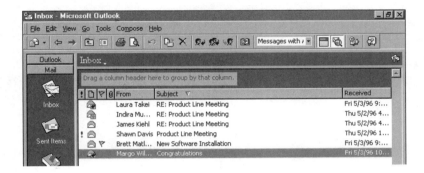

2 Drag the Subject column header into the Group By box.

The messages in your Inbox are grouped by subject in descending sort order. Your screen should look similar to the following illustration.

Down arrow indicates a descending sort.

Collapsed categories

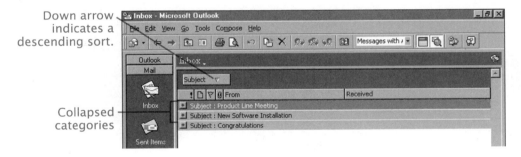

3 Click the plus sign (+) next to the "Subject: Congratulations" category.

The category expands and the message from Margo Wilson appears.

4 Click the minus sign (-) next to the "Subject: Congratulations" category.

The category collapses and the message is hidden.

5 Click the plus sign (+) next to the "Subject: Product Line Meeting" category.

The category expands to show four messages with the subject "Product Line Meeting." The messages are sorted in descending order by received date, based on the default settings. Your screen should look similar to the following illustration.

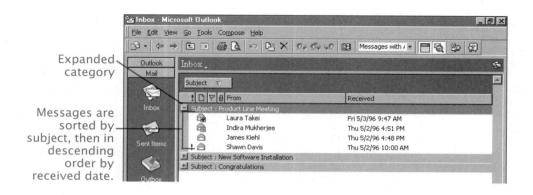

Expanded category

Messages are sorted by subject, then in descending order by received date.

TIP If you hide the Group By box, your messages will still be grouped.

Modify grouping criteria

In this exercise, you change the way the messages are grouped in your Inbox by adding another grouping criterion to the Group By box.

The Importance column heading is identified by an exclamation point (!) on it.

1 Drag the Importance column heading into the Group By box, and place it to the right of the Subject heading.

Your messages are grouped first by subject in descending order, and then by importance in descending order. Your screen should look similar to the following illustration.

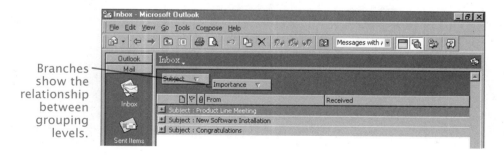

Branches show the relationship between grouping levels.

2 Click the plus sign (+) next to the "Subject: Product Line Meeting" category.

The category expands to show two importance grouping categories, "Importance: High" and "Importance: Normal."

3   Click the plus sign (+) next to the "Importance: High" category.

A Product Line Meeting message from Shawn Davis with high priority appears.

4   Click the plus sign (+) next to the "Importance: Normal" category.

Three messages about the Product Line meeting with normal priority appear. Your screen should look similar to the following illustration.

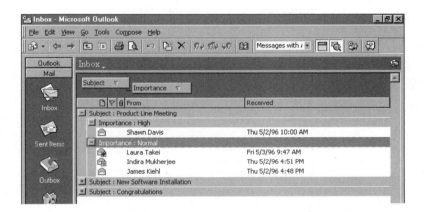

 TIP   You can create a personal view based on the groupings in your Inbox. To do this, choose the groups and sorts you want to apply to your messages, type a new view name in the Current View box on the Standard toolbar, and then press ENTER.

Restore the original view

You can also restore the default view by dragging the group column headings back into the message header.

In this exercise, you cancel the grouping in your Inbox by reapplying the default view, Messages With AutoPreview.

1   On the View menu, point to Current View, and then click Messages With AutoPreview.

A message appears, asking if you want to save or discard the current view settings.

2   Be sure that the Discard The Current View Settings And Reapply The View "Messages With AutoPreview" option button is selected, and then click OK.

The groups are removed, the Group By box is hidden, and the Messages With AutoPreview view is reapplied to your Inbox.

59

TROUBLESHOOTING If you accidentally save changes to a standard view, you can easily reset it. On the View menu, click Define Views. In the Views For Folder box, select the view you want to restore, and then click Reset.

Displaying Specific Files by Using Filters

If you want to display only certain messages in a folder, you can apply a *filter* to it. Any messages that do not match the filter conditions are hidden temporarily. For example, if you want to show only messages from your manager in your Inbox, you can filter the messages by sender. This can be especially useful if you receive many messages in the course of a day, and you need to find individual messages quickly.

When a filter is applied to a folder, the words "Filter Applied" appear on the Folder Banner and on the status bar in the lower-left corner of the screen. If a view includes a filter, it is applied to the folder first, before any other criteria. For example, if messages in a folder are sorted or grouped, and a filter is applied, the messages are filtered first and then sorted or grouped. You can easily remove the filter to show all messages again. Filtering messages is similar to sorting and grouping messages, except that the messages you filter out are hidden from view.

Filter messages

In this exercise, you apply a filter to your Inbox so that only the messages related to the Product Line Meeting are visible.

1 Be sure that the contents of your Inbox appear in the Information viewer.

2 On the View menu, click Filter.

The Filter dialog box appears.

3 In the Search For The Word(s) box, type **meeting**

4 Click the In down arrow and select Subject Field And Message Body.

The filter will search for the word "meeting" anywhere in a message.

5 Click OK.

The filter is applied, and only messages about the Product Line Meeting appear in the Inbox. Your screen should look similar to the following illustration.

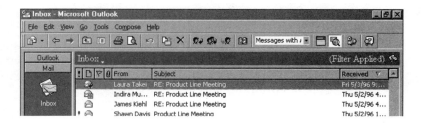

Remove the filter

Now that you have viewed your test messages, you want to remove the filter.

1 On the View menu, click Filter.

The Filter dialog box appears.

2 Click Clear All and then click OK.

The filter is removed and all the messages appear in the Inbox again.

Printing Messages

Any message in any folder can be printed. You can print several messages at once, as well as print more than one copy of a message. When you print multiple messages, you can print one message per page or print them all in a row on the same page(s).

You will learn more about working with message attachments in Lesson 9.

You can also print messages with attachments, such as other documents, if your computer recognizes the file format and if the original application used to create the attachment is installed on your computer.

 IMPORTANT You must have a printer installed to complete the following exercise. If you don't have access to a printer, skip to the "Working with Folders" section.

Print a message

In this exercise, you print the message from Margo Wilson, because you want to have a hard copy of the message to post in your office.

1 Click the Congratulations message from Margo Wilson.

You do not need to open a message in order to print it.

2 On the Standard toolbar, click the Print button.

Print

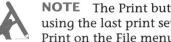 **NOTE** The Print button can be used to quickly print messages using the last print settings. To modify the print settings, click Print on the File menu.

Working with Folders

If you have received numerous messages that deal with a specific topic, such as a particular project, you can place those messages into their own folder. When you are finished with the project, you can easily delete the folder to streamline your work environment.

You can also display the folder list by clicking the Show/Hide Folder List button on the Standard toolbar.

You can create your own personal folders in Outlook, and then move or copy messages into them. You can also create a subfolder within a folder, such as your Inbox, to further organize your messages. All of your personal folders are shown in the Folder List. You can click the plus sign (+) next to a top-level folder to display subfolders.

You can easily delete any folders that you create. However, when you delete an entire folder, you also delete all the subfolders and items it contains. Just as with messages, if you accidentally delete a folder, you can recover the folder and its contents from the Deleted Items folder before you log off from Outlook. Built-in folders, such as the Inbox folder and Sent Items folder, cannot be deleted.

Create a folder

In this exercise, you create a subfolder in your Inbox folder to store messages concerning the upcoming Product Line meeting.

1 Be sure that the contents of your Inbox appear in the Information viewer.

You can also point to Folder, and then click Create Subfolder.

2 On the File menu, point to New, and then click Folder.

The Create New Folder dialog box appears.

3 In the Name box, type **Product Line**

This is the name for your new folder.

4 Click in the Description box, and then type **Messages regarding the Margo Tea Company product line**

5 Be sure that the Create A Shortcut To This Folder In The Outlook Bar check box is selected, and then click OK.

The Product Line subfolder is created and a shortcut icon to the subfolder appears in the Mail group on the Outlook Bar.

6 Scroll down to see the Product Line shortcut icon in the Mail group.

Your screen should look similar to the following illustration.

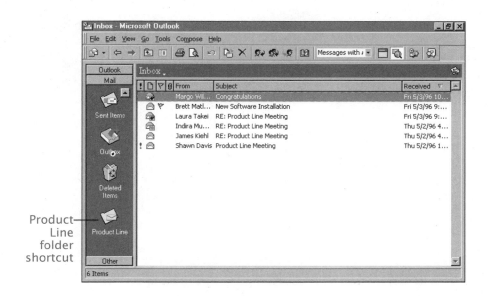

Product— Line folder shortcut

View the Folder List

In this exercise, you display the Folder List to see the relationship between the new subfolder and your other Outlook folders.

1 On the Folder Banner, click the word "Inbox."

The Folder Banner List appears.

Minus sign indicates that subfolders appear.

Plus sign indicates collapsed folder with subfolders that do not appear.

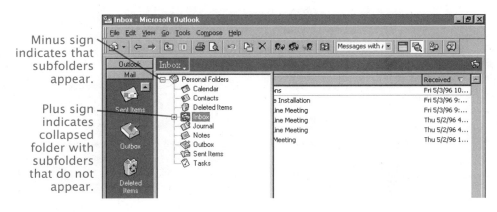

2 Click the plus sign (+) next to the Inbox folder.

The Product Line subfolder appears. Your screen should look similar to the following illustration.

New— subfolder

3   Click the word "Inbox" again on the Folder Banner.

The Folder List closes.

Move a group of messages to a folder

Now that you have a folder for storing messages related to the Margo Tea Company's product line, you can move messages into it. In this exercise, you sort messages by subject, and then move the appropriate messages to the Product Line subfolder you created.

1   Be sure that the contents of your Inbox appear in the Information viewer, and then click the Subject column heading.

The messages are sorted in ascending order by subject.

2   Drag the "RE: Product Line Meeting" message from Laura Takei onto the Product Line shortcut icon on the Outlook Bar.

The message is moved to the Product Line folder.

Hold down SHIFT to select multiple consecutive messages; hold down CTRL to select multiple non-consecutive messages.

3   Repeat step 2 to drag the other messages about the Product Line Meeting into the Product Line folder.

4   On the Outlook Bar, click the Product Line shortcut icon.

All messages regarding the upcoming Product Line meeting are now located in one folder.

TIP   You can have incoming messages with a particular subject or sender moved to a specific folder automatically, if you are using Outlook with a Microsoft Exchange Server. To do this, on the Tools menu, click Inbox Assistant, and then click Add Rule. Select options in the dialog box to determine when you want to apply the rule, what message conditions you want to be used, what you want to happen to the message, and any exceptions to the rule. You will learn more about automating message handling in Lesson 12, "Working Remotely."

Deleting Messages

When you have finished reading and taking actions, such as replying to or forwarding messages, it is a good idea to decide whether you want to save or delete your messages. If you save all the messages that you receive, they will require a lot of storage space, and they will be harder to organize. If you no longer need a message, you should delete it.

Because deleted messages are moved to the Deleted Items folder temporarily, if you change your mind about deleting a message, you can still retrieve it. By default, messages will remain in the Deleted Items folder until you choose to delete them permanently or empty the entire folder.

Delete a message

In this exercise, you delete messages that you no longer need from your Inbox.

1   On the Outlook Bar, click the Inbox icon.

2   Click the Congratulations message from Margo Wilson.

    You do not need to open a message to delete it.

Delete

3   On the Standard toolbar, click the Delete button.

    The message is moved from the Inbox folder to the Deleted Items folder.

Delete a folder

Now that the product line meeting has taken place, and all the issues have been addressed, you don't need to keep the messages relating to it anymore. In this exercise, you delete the Product Line subfolder from your Inbox.

Folder List

1   On the Standard toolbar, click the Folder List button.

    The Folder List appears to the left of the Information viewer. Your screen should look similar to the following illustration.

Drag this border to see more or less of the Folder List.

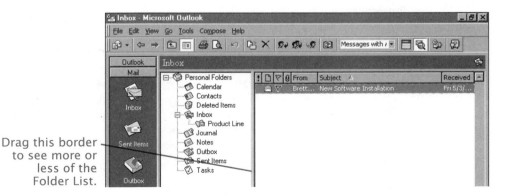

2   In the Folder List, click the Product Line subfolder.

3   On the Standard toolbar, click the Delete button.

The Product Line folder and its contents are placed in the Deleted Items folder.

4   Click the plus sign (+) next to the Deleted Items folder.

The folder expands to show the deleted Product Line folder within the Deleted Items folder.

5   On the Outlook Bar, use the right mouse button to click the Product Line shortcut icon.

A shortcut menu appears.

6   Click Remove From Outlook Bar.

A message appears, asking you to confirm the deletion.

7   Click Yes.

The folder shortcut is removed from the Outlook Bar.

8   Click the Folder List button again to hide the folder list.

Folder List

Empty the Deleted Items folder

In this exercise, you delete the contents of the Deleted Items folder.

1   On the Outlook Bar, click the Deleted Items icon.

The items that you deleted earlier appear in the Deleted Items folder.

2   On the Outlook Bar, use the right mouse button to click the Deleted Items icon.

A shortcut menu appears.

You can also click Empty "Deleted Items" Folder on the Tools menu.

3   Click Empty "Deleted Items" Folder.

A message appears, asking you to confirm the deletion of all items and subfolders.

4   Click Yes.

The contents of the Deleted Items folder are permanently deleted.

 TIP   You can set the Deleted Items folder to empty automatically each time you exit from Outlook. On the Tools menu, click Options. On the General tab, select the Empty The Deleted Items Folder Upon Exiting check box, and then click OK.

Conducting a Vote with a Message

Suppose you want to conduct a quick, informational survey of your co-workers. For example, you want to know what everyone thinks about adopting a new company recycling program. You could walk around the office asking everyone's opinion of the program, record their answers, and add up the results, but this would be fairly time-consuming. With Outlook, you can conduct a vote using an e-mail message. Recipients simply click a button to indicate a response, and the results are tabulated for you in the copy of the original message located in your Sent Items folder.

In the following exercises, you ask several co-workers to participate in a community fund-raiser, and then use the voting options in Outlook to collect their responses.

IMPORTANT Because this section requires you to collect voting results, you'll need to recruit some help from at least two other people on your network who are willing to cooperate by reading and responding to your message. If your computer is only connected to the practice workgroup postoffice, use names from the Postoffice Address List to address your message.

Create a new message

In this exercise, you create a message and address it to several co-workers.

1   On the Outlook Bar, click the Inbox icon.

New Mail Message

2   On the Standard toolbar, click the New Mail Message button.

A blank Mail Form appears.

3   Click the To button.

4   Click the Show Names From The down arrow, and then select Global Address List.

The names of people in your organization's global address list appear.

You can hold down CTRL to select multiple non-consecutive names.

5   Select the names of the people helping you with this exercise, click To, and then click OK.

6   In the Subject box, type **Walk For Kids**

7   In the message area, type **I'm looking for volunteers to join me in this year's 10-K walk to benefit local schools. Would you like to be a member of the Margo Tea Company corporate team?**

Add voting buttons to your message

In this exercise, you include voting buttons in your message so that recipients can respond easily.

1 Click the Options tab.

2 In the General Options area, select the Use Voting Buttons check box.

Sample button text appears in the list box to the right.

3 Click the button text down arrow to display the different text options.

4 Click the "Yes; No; Maybe" option button.

A Yes button, a No button, and a Maybe button will appear on the message in the recipients' mailboxes.

5 Be sure that the Save Sent Message To check box is selected, and that Sent Items appears in the Save Sent Message To box.

The survey responses will be tracked on your copy of the original message located in your Sent Items folder.

6 Click the Send button.

The message with voting buttons is sent to your co-workers.

IMPORTANT To complete the next exercise, be sure that the recipients respond to the message by opening it in their respective Inboxes, and clicking Yes, No, or Maybe. The recipients are then prompted to send their responses back to you. A note is added to each recipient's message in his or her mailbox. If you addressed your message to practice workgroup postoffice names, skip this exercise.

Track survey results

When you send out a voting message, the recipients' responses are delivered to your mailbox and their answers, such as "Yes", "No", or "Maybe", appear in the Subject column so that you can assess the responses at a glance. However, if you are tracking a large number of responses, you can also check your copy of the original message in the Sent Items folder. All voting responses are recorded in a single place. In this exercise, you review the responses to your survey in your Inbox folder and in your Sent Items folder.

1 On the Tools menu, click Check For New Mail.

This ensures that all responses have been delivered to your Inbox. Your screen should look similar to the following illustration.

The names and responses on your screen will be different from the names in this illustration.

Responses appear in the Subject column.

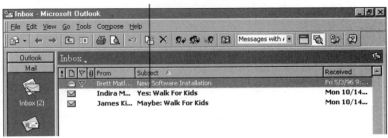

2 Open and close each response.

You must open voting messages to record their results on the Tracking tab on the original message.

3 On the Outlook Bar, click the Sent Items icon.

The contents of the Sent Items folder appear. Your screen should look similar to the following illustration.

Icon indicates that information has been added to the Tracking tab on the message.

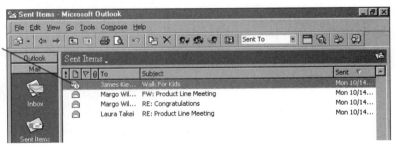

4 Double-click the "Walk For Kids" message.

5 Click the Tracking tab.

The reply totals appear in the comment area, and the message status for each recipient is displayed. Your message should look similar to the following illustration.

Individual responses

Reply Totals

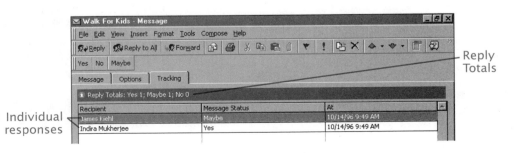

6 Click the Close button on the "Walk For Kids" message.

Finish the lesson

You can also click the Delete button.

1 Select the practice messages you used in this lesson in your Inbox folder, Sent Items folder, and Deleted Items folder, and then press DELETE.

2 To continue to the next lesson, on the Outlook Bar, click the Contacts shortcut icon in the Outlook group.

3 If you are finished using Outlook for now, on the File menu, click Exit And Log Off.

Lesson Summary

To	Do this	Button
Open a message	Double-click the message.	
Browse through multiple messages	Open a message, and then, click the Next Item button or the Previous Item button on the Standard toolbar.	
Flag a message	Open the message. On the Standard toolbar, click the Message Flag button. Type your message flag text. Select a due date, if necessary, and then click OK.	
Flag a message as completed	Open the message. On the Standard toolbar, click the Message Flag button. Select the Completed check box, click OK, and then click Yes.	
Reply to a message	Click or open the message. On the Standard toolbar, click the Reply button.	
Reply to all recipients	Click or open the message. On the Standard toolbar, click the Reply To All button.	
Forward a message	Click or open the message. On the Standard toolbar, click the Forward button.	
Check names	Type a recipient name. On the Standard toolbar, click the Check Names button.	

To	Do this	Button
Sort messages in a folder	In the Information viewer, click the column heading for a category.	
Group messages in a folder	On the Standard toolbar, click the Group By Box button. Drag the column headings you want to group by into the Group By box.	
Reset the current view	In the Current View box on the Standard toolbar, select the name of the view you want to apply. Discard the current view settings.	
Print messages	Click the message. On the Standard toolbar, click the Print button.	
Create a new folder	Select the location for your folder. On the File menu, point to New, and then click Folder. Type a name and description for the new folder, and then click OK.	
Delete a message	Select the message you want to delete. On the Standard toolbar, click the Delete button.	
Conduct a vote with a message	Create a new message. On the Options tab, select the Use Voting Buttons check box. Select or enter text for the buttons, select a location where the results can be tabulated, and then send the message.	

For online information about	On the Help menu, click Contents And Index, click the Index tab, and then type
Viewing items in your Inbox	**Opening, mail**
Working with incoming messages	**Organizing**
Replying to messages	**Replying to mail**
Forwarding messages	**Forwarding, mail**

For online information about	On the Help menu, click Contents And Index, click the Index tab, and then type
Grouping messages	Groups, creating
Printing messages	Printing
Sorting messages	Sorting
Flagging messages	Flagging mail messages
Voting using messages	Voting in mail messages

Creating a Contact List

Estimated time
25 min.

In this lesson you will learn how to:

■ Add names and information to the Contacts folder.

■ Organize and display your contact list.

■ Communicate with your contacts using e-mail.

To communicate efficiently with their business associates, many people keep track of important phone and fax numbers, addresses, and other relevant information in an address book or a business card holder. With Outlook, you can create and maintain a directory of professional colleagues and personal friends in a *contact list*, which is stored in the Contacts folder. The contact list is integrated with the other areas of Outlook so that you can easily access it any time you need information about your contacts. For example, in addition to looking up names and addresses in the contact list, you can check e-mail addresses against it or merge contact addresses with a Microsoft Word file to create a form letter.

In the Contacts folder, basic information about each contact—name, mailing address, telephone numbers, and e-mail address—appears in *address cards* in the Address Cards view by default. The address cards are arranged in alphabetical order to help you easily locate information on any contact. You can move quickly to the address cards for a particular letter of the alphabet by clicking the appropriate letter tab. You will learn more about changing Contacts folder views later in this lesson.

Start the lesson

1 Start Outlook using the Shawn Davis profile.

The Information viewer window appears, and the Inbox folder is open.

2 On the Outlook Bar, click the Contacts icon in the Outlook group.

The contents of the Contacts folder appear in the Information viewer. By default, a sample contact based on your software registration name has been created. Your screen should look similar to the following illustration.

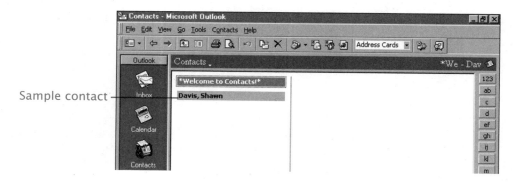

Sample contact

Set up the Contacts folder for this lesson

You will learn more about importing and exporting files in Lesson 10.

To better demonstrate the properties of the Contacts folder, it's best to have more than one or two items in the contact list. In this exercise, you import a contact list from the SBS Outlook Practice disk so that you can work with multiple contacts without having to enter all of them manually.

For a demonstration of how to import a contact list, double-click the Camcorder Files On The Internet shortcut on your Desktop or connect to the Internet address listed on p. xxx.

1 On the File menu, click Import And Export.

The Import/Export Wizard starts.

2 Be sure that Import From Schedule+ Or Another Application Or File is selected, and then click Next.

The file type options appear.

3 Select Comma Separated Values (Windows), and then click Next.

The file location and duplication options appear.

4 Click Browse.

The Browse dialog box appears.

5 Click the Look In down arrow, and then select drive C.

6   Double-click the Outlook SBS Practice folder, and then double-click the Lesson 4 folder.

The contents of the Lesson 4 folder appear.

7   Be sure that the Contacts file is selected, and then click OK.

8   In the Options area, click the Do Not Import Duplicate Items option button, and then click Next.

The destination options appear.

9   Be sure that the Contacts folder is selected, and then click Next.

10   Click Finish.

The file is imported from the practice disk into your contact list. Your screen should look similar to the following illustration.

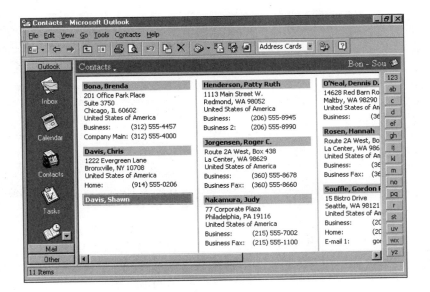

Creating a Contact List

It's very easy to enter a new contact in Outlook; you simply type the person's full name in a single box on the contact form. The full name is then divided automatically: by title, such as Mr. or Ms.; first, middle, and last names; and suffix, such as Ph.D., if any. These parts of a name can be used to sort and filter names. You can also choose how a contact appears in your contact list. By default, if you typed in "Ms. Claudia J. Daheim, Ph.D.," the entry would appear in your contact list as "Daheim, Claudia J." However, you can display the contact by full name, including any titles and suffixes, or by company, if you prefer.

In addition to entering contact names in a single box, you can also enter addresses that are then divided by column into street, city, state, postal code, and country sections. These sections can be used to help you organize your contacts, just as the parts of full names can.

As Operations Coordinator for the Margo Tea Company, you not only need to communicate with your fellow employees, but also with various outside contacts, such as Margo Tea Company clients, suppliers, and advertising agency. In this lesson, you will add some of these important individuals to your contact list, and then display the information in the ways that are most useful to you.

Navigate in the contact list

In this exercise, you practice moving around in the Contacts folder and displaying different address cards.

 NOTE The Information viewer displays as many address cards as will fit on the screen. Depending on the number of entries in your contact list, you might see more or fewer address cards than expected on a particular letter tab. For example, if you click the UV tab, but you have no contact entries that start with U or V, the Information viewer displays the surrounding alphabetical entries, such as R through W, and the next address card listed alphabetically is selected, in this case an entry beginning with the letter W.

1 Click the D tab to the right of the address cards.

Contact entries beginning with the letter D appear, and the first contact in that group, "Davis, Chris," is selected.

2 Click the ST tab.

The "Souffle, Gordon R." contact is selected.

3 Click the YZ tab.

There are no contact entries beginning with Y or Z in your contact list. The previous entry listed alphabetically in descending order, "Wing, Gretchen M.," is selected.

4 Click the AB tab.

There are no contact entries beginning with A; the next available entry, "Bona, Brenda," is selected.

 TIP To find a specific contact quickly, on the Tools menu, click Find Items. Type the name or text you want to search for in the Search For The Word(s) box, and then select the field or fields you want to search in the In box. Click Find Now.

Create a contact

In Lesson 2, you added an Internet e-mail address for Debbie Abdul, the Account Executive in charge of promoting the Margo Tea Company's new product line. In this exercise, you create a new contact for Debbie Abdul so that you can also reach her by e-mail or telephone when you need to.

New Contact

The New Mail Message button in Inbox becomes the New Contact button in the Contacts folder.

1 On the Standard toolbar, click the New Contact button.

A blank contact form appears.

2 Maximize the new contact form.

Your screen should look similar to the following illustration.

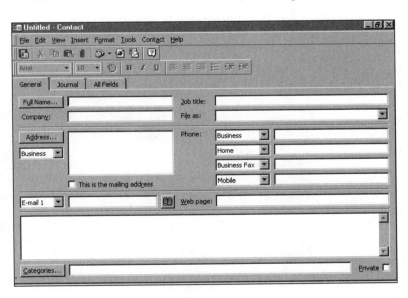

3 In the Full Name box, type **Ms. Debbie Abdul**, and then press TAB.

The insertion point moves to the Job Title box.

4 Type **Account Executive**, press TAB, and then type **Fitch & Mather.**

5 Click Address.

The Check Address dialog box appears.

6 Fill out the address details as follows. After each entry, press TAB.

In this box	Type
Street	511 54th Boulevard SE
City	Bellevue
State	WA

In this box	Type
ZIP/Postal Code	98531
Country	United States of America

7 Click OK.

The address appears in the Address box.

8 In the Business Phone box, type **(206) 555-1218**

9 On the Standard toolbar, click the Save And Close button.

> **NOTE** If the Location Information dialog box appears, fill in the information, and then click OK.

The address card for Debbie Abdul appears in your contact list. Your screen should look similar to the following illustration.

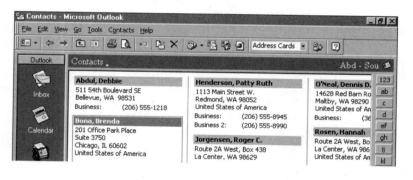

Save And New

> **TIP** If you are entering several contacts in a row, you can click the Save And New button to save a contact and then have a blank contact form appear. If you want to add a new contact from the same company as the selected contact, on the File menu, click Save And New In Company.

Editing Contacts

Contact names, titles, addresses, and phone numbers change frequently in the business world, but with Outlook you can easily keep your contact information up to date. You can edit it in an address card or open the contact entry to edit it in greater detail.

Change the view

In this exercise, you change the current view, Address Cards, to a more detailed view so that you can see at a glance all the pertinent information about each of your contacts.

You can also point to Current View on the View menu to select a different view.

1 On the Standard toolbar, click the Current View down arrow.

A list of available views appears.

2 Select Detailed Address Cards.

The address cards appear in Detailed Address Cards view. The information for each contact in your list is displayed in his or her address card. Your screen should look similar to the following illustration.

The amount of information varies depending on how many fields were completed in the contact form.

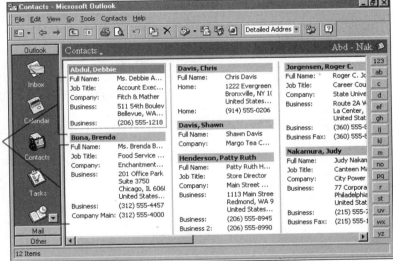

Edit an address card

In this exercise, you make changes to a contact entry by typing information directly into an address card in your contact list.

1 In the Information viewer, click the "Jorgensen, Roger C." contact entry.

The address card is selected.

2 In the address card, click the Job Title box.

A dotted line appears around the Job Title box on the address card and the pointer changes to an insertion point. Your screen should look similar to the following illustration.

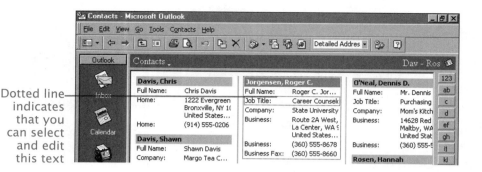

Dotted line
indicates
that you
can select
and edit
this text

*You might need
to scroll to the
right to see
the entire
address card.*

3 Drag to select the text "Career Counselor."

If you double-click the text, you will open the contact entry.

4 Type **Employment Services Director**, and then press ENTER.

The address card is updated.

TROUBLESHOOTING If you are unable to edit fields directly in an address card, click Format View on the View menu. Select the Allow In-cell Editing check box, and then click OK.

Add information to a contact

In this exercise, you open a contact entry and add information using the contact form.

1 Double-click the "O'Neal, Dennis D." address card.

The Dennis D. O'Neal contact form opens. Your screen should look similar to the following illustration.

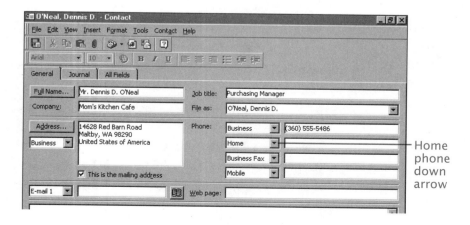

Home
phone
down
arrow

2 Click the Home Phone down arrow.

A list of phone number types appears.

3 Select Company Main.

The text in the list box changes to Company Main.

4 Type **(360) 555-9866**, and then press TAB twice.

The insertion point moves to the Business Fax box.

5 Type **(360) 555-9000**

6 On the Standard toolbar, click the Save And Close button.

The changes to the address card are saved. The Company Main and Business Fax phone numbers appear in Dennis O'Neal's address card. Your screen should look similar to the following illustration.

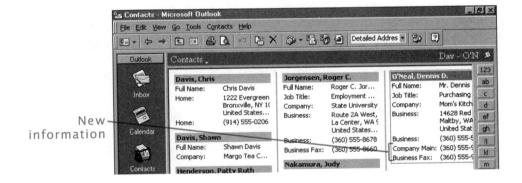

New information

TIP If your computer has the appropriate modem, phone, and phone line configuration, you can use your computer to automatically place telephone calls to your contacts. To do so, in the Contacts folder, select the contact you want to call, and then click the AutoDialer button on the Standard toolbar. In the New Call dialog box, click Start Call; your computer will dial the contact's default phone number automatically. You can also click the drop-down arrow next to the AutoDialer button, to choose from a variety of phone numbers and dialing options. For help configuring your computer, see your system administrator.

AutoDialer

Add an e-mail address for a contact

You can add e-mail addresses from your Address Book to contact entries without leaving the Contacts folder. In Lesson 2, you added an Internet e-mail address for Debbie Abdul to your Address Book. In this exercise, you add that e-mail address to the contact entry for Debbie Abdul.

1 Double-click the "Abdul, Debbie" address card.

You might need to click the AB tab to display the card. The Ms. Debbie Abdul contact form opens. Your screen should look similar to the following illustration.

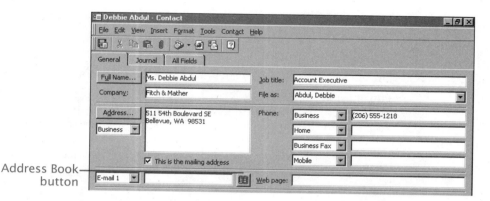

Address Book button

Address Book

2 Click the Address Book button to the right of the E-mail 1 box.

The Select Name dialog box appears.

3 Click the Show Names From The down arrow, and then select Personal Address Book.

The names in your personal address book appear.

> **IMPORTANT** If you have not completed Lesson 2, you can create a new entry for for Debbie Abdul. Click New and type **dabdul@fitch_mather.com** as an Internet address.

4 Click Debbie Abdul, and then click OK.

The underlined name "Debbie Abdul" appears in the E-mail 1 box. The name is underlined because it was checked against the names in the Address Book and is a valid e-mail address. Your screen should look similar to the following illustration.

5 In the E-mail 1 box, use the right mouse button to click Debbie Abdul.

A shortcut menu appears.

6 Click Properties.

The Debbie Abdul Properties dialog box appears. Debbie Abdul's Internet address appears. Your screen should look similar to the following illustration.

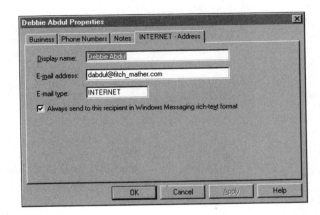

7 Click OK to close the dialog box.

8 On the Standard toolbar, click the Save And Close button.

The contact form closes. The e-mail address for Debbie Abdul is added to her address card.

Adding Personal Information About a Contact

When you fill out a contact entry, you use the fields provided on the General tab to enter the most basic contact information, such as name, job title, and address. But you can also add more personal information to a contact entry, from birthdays and anniversary dates to your own notes about a particular person. You can then decide whether or not you want to display that information in the address card.

Add notes to a contact

In this exercise, you add some notes to the contact entry for Patty Ruth Henderson, the Store Director for the Main Street Market.

1 Double-click the "Henderson, Patty Ruth" address card.

The contact form for Patty Ruth Henderson opens.

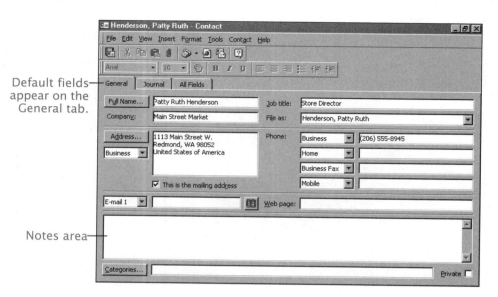

Default fields appear on the General tab.

Notes area

2 In the Notes area at the bottom of the form, type **Unavailable on Mondays**

3 On the Standard toolbar, click the Save And Close button.

The contact form closes. Because the notes area is one of the default fields available on the General tab, your note about Patty Henderson appears at the bottom of her address card. Your screen should look similar to the following illustration.

The Detailed Address Cards view displays the first 256 characters of a note for a contact.

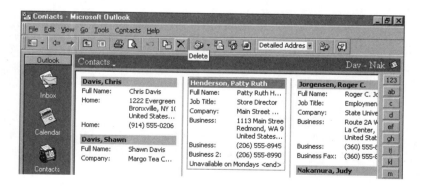

Add a personal date to a contact

In this exercise, you display the personal fields available for a contact and add a birthday.

1 Double-click the "Davis, Chris" address card.

2   Click the All Fields tab.

3   Click the Select From down arrow, scroll down, and then select Personal Fields from the list.

   The available fields for personal information about a contact appear in a table format. Your screen should look similar to the following illustration.

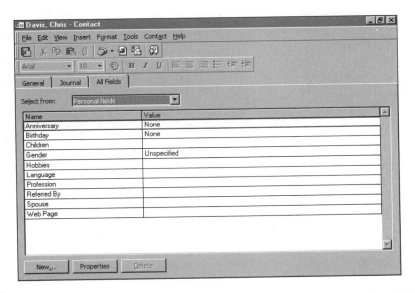

4   In the Birthday field row, double-click the word "None" in the Value column to select it.

5   Type **June 6, 1964**

6   On the Standard toolbar, click the Save And Close button.

   The contact form closes. Because the Birthday field is not one of the default fields on the General tab, Chris Davis' birthday does not appear in the address card.

 NOTE   When you enter a birthday or an anniversary date for a contact, that date is automatically added to your Calendar as an event. You will learn more about using Calendar in Lesson 5, "Organizing Your Schedule with Calendar."

For a demonstration of how to display additional fields in the address cards, double-click the Camcorder Files On The Internet shortcut on your Desktop or connect to the Internet address listed on p. xxx.

Display additional fields in the address cards

Since you're planning on adding more of your contacts' birthday dates, you want to be able to see them when you view your address cards. In this exercise, you add the Birthday field to the list of fields displayed.

1 On the View menu, click Show Fields.

The Show Fields dialog box appears.

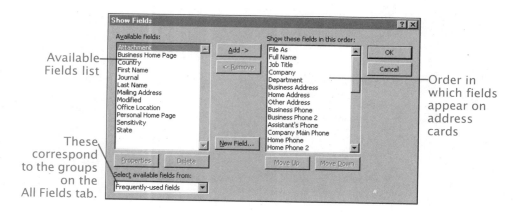

Available Fields list

Order in which fields appear on address cards

These correspond to the groups on the All Fields tab.

2 Click the Select Available Fields From down arrow, and then select Personal Fields.

A list of all the fields available for personal information about a contact appear.

3 In the Available Fields list, click Birthday.

4 Click Add.

The Birthday field is added to the bottom of the Show These Fields In This Order list. Your screen should look similar to the following illustration.

You can rearrange the field order on address cards with the Move Up and the Move Down buttons.

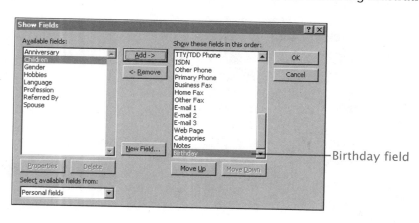

Birthday field

5 Click OK.

The Birthday field now appears in the "Davis, Chris" address card with the other default fields and contains the date "Sat 6/6/1964." Your screen should look similar to the following illustration.

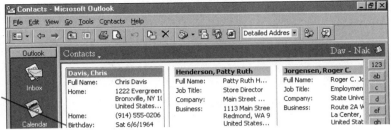

Birthday field

> **NOTE** If no information has been entered for a field, the field does not appear on the address card. Therefore, the Birthday field only appears in the Chris Davis address card since this is the only contact for which you have entered a birthday.

Organizing Contacts

Just as you can sort and organize your e-mail messages in a way that best suits your needs, you can also customize the way your contact information is arranged. For example, you can choose to only display certain information about your contacts, or you can file contacts by the company name instead of the individual's name if there are several people at a single company that you need to communicate with frequently.

In the previous exercise, you added the Birthday field to the default fields displayed on the address cards in Detailed Address Cards view. This change is only temporary; if you change views in the Contacts folder, the Birthday field will no longer appear, even though you selected it as an additional field to be displayed. If you want the Birthday field to always appear on your address cards, you can create a custom view. In the following exercises, you will experiment with applying, modifying, and restoring views, as well as displaying your contact information according to different criteria.

For a demonstration of how to save a custom view, double-click the Camcorder Files On The Internet shortcut on your Desktop or connect to the Internet address listed on p. xxx.

Save a custom view

In this exercise, you save the changes to the Detailed Address Cards view as a custom view so that the Birthday field always appears when you apply the custom view.

1   On the Standard toolbar, click in the Current View box to highlight the text.

2   Type **Personal Dates,** and then press ENTER.

This is the name for the custom view you've created. The Copy View dialog box appears.

3 In the Can Be Used On area, click the "This Folder, Visible Only To Me" option button.

Only you will be able to use the Personal Dates view and only in the Contacts folder.

4 Click OK.

The new custom view named Personal Dates is saved.

 NOTE To see a list of all available views and their descriptions for a particular folder, on the View menu, click Define Views. In the Define Views dialog box, you can apply existing views, modify and copy views, or create new ones.

Switch views

In this exercise, you test the Personal Dates custom view you created by switching to another view, and then switching back.

1 On the Standard toolbar, click the Current View down arrow, and then select Phone List.

Your contact information appears in a list format.

2 Click the Current View down arrow again, and then select Personal Dates.

Your contact information appears in the Personal Dates view and the Birthday field appears on the "Davis, Chris" address card.

 TIP You can organize your contacts by categories, such as Business and Personal, to make specific entries easier to find. In the Contact form, click the Categories button, and then select one or more check boxes from the Master Category List. You can also type your own category names in the Category box on the form. Once you have entered categories for your contacts, you can use those categories to help group your contact list. You will learn more about categories in Lesson 6, "Managing Your Tasks."

You can learn more about grouping items in either Lesson 3 or Lesson 6.

For a demonstration of how to rearrange columns in a table view, double-click the Camcorder Files On The Internet shortcut on your Desktop or connect to the Internet address listed on p. xxx.

Rearrange columns in a table view

In this exercise, you view your contacts in a table format, and then rearrange the available columns because you want your contacts' phone numbers to appear directly adjacent to their names.

1   On the Standard toolbar, click the Current View down arrow, and then select Phone List.

     Your contacts appear in Phone List view.

2   Scroll to the right until the Business Phone column is visible.

3   Drag the Business Phone column heading to the left, and then place it to the right of the Full Name column heading.

     As you drag, red arrows appear above and below the Business Phone column heading, indicating where it will be placed when you release the mouse button. Your screen should look similar to the following illustration.

Release the mouse button when the red arrows are pointing to this line.

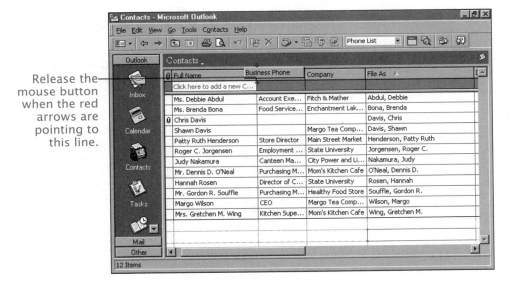

4   Release the mouse button.

     The Business Phone column now appears to the right of the Full Name column.

Restore a standard view

In this exercise, you restore the default settings to the Phone List view.

1   On the Standard toolbar, click the Current View down arrow, and then reselect Phone List.

     A message appears, asking if you want to save or discard the current view settings.

2   Be sure that the Discard The Current View Settings option button is selected.

The columns are restored to their original order.

Delete a custom view

If you decide you no longer need a custom view, you can always delete it. In this exercise, you delete the Personal Dates custom view.

1   On the View menu, click Define Views.

The Define Views For Contacts dialog box appears.

2   In the Views For Folder "Contacts" box, click the Personal Dates view.

3   Click Delete, and then click OK to confirm the deletion.

The Personal Dates custom view is deleted.

4   In the Views For Folder "Contacts" box, be sure that Address Cards is selected.

5   Click Apply View.

The dialog box closes, and your contacts appear in Address Cards view.

NOTE   You cannot delete one of the standard Outlook views, even if you have made changes to it. However, you can undo the changes that you've made to a view. To do so, on the View menu, click Define Views. Select the modified view in the Views For Folder list, and then click Reset.

File an address card differently

In this exercise, you file several address cards under a company name instead of the people's names because you have more than one contact at a specific company and you want to be able to find them quickly in one place.

1   Click the "Jorgensen, Roger C." address card to select it.

2   Hold down CTRL, and then use the right mouse button to click the "Rosen, Hannah" address card.

Both address cards are selected, and a shortcut menu appears.

3   Click Open.

The contact form for each card opens. The last card selected, Hannah Rosen, appears on top and buttons for both address cards appear on the taskbar. Your screen should look similar to the following illustration.

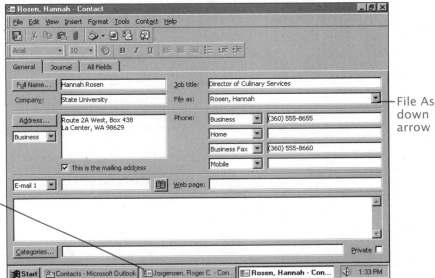

File As down arrow

Roger C. Jorgensen's entry is open underneath Hannah Rosen's form.

You can select multiple non-consecutive items by holding down the CTRL key.

If none of the File As fields suit your needs, you can also type in a new File As name, such as "Mom."

4 Click the File As down arrow on the General tab.

A list of file options appears.

5 Select State University.

6 On the Standard toolbar, click the Save And Close button.

The Hannah Rosen contact form closes, and the Roger C. Jorgensen contact form appears.

7 Click the File As down arrow, and then select State University.

8 Save and close the contact form.

The contact list appears, containing two entries for State University. You might need to click the ST tab, to the right of the address cards, to see both entries.

TIP Instead of changing the way each individual contact is filed, you can sort all contacts by company name, or by any other field on the contact form. On the View menu, click Sort. Click the Sort Items By down arrow, and then select the field you want to sort by.

Printing a Contact List

If you want a copy of your contact list to carry with you, you can print some or all of the contact information for your entire contact list or for specific contacts only. You can also choose from a variety of print formats so that your contact information appears in a way that is most useful for you. For example, you can use the Card Style to print contact information as it appears in Address Cards or Detailed Address Cards view, or you can simply print a list of contacts and their phone numbers using the Phone Directory Style.

Print a copy of your contact list

In this exercise, you choose a print style and print a copy of your entire contact list to keep with you when you are out of the office.

You can also press CTRL+P.

1   On the File menu, click Print.

The Print dialog box appears.

2   In the Print Style area, scroll down and select Phone Directory Style.

You want to print a list containing only contact names and phone numbers.

3   In the Print Range area, be sure that the All Items option button is selected, and then click OK.

The contact list prints.

Communicating with Contacts

If you have entered e-mail addresses for some of your contacts, you can easily send them e-mail messages without leaving the Contacts folder. You can start a new message addressed to a contact either by dragging the contact name onto the Inbox icon on the Outlook bar from any view, or by using a toolbar button. You can also display contact e-mail addresses and fax numbers in the Outlook Address Book.

Send a message to a contact

In this exercise, you create and send a message addressed to Debbie Abdul, the Account Executive managing Margo Tea Company's advertising campaign.

1   Select the "Abdul, Debbie" address card.

2   On the Standard toolbar, click the New Message To Contact button.

A Mail form addressed to Debbie Abdul appears.

New Message To Contact

3   In the Subject box, type **Packaging Designs**

4 In the message area, type **I'd like to incorporate our newest logos into the print ads you're working on. Should I send them to you?**

5 On the Standard toolbar, click the Send button.

The message is sent. Because you are using a fake Internet address for Debbie Abdul, you will receive an Undeliverable message from your system administrator in your Inbox.

View the Outlook Address Book

In this exercise, you open your Address Book and view the Contacts folder in the Outlook Address Book to make sure that all the appropriate contact information appears.

1 On the Outlook Bar, click the Inbox icon.

The contents of the Inbox appear in the Information viewer.

2 On the Standard toolbar, click the Address Book button.

The Address Book dialog box appears.

Address Book

Contacts is a subfolder of the Outlook Address Book

3 Click the Show Names From The down arrow, and then select Contacts.

The contents of the Contacts folder appear. Your screen should look similar to the following illustration.

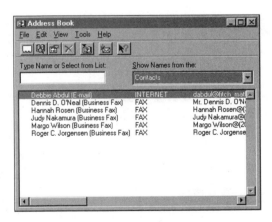

4 Close the Address Book dialog box.

TIP You can use contact information to create letters, envelopes, or mailing labels with the Microsoft Word 97 Mail Merge feature. Use the Outlook Address Book as your data source.

Viewing a Contact's Web Page

If one of your contacts has a Web page on the Internet, you can add the Web page address to the contact entry in your Contacts folder. Adding the Web page address is similar to adding an e-mail address. You can then view the Web page without leaving the Contacts folder by simply clicking a button.

 IMPORTANT You must have Microsoft Internet Explorer installed to view a contact's Web page. If you do not have Internet Explorer on your computer, skip to Finish the Lesson.

Add a Web page address for a contact

In this exercise, you open an existing contact and add a Web page address.

1 On the Outlook bar, click the Contacts icon.
2 Double-click the Debbie Abdul address card.
3 In the Web Page box, type **http://www.microsoft.com/mspress/fnm**
4 On the File menu, click Save.

Do not close the contact entry.

View a contact's Web page

In this exercise, you view Debbie Abdul's home page without leaving the contact entry.

1 Be sure that the Debbie Abdul contact entry is open.
2 On the Standard toolbar, click the Explore Web Page button.

Internet Explorer starts. After a moment, the Fitch & Mather home page appears. Your screen should look similar to the following illustration.

Explore Web Page

Current Web page address for contact

3 Close the Web browser window.

The contact entry for Microsoft Corporation appears.

4 Close the Debbie Abdul contact window.

 TIP You can manage important Web page addresses by adding them to your Favorites folder. In the Microsoft Internet Explorer window, be sure that the Web page address you want to save as a favorite is displayed, and then click the Favorites button. Click Add To Favorites, and then click OK. To use a shortcut to a favorite Web page, on the Outlook Bar, click the Other shortcut bar, and then click the Favorites folder. Double-click a shortcut from your list of shortcuts to start Internet Explorer and open the page.

Finish the lesson

1 To continue to the next lesson, on the Outlook Bar, click the Inbox shortcut icon in the Outlook group.

2 If you are finished using Outlook for now, on the File menu, click Exit And Log Off.

Lesson Summary

To	Do this	Button
Navigate in the Contacts folder	Click a letter tab to the right of the address cards to display entries beginning with that letter.	
Open existing contact information	Double-click the address card for the contact.	
Create a new contact	On the Standard toolbar, click the New Contact button. Enter the contact information in the appropriate fields.	
Change the view	On the Standard toolbar, click the Current View down arrow, and then select the view you want.	
Edit in an address card	In the address card, click the field you want to edit. Select the existing text, and then type the replacement text.	

To	Do this	Button
Add an e-mail address from the Address Book to a contact	Open the contact form. Click the Address Book button next to the E-mail box. Select the contact's name from one of the address lists in the Address Book and click OK.	
Add notes to a contact	Open the contact form. Click in the notes area at the bottom of the contact form, and then type your text.	
Add a personal date to a contact	Open the contact form, and then click the All Fields tab. Click the Select From down arrow, and then choose Personal Fields. Click in the Value column for the field of your choice, and then type the date.	
Display additional fields in the address cards	On the View menu, click Show Fields. Click the Select Available Fields From down arrow, and then select a group of fields. In the Available Fields column, select the field you want to display, and then click Add. Click OK.	
Save a customized view	On the Standard toolbar, click in the Current View box. Type a name for your view, and then press ENTER. Select a usage option for the view, and then click OK.	

To	Do this	Button
Delete a custom view	On the View menu, click Define Views. In the Views For Folder list, select the view you want to delete, and then click Delete.	
File an address card differently	Open the contact entry. Click the File As down arrow, and then select a filing option from the list.	
Send a message to a contact	Select the contact you want to address the message to. On the Standard toolbar, click the New Message To Contact button.	
View a contact's Web page	Open the contact. Be sure that a Web page address appears in the Web Page box, and then click the Explore Web Page button.	

For online information about	On the Help menu, click Contents And Index, click the Index tab, and then type
Creating contacts	**Contacts**
Viewing contact information	**Contacts, views**
Sending e-mail to contacts	**Addresses**
Viewing a contact's Web page	**Web**

Review & Practice

You will review and practice how to:

Estimated time

20 min.

- Create, address, and send a message.
- Move between Outlook folders.
- Reply to and forward messages.
- Sort messages.
- Add a contact to the contact list.

Before you move on to Part 2, which covers maintaining a daily schedule and personal task list, you can practice the skills you learned in Part 1 by working through this Review & Practice section. You will explore different Outlook folders, and create and send a message. You will also read, respond to, and organize the messages in your Inbox. Finally, you will add a new contact to your Contacts folder.

Scenario

As the Margo Tea Company's Operations Coordinator, you organize most events for the corporate office. The quarterly budget meeting is coming up, and you need to begin making the necessary arrangements (such as finding a location and ordering refreshments). You decide to ask several of your colleagues for suggestions. You'll read and organize their responses, and add the name of a suggested caterer to your contact list.

99

Step 1:   Create, Address, and Send a Message

You're looking for a new caterer to provide food for the quarterly budget meeting. You e-mail several of your co-workers to see if they have any recommendations.

1   Create a new message and address it to Laura Takei and Brett Matlock. Send a carbon copy to Margo Wilson.

2   Type **Catering References** as the message subject.

3   Type the following text as the message text:

Could either of you recommend a caterer to provide brunch for the budget meeting? I thought a change would be nice.

4   Format the message text as italic and change the color to purple.

5   Check the spelling, and then send the message.

For more information about	See
Creating messages	Lesson 2
Addressing messages and sending carbon copies	Lesson 2
Formatting text	Lesson 2
Checking spelling	Lesson 2
Sending messages	Lesson 2

Step 2:   Move Between Outlook Folders

You want to check the folders in the Mail group to make sure that your message was sent to all recipients. You also look for their responses in your Inbox.

1   Switch to the Mail folders group.

2   Open the Sent Items folder and make sure your Catering References message was sent. Switch to the Inbox folder.

3   Drag the messages contained in the Review & Practice 1 folder to your Inbox folder. (Hint: For more detailed instructions on setting up your Inbox with practice messages, see the beginning of Lesson 3.)

For more information about	See
Switching folder groups	Lesson 1
Opening folders	Lesson 1

Step 3: *Reply To and Forward Messages*

You read your messages, including the responses to your request about catering references. Then you decide to have pastries delivered from Main Street Market. You respond to the original recipients to inform them of your decision, and then forward Brett Matlock's message to Margo Wilson.

1 Open the message from Laura Takei and read it. Then, browse through all other messages in your Inbox.

2 Reply to the message from Brett Matlock, and send a carbon copy to Laura Takei. In the message area, type **Thanks, Brett. I'll give them a call.** Send the message.

3 Forward Brett Matlock's message to Margo Wilson. In the message area, type **I'm going to e-mail Ms. Stone this afternoon. I'll get you an expense statement as soon as I can.** Send the message.

4 Flag the message from Indira Mukherjee. Select the "Call" message flag. For the due date, display the drop-down calendar, and then select Wednesday of the next week. Close all open messages.

For more information about	See
Browsing through messages	Lesson 3
Replying to messages	Lesson 3
Forwarding messages	Lesson 3
Flagging messages for action	Lesson 3

Step 4: *Sort and Group Messages*

Now that you have read and responded to your messages, you organize them in your Inbox.

1 Sort messages in your Inbox in ascending order by sender.

2 Sort messages in your Inbox by received date in descending order.

3 Group the messages in your Inbox by subject. (Hint: Use a toolbar button to display the Group By box.)

For more information about	See
Sorting messages	Lesson 3
Grouping messages	Lesson 3

Step 5: *Add a Contact to the Contact List*

Now that you have chosen a caterer, you add her name, address and phone number to your contact list so that you can find the information easily.

1   Switch to the Contacts folder. Display the contact list in Detailed Address Cards view.

2   Create and save a new contact entry, using the following data.

Field	Data
Full Name	**Ms. Jo-lynn Stone**
Job Title	**Delivery Manager**
Company	**Main Street Market**
Address	**1113 Main Street W.** **Redmond, WA 98052**
Business Phone	**(206) 555-8600**
E-mail 1	**jolynn@mainstmkt.com**

3   Select the "Stone, Jo-lynn" address card. Edit the Job Title field within the address card, changing her job title to **Delivery Coordinator**

4   Start a new message to Jo-lynn Stone. In the Subject box, type **Catered Brunch**. In the message area, type **I'm interested in ordering a selection of pastries for an upcoming meeting. Could you give me some more information about your services?**

5   Send the message.

For more information about	See
Viewing contacts	Lesson 4
Creating new contacts	Lesson 4
Editing contacts	Lesson 4
Addressing messages to contacts	Lesson 4

Finish the Review & Practice

Follow these steps to delete the practice items you created in this Review & Practice, and then quit Outlook.

1   Select all address cards, and then click Delete.

2   Switch to the Inbox. Reapply the Messages With AutoPreview view to your Inbox and discard the current view settings.

3   Delete all the practice messages you used in this Review & Practice.

4   If you want to continue to the next lesson, on the Outlook Bar, click the Calendar icon.

5   If you are finished using Outlook for now, on the File menu, click Exit And Log Off.

Part 2

Managing Your Time

Organizing Your Schedule Using Calendar

Estimated time
30 min.

In this lesson you will learn how to:

- Create and edit appointments.
- Set recurring appointments.
- Add events to your calendar.
- Print your schedule.

Keeping track of all the appointments you make can be difficult. Is the team meeting on Thursday or Friday? Ten o'clock or two? Many people use an appointment book, a desk calendar, or a daily planner to keep track of their schedules. In Microsoft Outlook, Calendar acts as an electronic appointment book. You can use Calendar to record appointments, set reminders for upcoming appointments and events, and even coordinate meetings electronically with other people.

In Calendar, you can view your appointments for a single day, a week, or a month at a time. You can create a task list to help you monitor your progress on various projects, schedule tasks at specific times, and then cross them off as you complete them.

As the Operations Coordinator for Margo Tea Company, it is vital that you manage your time efficiently. In this lesson, you'll learn how to keep your own schedule up to date in Outlook, and you'll use Calendar to record all of your business and personal appointments. After you have mastered these skills with your own schedule file, you can begin coordinating schedules with other people.

Start the lesson

In this exercise, you start Outlook using the Shawn Davis profile, and then switch to the Calendar folder.

1 Start Outlook using the Shawn Davis profile.

2 On the Outlook Bar, click the Calendar icon.

The contents of the Calendar folder appear in the Information viewer. The current date appears in the Folder Banner.

IMPORTANT When you install Outlook, a sample appointment and a sample task are automatically added to your Calendar on the date the program is installed. These items will be placed on different areas of your Calendar depending on when you install Outlook and create your profile.

Creating and Editing Appointments

When you open your Calendar folder, the Day view of your schedule appears by default. Day, Week, and Month views are available to help you keep track of scheduled appointments. In Day view, the appointment area resembles a lined daily planner. Each day is divided into 30-minute time slots in which you can enter appointments. By default, the workday starts at 8 A.M. and ends at 5 P.M. The time slots outside this workday period appear shaded. In Week and Month views, the appointment areas resemble a calendar grid.

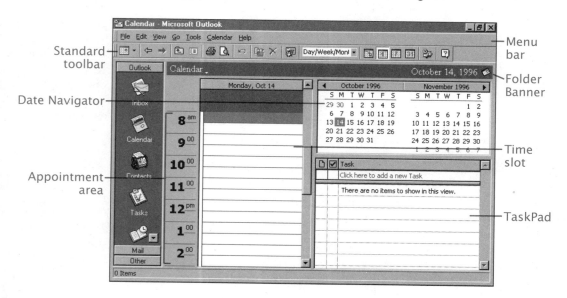

The Date Navigator appears to the right of the appointment areas in Day and Week views. The Date Navigator shows the current calendar month and either the previous or following month, depending on how you move from date to date. You can use the Date Navigator to scroll to different dates so that you can add future appointments or refer to past ones. Bold dates indicate that at least one appointment is scheduled for that date. Below the Date Navigator is the TaskPad, which displays tasks assigned to the current date.

You want to add the upcoming meetings to your schedule. You also want to schedule some personal appointments and make sure that they do not interfere with your work as Operations Coordinator.

Navigating in Calendar

In Day view, the easiest way to change dates is by using the Date Navigator. The months in the Date Navigator appear as small calendars, and you can simply click a date to display that date's appointments. You can also use the scroll bar at the top of the Date Navigator to display different months.

Change the date

Changing the year to 1999 for these exercises prevents confusion with your real appointments.

For the purposes of this lesson, you will change the year to 1999 so that your Calendar will match the illustrations in this book. In this exercise, you practice changing dates using different navigation methods.

1 On the Go menu, click Go To Date.

The Go To Date dialog box appears.

2 Be sure the text in the Date box is selected, and then type **5/14/99**

You can type dates in any style—such as 5-14-99 or May 14, 1999—to change them.

3 Click OK.

The appointment area and the Date Navigator display the date Friday, May 14, 1999.

Date Navigator scroll bar

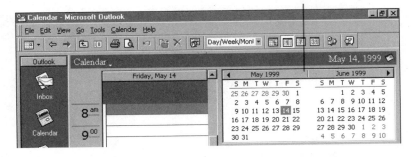

You can also click the name of a month to display a list of months to switch to.

4 On the Date Navigator scroll bar, click the right arrow.

June 1999 and July 1999 appear in the Date Navigator, and June 14 is selected. When you change months, the selected day of the month stays the same.

5 Click the left scroll arrow four times.

February 1999 and March 1999 appear, and March 14 is selected.

6 In the Date Navigator, click February 16.

The date changes to Tuesday, February 16, 1999.

Adding an Appointment to Your Schedule

It's very easy to add appointments to your schedule in Calendar. You can select a block of time in the appointment area, and simply type the appointment details into the time slots. Or, if you want to schedule a more detailed appointment, you can open an appointment form and enter the information. In the following exercises, you will create appointments using two different scheduling methods.

Add an appointment

In this exercise, you add an appointment to your schedule by typing the appointment description directly into the appropriate time slot.

1 In the appointment area, drag the pointer over the time slots from 11:00 A.M. to 12:30 P.M. to select them.

Three time slots are highlighted.

2 Type **Product Line meeting**, and then press ENTER.

The new appointment appears. Your screen should look similar to the following illustration.

Bold date indicates appointment scheduled on this day.

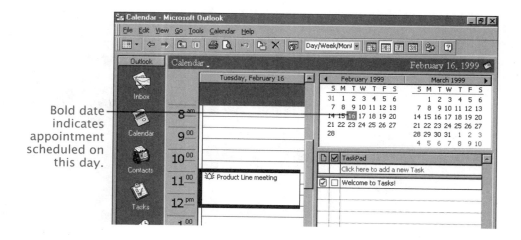

Create a detailed appointment

In this exercise, you use the New Appointment button to add a more detailed appointment to your schedule.

1 In the appointment area, drag to select the 2:30 P.M. to 4:00 P.M. time period.

You are creating an appointment with a 90-minute duration.

New Appointment

2 On the Standard toolbar, click the New Appointment button.

A new appointment form appears. The time period you selected is converted into start and end times on the form. Your screen should look similar to the following illustration.

The New Mail Message button in the Inbox becomes the New Appointment button in Calendar.

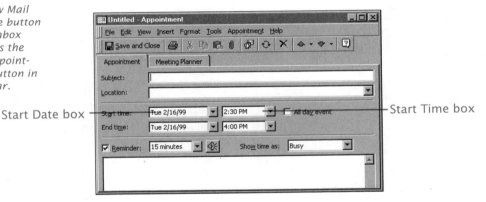

3 In the Subject box, type **Team strategy meeting**, and then press TAB.

The insertion point moves to the Location box.

4 In the Location box, type **Conference Room B**

5 Click the Start Time down arrow.

A list of times in half-hour increments appears.

You can also enter a new time by typing the number in the Start Time box.

6 Select 3:30 P.M.

The new start time for the meeting is entered, and the end time changes from 4:00 to 5:00 to preserve the 90-minute duration of the meeting.

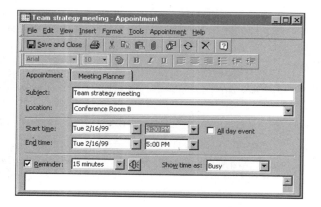

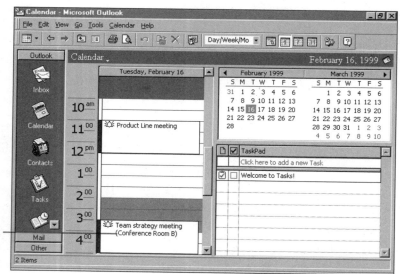

Save and Close

7 On the Standard toolbar, click the Save And Close button.

The appointment is added to your schedule. Your screen should look similar to the following illustration.

Location is indicated in parentheses.

Editing Appointments

You can quickly and easily change an appointment in Calendar. For example, you can move an appointment to a new date or time, or change its duration. You can schedule several similar appointments by copying an appointment to the Clipboard, and then pasting it to another date. You can also set appointments to recur over a long period of time. You can select and edit an appointment directly in the appointment area, or, if you want to make detailed changes to an appointment, you can open the appointment form. You can use the Delete button to cancel an appointment.

Outlook includes an *Autodate* function that makes it even easier to select dates and start and end times for your appointments. The Autodate fields are text-sensitive, which means that instead of typing "12:00 P.M." in the Start Time box, you can type "noon," and Calendar will recognize and insert the appropriate time. In the same way, you can type text such as "next Wednesday" to insert the appropriate date.

IMPORTANT When you enter Autodate text in date fields, the selected dates correspond to the date and time set on your computer, not necessarily the date you are working on in Calendar. For example, although you are scheduling appointments for 1999 in this lesson, if you typed "this Tuesday" as a start date in the appointment form, the start date would be entered as Tuesday of the current week on your system.

As Operations Coordinator for Margo Tea Company, you have many different responsibilities. You need to make frequent changes to your schedule to accommodate the needs of both your co-workers and your outside clients.

Change an appointment

In this exercise, you make changes to an appointment in the appointment area.

1   Click the "Team strategy meeting" to activate it.

    Blue top and bottom borders appear on an active appointment and the mouse pointer changes to an insertion point.

2   Double-click to select the word "Team."

    The text is highlighted.

3   Type **Campaign**, and then press ENTER.

    The text is replaced as you type.

4   Point to the top border of the "Campaign strategy meeting" appointment.

    The pointer changes to a two-headed arrow.

5   Drag the top border up one time slot to 3:00 P.M.

    The appointment start time changes to 3:00 P.M. The duration is now two hours.

6   Point to the bottom border, and then drag the bottom border up two time slots to 4:00 P.M., and then press ENTER.

    The appointment duration changes to one hour. Your screen should look similar to the following illustration.

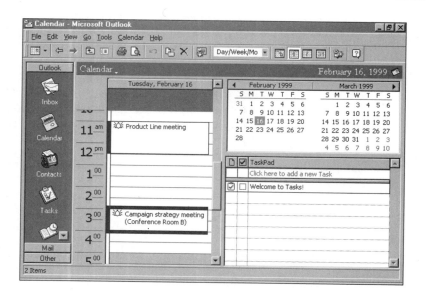

Add information to an appointment

In this exercise, you modify an appointment by opening the appointment form.

1   Double-click the "Product Line meeting" appointment to open it.

The "Product Line meeting" appointment entry form appears.

2   Click in the Location box, and then type **Margo's Office**

3   In the Start Time box, select the current text, "11:00 A.M."

4   Type **noon**, and then press ENTER.

The time is entered as 12:00 P.M. The end time changes to 1:30 P.M.

5   Click the End Time down arrow.

A list of end times and durations appears.

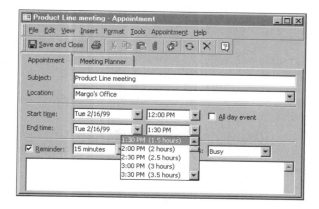

6 Scroll up, and then select "1:00 P.M. (1 Hour)."

The end time and duration are changed.

7 On the Standard toolbar, click the Save And Close button.

The start and end times of the "Product Line meeting" appointment change, and a location is added to the appointment.

Move an appointment

In this exercise, you use the Date Navigator to quickly move an appointment to a different day.

1 Position the pointer over the left border of the "Campaign strategy meeting" appointment.

The pointer changes to a four-headed arrow.

2 Drag the appointment onto February 12 in the Date Navigator.

The appointment is moved to Friday, February 12, 1999, and that date appears in the appointment area. The start time, 3:00 P.M., and the end time, 4:00 P.M., do not change. Your screen should look similar to the following illustration.

Reminder symbol ———

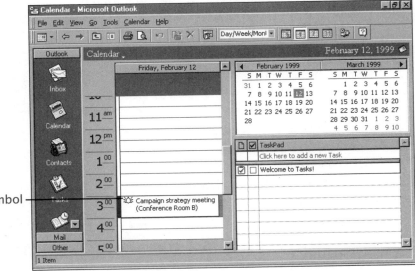

Setting Reminders

You can set a reminder for any appointment. When you have set a reminder, a message appears to notify you of the upcoming appointment. You can set the timing on a reminder to control how far in advance of the appointment it appears. The following illustration shows a sample reminder message.

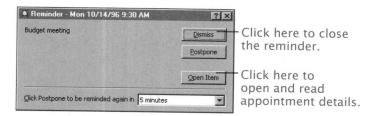

Click here to close the reminder.

Click here to open and read appointment details.

A reminder is automatically set for each new appointment you create; the default timing on a reminder is 15 minutes. When an appointment has a reminder, a reminder symbol appears with the appointment description in the appointment area.

Change a reminder

In this exercise, you change the timing for the reminder for the "Product Line meeting" so that you will get the reminder early and have enough time to set up your presentation materials.

1   In the Date Navigator, click February 16.

The date changes to Tuesday, February 16, 1999. The "Product Line meeting" appointment appears.

2   Double-click the "Product Line meeting" appointment.

The appointment form opens.

You can also type a number into the Reminder box to set the timing.

3   Be sure that the Reminder check box is selected, and then click the Reminder down arrow.

A list of timing increments appears.

4   Select 30 minutes.

5   On the Standard toolbar, click the Save And Close button.

The reminder is set for 30 minutes before the appointment.

NOTE   The time setting for a reminder does not appear anywhere in the appointment area. To check a time setting, you need to open the appointment form.

Setting Tentative Appointments

You can use Calendar in Outlook to view your co-workers' schedules, and to co-ordinate meetings and appointments with them. You can set or change user access *permissions* to your schedule at any time, which gives you control over who has access to your schedule. The different access permissions control the ability of your co-workers to view or change part of your schedule. You will learn more about setting access permissions and using Outlook over a network in Lesson 7, "Coordinating Schedules with Other Users."

Suppose you want to remind yourself of an appointment, but you're not really sure that you'll be able to keep it. For example, a friend has invited you to lunch, but you think you might need to stay in the office to attend a project meeting. You can schedule *tentative* appointments that are listed in your schedule, but do not appear when others use your Calendar. You can finalize tentative appointments in your schedule or change them to another time if a colleague schedules a conflicting priority appointment. Tentative appointments appear in gray in your schedule.

Make an appointment tentative

In this exercise, you make the "Campaign strategy meeting" appointment tentative because you are not sure that the invitees outside of your company will be able to attend.

1   In the Date Navigator, click February 12.

The date changes to Friday, February 12, 1999. The "Campaign strategy meeting" appointment appears.

2   Double-click the "Campaign strategy meeting" appointment.

The appointment form opens.

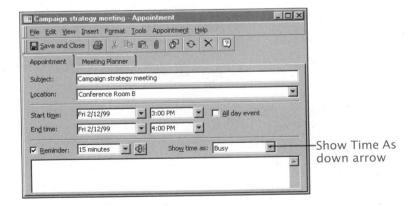

3   Click the Show Time As down arrow, and then select Tentative.

The appointment will appear as tentative in your schedule.

4 On the Standard toolbar, click the Save And Close button.

The "Campaign strategy meeting" appointment appears in gray in your schedule. Your screen should look similar to the following illustration.

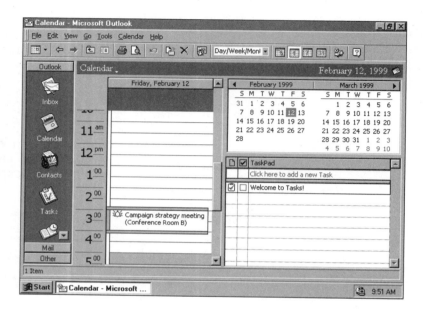

Making Appointments Private

You can coordinate schedules with others by allowing them access to your Calendar, but still protect your own confidential information. You can designate your personal appointments as *private* so that they cannot be read by other Outlook users. A private appointment appears as a busy time in the scheduled time slots when others view your schedule, but the details of the appointment are not visible.

Schedule a private appointment

In this exercise, you schedule a dentist appointment. Because this appointment is personal in nature, you want to designate it as private.

1 Be sure that Friday, February 12, 1999, appears in the Information viewer.

2 Drag to select the 10:30 A.M. to 11:30 A.M. time period.

3 Type **Dentist**, and then press ENTER.

The appointment is added to your schedule.

4 Use the right mouse button to click the "Dentist" appointment.

A shortcut menu appears.

5 Click Private.

A key symbol appears, indicating that the appointment is private. Your screen should look similar to the following illustration.

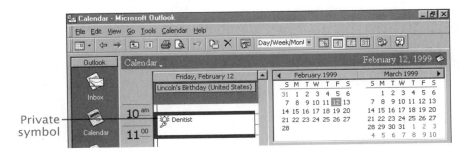

Private symbol

Scheduling Time Out of the Office

In addition to recording your busy times, you can mark specific time periods or appointments to indicate that you are actually out of the office at that time. When other users view your schedule, they will know that you are definitely unavailable during those periods. Out of office times appear in dark blue in your schedule.

Mark an appointment as out of office

In this exercise, you set the "Dentist" appointment to show that you are out of the office so that any co-workers who view your schedule know that you are not available at that time.

1 Double-click the "Dentist" appointment.

The appointment form opens.

2 Click the Show Time As down arrow.

A list of display options appears.

3 Select Out Of Office.

4 On the Standard toolbar, click the Save And Close button.

The appointment appears in your schedule with a dark blue border, indicating that you will be out of the office at this time.

117

Setting Recurring Appointments

As your team continues its work on developing and marketing Margo Tea Company's new product, you want to schedule a weekly meeting to monitor everyone's progress and make sure that each team member is kept up to date on the project's status. You can schedule recurring appointments in Calendar so that you do not have to enter the meeting information each week.

Set a recurring appointment

In this exercise, you schedule a recurring bi-weekly appointment with the product line team.

1 In the Date Navigator, click February 15.

2 Select the 9:00 A.M. to 10:00 A.M. time period.

3 Type **Team update**, and then press ENTER.

The appointment is added to your schedule.

4 Double-click the "Team update" appointment.

The appointment form opens.

Recurrence

5 On the Standard toolbar, click the Recurrence button.

The Appointment Recurrence dialog box appears.

Set frequency of recurrence here.

Set recurrence dates here.

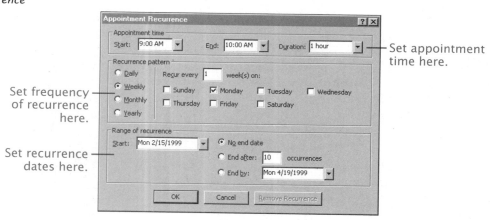

Set appointment time here.

6 In the Recurrence Pattern area, be sure that the Weekly option button is selected and that 1 is selected in the text box between Recur Every and Week(s) On.

7 In the Recurrence Pattern area, be sure that the Monday check box is selected, and then select the Wednesday check box.

The "Team update" appointment is set to recur twice a week, on Monday and Wednesday mornings from 9:00 A.M. to 10:00 A.M.

8 In the Range Of Recurrence area, click the End By option button.

You use this option to set a specific end date for the recurrence.

9 In the End By box, select the current text, and then type **6/16/99**

The appointment will recur until Wednesday, June 16, 1999.

10 Click OK.

The recurrence information appears on the Appointment tab of the "Team update" appointment form. Your screen should look similar to the following illustration.

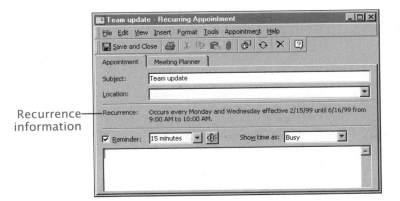

Recurrence information

11 On the Standard toolbar, click the Save And Close button.

The appointment form closes. A recurring symbol appears with the appointment description in the appointment area. Your screen should look similar to the following illustration.

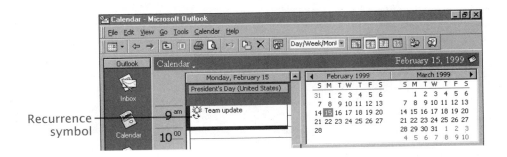

Recurrence symbol

NOTE You can also change an existing appointment to a recurring appointment. Simply open the appointment form, and then click the Recurrence button on the Standard toolbar.

Cancel an appointment

In this exercise, you cancel one of the recurring "Team update" appointments because you will be out of the office at a seminar all day.

1   In the Date Navigator, click February 17.

    The date changes to Wednesday, February 17, 1999.

2   Click the "Team update" appointment to activate it.

3   On the Standard toolbar, click the Delete button.

    A message appears, asking if you want to delete all instances of the recurring appointment or just one.

4   Be sure that the Delete This One option button is selected, and then click OK.

    Only the "Team update" appointment on February 17 is canceled.

Delete

IMPORTANT   You cannot delete an appointment by pressing DELETE on your keyboard. You must first select the appointment, and then use the Delete button on the Standard toolbar.

Adding Events

You can add an *event*, such as a seminar or a vacation, to your schedule by using the Event command or by simply typing the event information into the *banner* that appears at the top of the appointment area. When you add an event, a message appears in your schedule on the date of the event, but the event is not scheduled for a particular time.

You can also insert annual events, such as holidays or birthdays, in your schedule. An annual event will recur automatically in your Calendar each year.

Add an event

In the previous exercise, you canceled one of your appointments with the product line team because you plan to be out of the office that day. In this exercise, you add a two-day seminar to your schedule as an event.

1   Be sure that Wednesday, February 17, 1999, appears in the Information viewer.

2   On the Calendar menu, click New Event.

    A blank event entry form appears.

3   In the Subject box, type **Personal Empowerment Seminar**, and then press TAB.

4   In the Location box, type **Convention Center**

5   Be sure that Wed 2/17/99 appears in the Start Time box and that the All Day Event check box is selected.

6   Click the End Time down arrow.

A calendar appears.

7   Select February 18.

The End Time is set for Thu 2/18/96.

8   Clear the Reminder check box.

Since you will be out of the office to attend the seminar, you won't be there to receive a reminder.

9   On the Standard toolbar, click the Save And Close button.

The event appears in the banner at the top of the appointment area. Your screen should look similar to the following illustration.

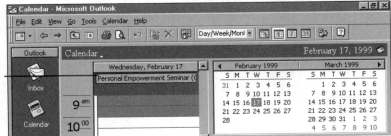

Event appears in banner.

Importing Holidays

In Outlook, holidays are considered all-day annual events. You can easily add holidays to your schedule by importing them from one of the holiday folders included with Outlook. Each folder contains a package of holidays observed by a specific country or by a religious group. For example, July 4, Independence Day, is included in the United States folder, while Passover is included in the Jewish Religious Holidays folder. When you import holidays from one of these folders, the name of the holiday appears in the Subject box on the event form, and the religion or country of origin appears in the Location box. You can import any combination of holidays you choose.

Import a set of holidays

In this exercise, you import the set of holidays located in the United States folder to add them to your calendar.

121

1   On the Tools menu, click Options.

The Options dialog box appears, and the Calendar tab is active.

2   Click Add Holidays.

The Add Holidays To Calendar dialog box appears.

3   Be sure the United States check box is selected, and then click OK.

The holiday files are imported.

4   Click OK to close the Options dialog box.

5   In the Date Navigator, click February 14.

Valentine's Day, a United States holiday that occurs on February 14, appears in the event banner at the top of the appointment area. Your screen should look similar to the following illustration.

Text in parentheses indicates where holiday is observed.

 TIP   You can delete individual holidays from your Calendar or delete them all at once. To delete holidays, on the Standard toolbar, click the Current View down arrow, and then select Annual Events. Select the holidays you want to delete, and then click the Delete button.

Delete

Printing Schedules

You can print a copy of any portion of your schedule file so that you can carry the information with you or incorporate it into a report. You can determine how the printed copy appears on the page by choosing from a variety of page layouts. You can also change the attributes of the printed text, such as the font size.

NOTE You cannot hide private items when you print your schedule. If you do not want private items to appear in the printed copy, you can filter them out before you print. To do so, on the View menu, click Filter, and then click the Advanced tab. Click the Field button, point to Frequently-used Fields, and then click Sensitivity. Click the Value down arrow, select Private, click OK, and then print your schedule.

While you are attending the Personal Empowerment Seminar as a representative of Margo Tea Company, you want to have a printed copy of your schedule at hand so that you can refer to the rest of your appointments for the week and write down any new appointments immediately, instead of waiting until you return to the office.

Print a schedule

In this exercise, you choose a print setting, and then preview and print one week of your schedule.

1 On the File menu, click Print.

The Print dialog box appears; it is set to print the current schedule date, February 14, 1999, by default.

Select the appearance of your printed schedule here.

Select the dates you want to print here.

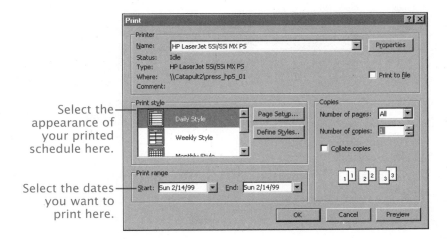

2 In the Print Style area, select Weekly Style.

A week of your schedule will be printed on a single page.

3 In the Print Range area, click the Start down arrow.

A small calendar appears.

4 Click February 15.

5 In the Print Range area, click the End down arrow, and then click February 21.

6 Click Preview.

The Print Preview window opens. Your screen should look similar to the following illustration.

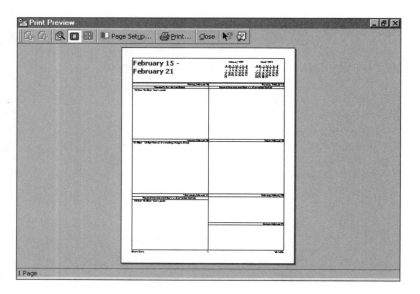

7 Click the Print button.

The Print dialog box appears again.

8 Click OK.

A copy of your schedule for the week of February 15 through February 21, 1999, prints.

Customizing Your Calendar Display

You can customize most of the Calendar options. For example, you can set the default display so that the workday in the appointment area starts at 9:00 A.M. instead of 8:00 A.M., or change it so that the work week starts on Tuesday. You can change the dimensions of the appointment area to display more appointment text or show a different number of months in the Date Navigator.

At Margo Tea Company, the typical workday begins at 8:30 A.M. and ends at 5:30 P.M. You want to change the Calendar settings to reflect your workday. You also want to resize the appointment area to view your appointments in more detail.

Change Calendar default options

In this exercise, you change the start and end times of your workday.

1 On the Tools menu, click Options.

The Options dialog box appears, with the Calendar tab in front.

2 In the Calendar Working Hours area, click the Start Time down arrow.

A list of available times appears.

3 Select 8:30 A.M.

4 Click the End Time down arrow, select 5:30 P.M., and then click OK.

The change does not take place until you leave the Calendar folder, and then return to it.

5 On the Outlook Bar, click the Inbox icon.

The contents of your Inbox appear in the Information viewer.

6 On the Outlook Bar, click the Calendar icon.

The current date appears in the Information viewer, and the workday begins at 8:30 A.M.

Resize the appointment area

In this exercise, you resize the appointment area so that more space is available for appointment details.

1 Position the pointer over the right border of the appointment area until the pointer changes to a two-headed arrow.

Your screen should look similar to the following illustration.

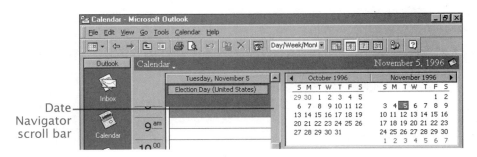

Date Navigator scroll bar

2 Drag the appointment area border to the right until a gray line appears in the middle of the Date Navigator, and then release the mouse button.

The appointment area has doubled in width, and the Date Navigator contains only the current month. Your screen should look similar to the following illustration.

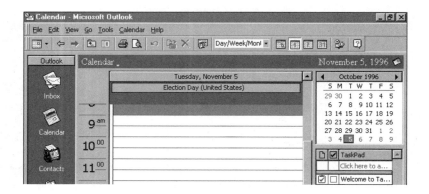

 TIP To display multiple consecutive days in the appointment area, hold SHIFT and click the adjacent days you want to see in the Date Navigator. To display non-consecutive days, hold CTRL and click the appropriate dates in the Date Navigator.

Finish the lesson

Follow these steps to delete the practice appointments you created in this lesson.

1   On the Go menu, click Go To Date.

2   Type **2/15/99**, and then click OK.

3   Click the "Team update" appointment, and then click the Delete button.

A message appears, asking if you want to delete all occurrences of this appointment.

4   Click the Delete All Occurrences option button.

The appointments are deleted.

5   Delete the "Dentist" appointment and the "Campaign Strategy meeting" on February 12, 1999, and the "Product Line meeting" on February 16, 1999.

6   Delete the Personal Empowerment Seminar event on February 17, 1999.

7   On the Tools menu, click Options. On the Calendar tab, reset the Start Time to 8:00 A.M. and the End Time to 5:00 P.M.

8   If you want to continue to the next lesson, on the Outlook Bar, click the Tasks icon.

9   If you are finished using Outlook for now, on the File menu, click Exit And Log Off.

Lesson Summary

To	Do this	Button
Change the date	On the Go menu, click Go To Date. Type the new date, and then click OK.	
Add an appointment to your schedule	On the Standard toolbar, click the New Appointment button. In the appointment form, type the appropriate information.	
Edit an appointment	Double-click the appointment in the appointment area. Make changes in the appointment form.	
Move an appointment	Drag the appointment to a new date in the Date Navigator.	
Change a reminder	Open the appointment form. Click the Reminder down arrow, and then select a new timing increment.	
Make an appointment tentative	Open the appointment form. Click the Show Time As down arrow, and then select Tentative.	
Make an appointment private	Use the right mouse button to click the appointment in the appointment area, and then click Private.	
Schedule time out of the office	Open the appointment form. Click the Show Time As down arrow, and then select Out Of Office.	
Schedule a recurring appointment	Open the appointment form. On the Standard toolbar, click the Recurrence button. Choose a recurrence pattern and range.	
Add events	On the Calendar menu, click New Event. Type in the appropriate information.	
Import holidays	On the Tools menu, click Options. Click Add Holidays, select the holiday folders from which you want to import, and then click OK.	

To	Do this
Print schedules	On the File menu, click Print. Select a print style and the date or dates you wish to print, and then click OK.
Change Calendar default options	On the Tools menu, click Options. On the Calendar tab, make the changes you want, and then click OK.

For online information about	On the Help menu, click Contents And Index, click the Index tab, and then type
Creating appointments	**Creating appointments** *or* **appointments, scheduling**
Editing appointments	**Appointments, editing**
Setting reminders	**Reminders**
Displaying free and busy times	**Busy times in calendar** *or* **free time in calendar**
Making appointments private	**Security, overview**
Setting recurring appointments	**Recurring appointments**
Scheduling events	**Events** *or* **annual events**
Printing schedules	**Printing, appointments**
Customizing Calendar	**Customizing Calendar**

Managing Your Tasks

Estimated time
40 min.

In this lesson you will learn how to:

- Create a task list.
- Organize and prioritize tasks.
- Track task status.
- Schedule tasks in Calendar.

You have learned how to use Calendar in Microsoft Outlook to organize your daily appointments, but what about the various duties you have and the projects that you work on each day? Outlook includes a Tasks folder that you can use to keep track of all your daily tasks. You can use it to record your tasks and to set task priorities and due dates. You can also sort your tasks into different categories and view them in the order that is most useful to you. For example, you can display your tasks by project, in order of priority, or both. You can set reminders for individual tasks and add tasks to your schedule in Calendar.

In this lesson, you create and organize a list of tasks related to the upcoming Product Line meeting to monitor your progress and take care of all the necessary preparations for a successful meeting.

Start the lesson

When you install Outlook, a sample task is automatically added to your task list. Because this task has no due date, it appears in your task list until you delete it. In this exercise, you start Outlook, switch to the Tasks folder, and then delete the sample task. You will create and work with new tasks in this lesson.

1   Start Outlook using the Shawn Davis profile.

2   On the Outlook bar, click the Tasks icon.

The contents of the Tasks folder appear in the Information viewer.

3   In the task list, click the "Welcome to Tasks!" task.

The entire task is selected.

Delete

4   On the Standard toolbar, click the Delete button.

The sample task is deleted. No other items appear in the task list.

Creating a Task List

You can view your entire task list in the Tasks folder. In addition to this list, an abridged version of the task list, the *TaskPad*, appears below the Date Navigator in the Calendar folder. Tasks with a specified due date appear as *active* tasks in the TaskPad on the appropriate day. Tasks without a specified due date are also considered active tasks, and appear daily in both the task list and the TaskPad until you complete or delete them.

The default view in the Tasks folder is the Simple List view, which displays only the subject and due date for each task. It also includes a Complete column in which you can select a check box to indicate that a task has been completed. You can apply different views to the task list to see more details. You will learn more about the different views later in this lesson. The following illustration shows a sample task list.

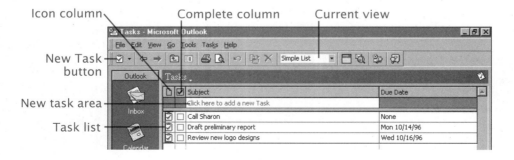

You can add tasks by simply typing them into the new task area at the top of the task list. You can also create more detailed tasks by opening up the task form and selecting the options you want.

Add tasks

In this exercise, you add several new tasks that need to be completed before your meeting into the new task area.

1 In the new task area, click the Click Here To Add A New Task box.

An insertion point appears in the Subject column of the new task area.

2 Type **Reserve overhead projector for presentation**, and then press ENTER.

The "Reserve overhead projector for presentation" task is added to the task list, and the insertion point reappears in the new task area. Your screen should look similar to the following illustration.

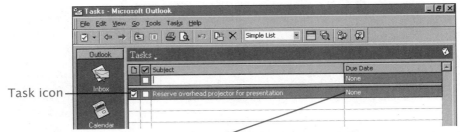

Task icon

The task has not been given a due date.

3 Type **Distribute corporate newsletter**, and then press ENTER.

The task is added to the task list, and the insertion point reappears in the new task area.

4 Type **Call caterer**, and then press TAB.

The Due Date column in the new task area becomes active.

5 Type **2/19/99**, and then press ENTER.

The task is added to the task list with a due date of Fri 2/19/99. Your screen should look similar to the following illustration.

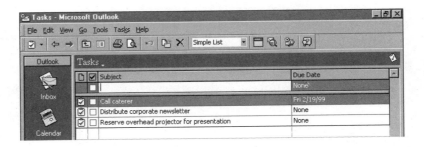

131

Insert a detailed task

In this exercise, you insert a more detailed task by specifying your progress on the task using the task form.

New Task

The New Mail Message button in the Inbox folder becomes the New Task button in the Tasks folder.

You will assign priorities and set other options later in this lesson.

1 On the Standard toolbar, click the New Task button.

A blank task form appears, and the insertion point appears in the Subject box.

2 Maximize the task form.

3 Type **Draft schedule for new product release**

4 Click the Due option button.

The current date appears in the Due box by default, and a note informing you that the task is due today appears in the Comment area above the Subject box. Your screen should look similar to the following illustration.

Comment area

The current date on your computer appears here.

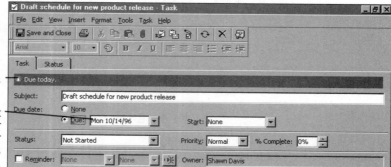

5 Press TAB to select the text in the Due box, type **2/17/99**, and then press ENTER.

The due date changes to Wed 2/17/99, and the note in the Comment area disappears. The insertion point moves to the Start box.

6 Be sure that the text in the Start box is selected, type **2/15/99**, and then press ENTER.

7 Click the Status down arrow, and then select In Progress.

8 On the Standard toolbar, click the Save And Close button.

You will learn how to sort tasks differently later in this lesson.

The "Draft schedule for new product release" task appears in your task list. Your tasks are listed in date order, with the most recent tasks at the top of the list. Your screen should look similar to the following illustration.

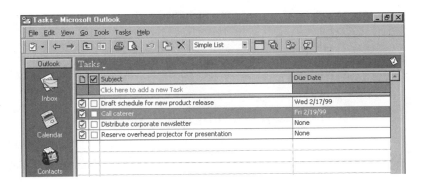

Editing Tasks

If the due date, priority, project, or subject of a task changes, you can edit the task to update the information. For example, if your weekly team meeting is postponed due to a holiday, you can extend the due date for your meeting report to reflect the change. To edit a task, you can type changes directly into the task list or open the task form and edit the information. You can also reorganize your tasks by dragging them to a different location in the task list.

Edit tasks

In this exercise, you edit the due dates for several tasks.

1   In the "Call caterer" task, click in the Due Date column.

The Due Date cell for the "Call caterer" task is selected and a down arrow appears in the cell. Your screen should look similar to the following illustration.

Dotted lines indicate that the cell is active.

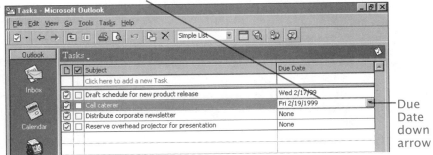

Due
Date
down
arrow

2   Click the Due Date down arrow.

A calendar appears, showing the month of February 1999.

133

3 In the calendar, select February 22, and then press ENTER.

The change to the task is saved, and the new due date appears as Mon 2/22/99.

4 In the task list, double-click the "Distribute corporate newsletter" task.

The task form opens.

5 In the Due Date area, click the Due option button.

The current date appears in the Due box by default.

6 On the Standard toolbar, click the Save And Close button.

The change to the task is saved, and the "Distribute corporate newsletter" task appears in your task list with the current date as its due date. Your screen should look similar to the following illustration.

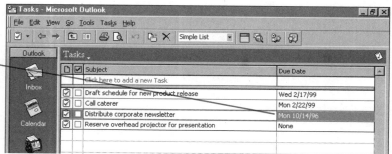

Your due date matches the current date setting on your computer.

7 In the "Distribute corporate newsletter" task, select the current date in the Due Date column.

You can edit tasks in the task list or by opening the task form.

8 Click the Due Date down arrow, select the next business day from the current date, and then press ENTER.

You are changing this date for the purpose of the following exercise so that the task will appear in the Next Seven Days view.

Changing Task Views

To see your tasks in greater detail or to display tasks for a particular period of time, you can apply a different view to your task list. For example, you can display a detailed list of all your tasks, including columns for status and percent complete. You can also view your tasks on a timeline for a more visual representation of how you should manage your time; or, you can show only those tasks for the upcoming week so that you don't need to search the entire task list for your most urgent duties.

Change views

In this exercise, you experiment with the different standard views available in the Tasks folder.

1 On the Standard toolbar, click the Current View down arrow.

A list of the available standard views appears.

2 Select Detailed List.

Your task list appears in Detailed List view, displaying several more columns. Your screen should look similar to the following illustration.

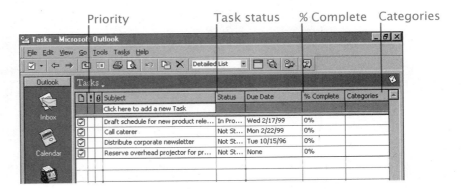

3 On the Standard toolbar, click the Current View down arrow, and then select Task Timeline.

Your task list appears in Task Timeline view.

Week

4 On the Standard toolbar, click the Week button.

The timeline changes to a week-at-a-glance format, and the "Distribute corporate newsletter" task appears for tomorrow's date. Your screen should look similar to the following illustration.

Your week dates correspond to the current date.

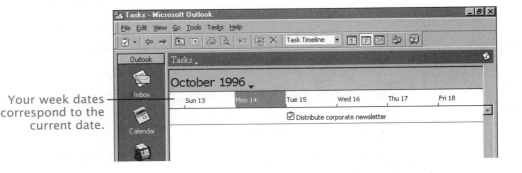

5 Click the Current View down arrow, and then select Next Seven Days. If you are prompted to save or discard the current view settings, click the Discard The Current View Settings option button.

Your task list appears in Next Seven Days view. The "Distribute corporate newsletter" task is the only task scheduled for the upcoming week. In the Folder Banner and on the status bar, the words "Filter Applied" appear, indicating that all appointments except those for the upcoming week are filtered out of this view. Your screen should look similar to the following illustration.

Filtered task list →

Folder Banner indicates that a filter is applied.

6 Click the Current View down arrow, and then select Simple List.

Your task list appears in Simple List view and the filter is removed.

Mark a task as completed

In this exercise, you check off a task in the Complete column, and then make the task active again.

1 Next to the "Distribute corporate newsletter" task, select the box in the Complete column.

A check mark appears in the Complete column, and a line appears through the task name, indicating that it is complete. Your screen should look similar to the following illustration.

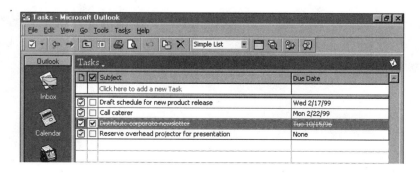

2 In the task list, double-click the "Distribute corporate newsletter" task.

The task form opens. The task status has been changed to Completed and 100% appears in the % Complete box. Your screen should look similar to the following illustration.

Task is 100% complete.

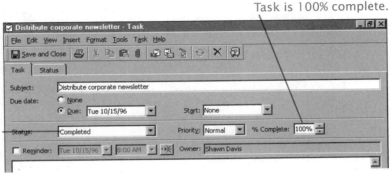

Task status is completed.

You can also use the arrow buttons to change the percentage.

3 In the % Complete box, select 100, type **50**, and then press ENTER.

The % Complete changes to 50%, the task status changes to In Progress, and a note appears in the Comment area, indicating that the task is due tomorrow.

4 On the Standard toolbar, click the Save And Close button.

The changes are saved and the task closes. It is no longer crossed out in the task list. Your screen should look similar to the following illustration.

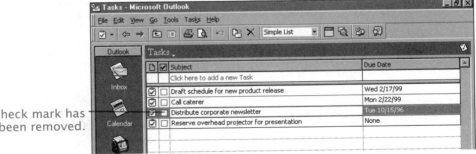

Check mark has been removed.

5 On the Standard toolbar, click the Current View down arrow, and then select Detailed List.

Your tasks appear in Detailed List view. The status of the "Distribute corporate newsletter" task appears as In Progress and 50% appears in the % Complete column.

137

Organizing Tasks

Now that you have created a task list and entered all the tasks that need to be accomplished to guarantee a successful meeting, you can organize them to make sure that all the tasks are completed on time. Setting priorities for each task allows you to focus on your tasks in order of importance. You can also group tasks and display them according to specific criteria. For example, you might want to view your tasks organized by project, by priority, or both. You can group tasks by up to four criteria at one time. You can also add a task, such as an appointment, to your Calendar folder and schedule it for a specific time.

On the task form, the fields on the Task tab correspond to the column headings that appear in the different views. The different options you select in these fields or the information you enter can be used as criteria for organizing your tasks. Some of the different field options from the Tasks tab are described in the following table.

Field	Option	Description
Status	Not started	Used when work has not yet begun on a task. 0% appears in the % Complete field.
	In Progress	Used when work on a task has been started, but not completed. Any percentage from 1% to 99% appears in the % Complete field.
	Completed	Used when all work on a task has been done. The % Complete field shows 100%.
	Waiting On Someone Else	Used when completion of the task depends on another person's involvement. Any percentage from 0% to 99% appears in the % Complete field.
	Deferred	Used when work on the task has been postponed. Any percentage from 0% to 99% appears in the % Complete field.
Priority	Low	Used for least important tasks.
	Normal	Used for tasks of average importance.
	High	Used for urgent tasks.
% Complete	N/A	Used to indicate the amount of work done on a task. Any percentage from 0% to 100% appears in this field, and the task status changes to reflect the percentage.

Setting Task Priorities

With Outlook, you can assign different task priorities so that you can easily decide which tasks require your attention first. The task priorities are just like the message priorities you use when sending messages; you can give tasks a Low, a Normal, or a High priority. In most views in the Tasks folder, a Priority column appears in the Information viewer. For tasks with a high priority, a red bold exclamation point appears in the Priority column; tasks with a low priority have a downward-pointing blue arrow. Normal priority tasks do not have a symbol in the Priority column. The priority symbols are shown in the following table.

Symbol	Priority level
❗	High priority
⬇	Low priority

You can set the priority when you create a new task or you can change the priority later. You can change a priority for a task in the task form or directly in the Priority column of the task list.

Set task priorities

In this exercise, you prioritize several tasks.

1 Double-click the "Draft schedule for new product release" task.

The task form opens.

2 In the Status area, click the Priority down arrow, and then select High.

The task is assigned a high priority.

3 On the Standard toolbar, click the Save And Close button.

A high priority symbol appears in the Priority column for the task. Your screen should look similar to the following illustration.

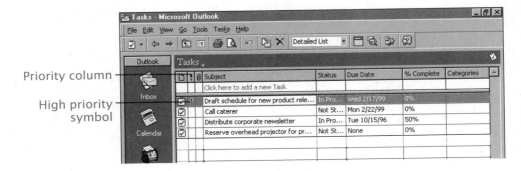

139

4 In the "Reserve overhead projector for presentation" task, click in the Priority column.

A list of priorities appears.

5 Select Low, and then press ENTER.

A low priority symbol appears next to the task name.

Assigning Tasks to Categories

For a demonstration of how to assign tasks to categories, double-click the Camcorder Files On The Internet shortcut on your Desktop or connect to the Internet address listed on p. xxx.

You can assign all Outlook items, including tasks, to different categories to make the items easier to find. A *category* is simply an identifying word or phrase that you can use as a criterion to organize or search for specific items. For example, you can assign your tasks to either the Business or the Personal category. You can then search those categories separately, depending on whether you want to look up your day's office duties or an errand you need to run after work. The Business and Personal categories are two of the many categories provided in Outlook's *Master Category List*. You can choose a category from the master list or you can create your own category. For example, you can create a category for the Company Expansion Project. Then, you can assign all tasks related to the Company Expansion Project to a single category in order to view them all at once.

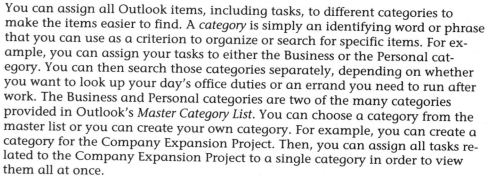

NOTE You can assign different types of items, such as mail messages, contacts, and tasks, to a single category. Assigning items from different folders to a single category is the only way to group different types of items together.

Assign tasks to a category

In this exercise, you assign several tasks to one of the categories from the Outlook Master Category List. You will use categories to group and find specific tasks later in this lesson.

1 Be sure that the "Reserve overhead projector for presentation" task is selected.

2 Hold down CTRL, and then click the "Call caterer" task.

Both tasks are selected.

3 On the Edit menu, click Categories.

The Categories dialog box appears.

4 Select the Phone Calls check box.

Phone Calls appears in the Items Belong To These Categories box at the top of the dialog box.

5 Click OK.

The tasks are added to the Phone Calls category, and "Phone Calls" appears in the Categories column for each task. Your screen should look similar to the following illustration.

Categories are added in this column.

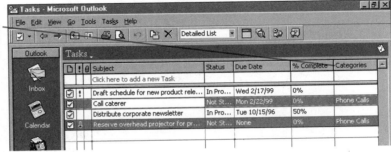

Add a category to the Master Category List

In this exercise, you create a category for items related to the new Product Line meeting, and add it to the Master Category List so that you can use it in any Outlook folder. You then apply this category to several tasks.

1 Hold down CTRL, and then, in the task list, select the "Draft schedule for new product release" task.

You should have three tasks selected: "Draft schedule for new product release," "Call caterer," and "Reserve overhead projector for presentation."

2 On the Edit menu, click Categories.

The Categories dialog box appears.

3 Click Master Category List.

The Master Category List dialog box appears.

4 In the New Category box, type **New Product Line**, and then click Add.

The New Product Line category is added to the Master Category List.

You can restore the Master Category List by clicking Reset in the Master Category List dialog box.

5 Click OK.

The Master Category List dialog box closes.

6 In the Categories dialog box, select the New Product Line check box.

This category will be applied to the three tasks you selected in step 1.

7 Click OK to close the Categories dialog box.

"New Product Line" appears in the Categories box for each of the selected tasks, and an ellipsis (...) appears in the Categories box for those tasks that are assigned to more than one category.

TIP You can also type a category name into the Categories column for a task, into the Categories box on an item form, or into the Items Belong To These Categories box in the Categories dialog box. However, category names entered using any of these methods will only appear for the specific item assigned to them; the names will not be added to the Master Category List.

View tasks by category

In this exercise, you apply the By Category view to your task list so that you can see what projects or activities your tasks are related to.

NOTE In the previous exercises, you assigned certain tasks to more than one category. When you view your tasks by category, copies of tasks assigned to multiple categories will appear under each category heading. However, the original task will still appear only once in your task list.

1 On the Standard toolbar, click the Current View down arrow, and then select By Category.

Your tasks appear in By Category view. The plus sign (+) next to each category heading indicates that the category is collapsed and entries in that category are hidden. Your screen should look similar to the following illustration.

2 Click the plus sign (+) for the New Product Line category.

The category expands, showing the tasks assigned to the New Product Line project. Your screen should look similar to the following illustration.

Plus sign (+) indicates category is collapsed.

Minus sign (-) indicates category is expanded.

			Subject	Status	Due Date	% Complete	Categories
			Click here to add a new Task				
+ Categories : (none)							
- Categories : New Product Line							
☑	↓		Reserve overhead projector for p...	Not St...	None	0%	New Produ...
☑	!		Draft schedule for new product rel...	In Pro...	Wed 2/17/99	0%	New Produ...
☑			Call caterer	Not St...	Mon 2/22/99	0%	New Produ...
+ Categories : Phone Calls							

3 Click the plus sign (+) for the Phone Calls category.

The category expands, showing the "Reserve overhead projector for presentation" and "Call caterer" tasks. These tasks have been assigned to more than one category.

4 Click the plus sign (+) for the None category.

The "Distribute corporate newsletter" task appears. This task has not been assigned to any category. Your screen should look similar to the following illustration.

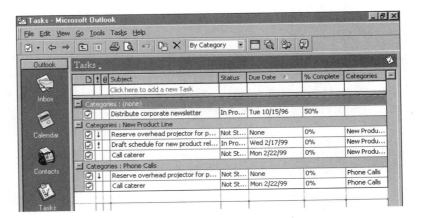

5 On the Standard toolbar, click the Current View down arrow, and then select Detailed List.

Your tasks appear in Detailed List view.

Arranging Tasks

If the available views in Tasks do not meet your needs, you can organize tasks according to your own criteria. In Lesson 3, you learned how to sort and group e-mail messages in your Inbox. You can sort and group the tasks in your task list the same way to arrange them in ways that are most useful to you. For example, you might arrange your tasks by priority, by end date, by duration, or by project. You can group tasks by specific criteria, sort them in a certain order, or filter tasks so that only certain ones appear in your task list.

Sort tasks

In this exercise, you experiment with different sort orders in your task list.

1 In the Information viewer, click the Subject column heading.

Your tasks are sorted in ascending alphabetical order, by subject. Your screen should look similar to the following illustration.

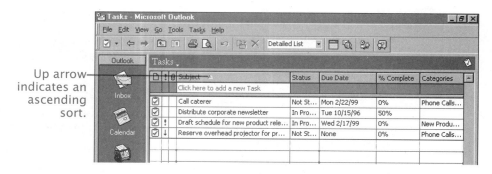

Up arrow indicates an ascending sort.

2 Click the Subject column heading again.

Your tasks are sorted in descending alphabetical order, by subject.

Tasks with no end date appear at the end of the list.

3 Click the Due Date column heading.

Your tasks are sorted in descending numerical order, by due date, with the furthest due date at the top of the list.

Group tasks

In this exercise, you group your task list to display your tasks according to several criteria.

Group By Box

1 On the Standard toolbar, click the Group By Box button.

The Group By box appears at the top of the task list in the Information viewer.

2 Drag the Status column heading into the Group By box.

Your tasks are grouped by status into two groups: "Status: Not Started," and "Status: In Progress." Your screen should look similar to the following illustration.

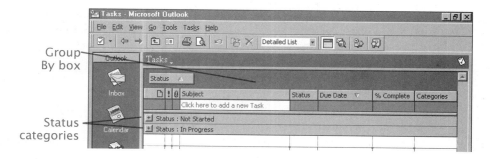

Group By box

Status categories

3 Click the plus sign (+) next to the "Status: Not Started" heading.

The tasks that you have not yet started to work on, "Call caterer" and "Reserve overhead projector for presentation," appear.

4 Click the plus sign (+) next to the "Status: In Progress" heading.

The tasks in progress, "Draft schedule for new product release" and "Distribute corporate newsletter," appear. Your screen should look similar to the following illustration.

Priority column —

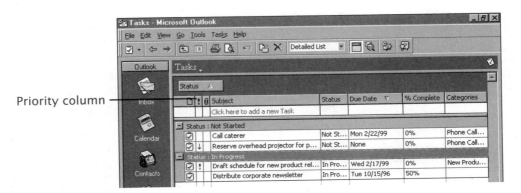

5 Drag the Priority column heading into the Group By box, to the right of the Status column heading.

The group headings are collapsed automatically, and your tasks are now grouped by status, and then by priority.

6 Click the plus sign (+) next to the "Status: In Progress" heading.

Two sub-group headings, "Priority: High" and "Priority: Normal," appear.

7 Click the plus sign (+) next to the "Priority: High" heading.

The high-priority task, "Draft schedule for new product release," appears. Your screen should look similar to the following illustration.

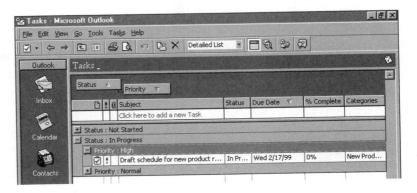

Restore the view

In this exercise, you remove your groupings and reapply a standard view to your task list.

1   On the Standard toolbar, click the Current View down arrow, and then click Detailed List.

A message appears, asking if you want to save or discard the changes you made to the current view settings.

2   Be sure that the Discard The Current View Settings And Reapply The View "Detailed List" option button is selected, and then click OK.

The Group By box is hidden, and your tasks appear in Detailed List view.

 TIP   You can also save your view settings as a custom view. To do so, on the View menu, click Define Views. Click New, and then type a name for the view you've created. To learn more about creating custom views, see Lesson 4, "Creating a Contact List."

Filter tasks

Suppose you want to display only those tasks related to the new product line so that you can quickly determine what needs to be done for that project alone. In this exercise, you apply a filter to your task list so that only tasks matching the filter criteria appear.

1   On the View menu, click Filter.

The Filter dialog box appears; the Tasks tab is active.

2   In the Search For The Word(s) box, type **product**

You will be applying a filter to display only those tasks related to the new product line.

3   Click the In down arrow, and then select Frequently-Used Text Fields.

You want to search all the text fields in the task list, not just the subject field, for the word "product."

4   Click OK.

The filter is applied, and tasks that do not refer to the new product line are filtered out. Your screen should look similar to the following illustration.

Folder Banner indicates that a filter is applied.

You used a filter to search for the word "product" in these fields.

5   On the View menu, click Filter.

The Filter dialog box appears.

6   Click Clear All, and then click OK.

The filter is removed and all tasks appear.

Scheduling Tasks

So far, you've only looked at your tasks in the Tasks folder. In the Calendar folder, your active tasks for the day also appear in the TaskPad list to the right of your schedule. You can easily add tasks to your schedule so that they are assigned to specific times and appear as appointments. This is a good way to make sure that you have enough time to complete a task during a particular day.

Create an appointment from a task

In this exercise, you create a Calendar appointment from a task, without leaving the Tasks folder.

1   Select the "Draft schedule for new product release" task, and then drag it onto the Calendar icon on the Outlook Bar.

After a moment, an appointment form appears.

2   Maximize the appointment form.

Scroll down to view all the details on the task.

"Draft schedule for new product release" appears automatically in the Subject box, and the task details appear in the notes area. Your screen should look similar to the following illustration.

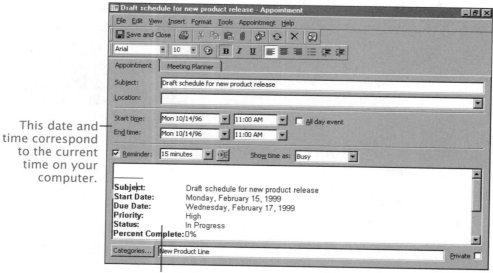

This date and time correspond to the current time on your computer.

Task details such as duration, priority, status, and percent complete appear here.

3 Click the Start Time down arrow, and then select 3:00 P.M.

4 Click the End Time down arrow, and then select 5:00 P.M.

The appointment has a duration of 2 hours.

5 On the Standard toolbar, click the Save And Close button.

The appointment is added to your schedule. Your task list reappears. If a message appears stating that the reminder cannot be set, click Yes.

View your scheduled task

In this exercise, you switch to the Calendar folder and view the appointment you just created from a task.

➤ On the Outlook Bar, click the Calendar icon.

The contents of the Calendar folder appear in the Information viewer, along with the current date. The appointment you scheduled from a task appears in the 3:00 P.M.-5:00 P.M. time period. Your screen should look similar to the following illustration.

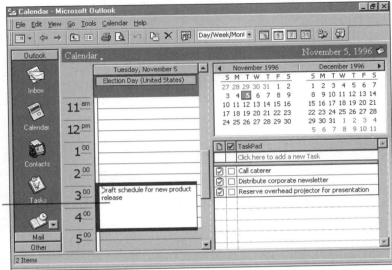

You might
need to scroll
down to see
the entire
appointment.

Schedule a task from the TaskPad

While you are in the Calendar folder, you can also drag tasks into the
schedule from the TaskPad. In this exercise, you schedule time to complete another task using the TaskPad.

1 In the appointment area, click the 1:00 P.M. to 1:30 P.M. time slot.

*Scroll down
to view all
the details
on the task.*

2 Drag the "Reserve overhead projector for presentation" task from the
TaskPad into the 1:00 P.M.-1:30 P.M. time slot.

An appointment form appears, with "Reserve overhead projector for presentation" in the Subject box; a start time of 1:00 P.M. and end time of
1:30 P.M. are entered automatically. Your screen should look similar to
the following illustration.

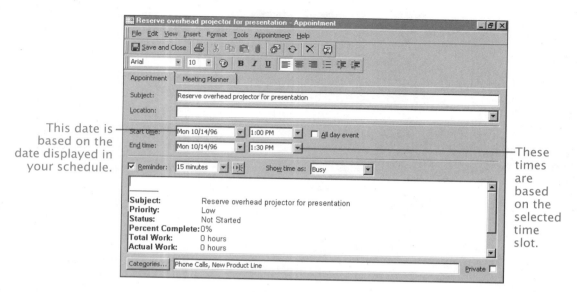

This date is based on the date displayed in your schedule.

These times are based on the selected time slot.

3 On the Standard toolbar, click the Save And Close button.

The appointment is added to your schedule.

Creating a Recurring Task

Suppose you have certain tasks that occur at regular intervals, such as "Submit monthly expense report" or "Type up weekly meeting minutes." You can create recurring tasks in Outlook, just as you can create recurring appointments. When you add a recurring task to your task list, only the initial occurrence appears in the list at first. When you have marked the initial occurrence of the task as complete, the next occurrence appears in the task list automatically.

Create a recurring task

In this exercise, you set the period and frequency of recurrence for a new task.

1 On the Outlook Bar, click the Tasks icon.

Your task list appears in the Information viewer.

New Task

2 On the Standard toolbar, click the New Task button.

A blank task form appears.

3 In the Subject box, type **Submit weekly progress report**

4 On the Standard toolbar, click the Recurrence button.

Recurrence

The Task Recurrence dialog box appears.

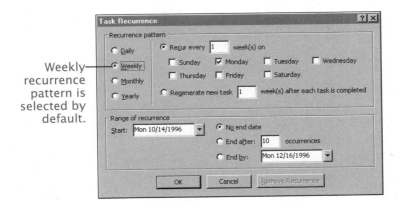

Weekly recurrence pattern is selected by default.

5   In the Recurrence Pattern area, be sure that the Weekly and Recur Every 1 Week(s) On option buttons are selected.

6   Select the Friday check box, and then clear the selection from all other check boxes.

    The task is set to recur weekly on Fridays.

7   Click OK.

    The next occurrence of the task and its recurrence information appear in the Comment area on the task form.

8   On the Standard toolbar, click the Save And Close button.

    The first occurrence of the task appears in your task list. Your screen should look similar to the following illustration.

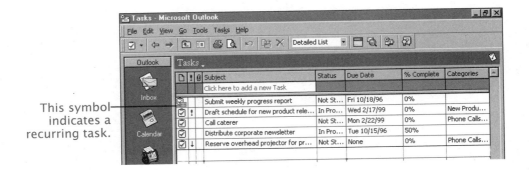

This symbol indicates a recurring task.

Mark a recurring task as completed

In this exercise, you mark the first occurrence of the "Submit weekly progress report" task as completed in your task list and verify that the next occurrence appears automatically.

151

1   On the Standard toolbar, click the Current View down arrow, and then select Simple List.

A message appears, asking if you want to preserve or discard the current view settings. This occurs because of the filter you applied earlier in this lesson.

2   Be sure that the Discard The Current View Settings option button is selected, and then click OK.

Your tasks appear in Simple List view.

You can also type 100% in the % Complete column.

3   In the "Submit weekly progress report" task, select the check box in the Complete column.

A strikethrough line appears through the task, indicating that it is complete. The next occurrence of the task, dated the Friday of the following week, automatically appears in your task list.

Finish the lesson

Follow these steps to delete the tasks and appointments you created in this lesson.

1   On the Edit menu, click Categories. Click Master Category List, and then click Reset to remove the New Product Line category from the list.

A message appears, asking you to confirm the deletion.

2   Click OK to delete the category name, and then click OK to close each dialog box.

3   Be sure that the task list appears in the Information Viewer, and then, on the Edit menu, click Select All.

All your tasks are selected.

Delete

4   On the Standard toolbar, click the Delete button.

A message appears, asking if you want to delete all occurrences of the "Submit weekly progress report" task.

5   Click the Delete All option button, and then click OK.

6   Switch to the Calendar folder. Delete the appointments you created for the current date.

Go To Today

7   To continue to the next lesson, be sure you are in the Calendar folder, and then, on the Standard toolbar, click the Go To Today button.

The current date appears in the Information viewer.

8   If you are finished using Outlook for now, on the File menu, click Exit And Log Off.

Lesson Summary

To	Do this	Button
Add a task	In the task list, click the Click Here To Add A New Task box, type the task information, and then press ENTER.	
Add a detailed task	On the Standard toolbar, click the New Task button. Type the task information into the appointment form.	
Edit a task	Double-click the task to open the task form, and then make your changes in the form.	
Change views	On the Standard toolbar, click the Current View down arrow, and then select the view you want to apply.	
Mark a task as completed	In Simple List or Detailed List views, select the check box in the Complete column for the task.	
Set priority for a task	In the task form, click the Priority down arrow, and then select a priority.	
Assign a task to a category	In the task list, select the task. On the Edit menu, click Categories. Select one or more categories from the list, and then click OK.	
Add a category to the Master Category List	In the Categories dialog box, click Master Category List. Type a name for the new category, and then click Add.	
Sort tasks	Click the column heading for the criteria you want to sort by.	
Group tasks	On the Standard toolbar, click the Group By Box button. Drag the column headings you want to group by into the Group By box, above the task list.	
Filter tasks	On the View menu, click Filter. Enter the filter criteria in the Filter dialog box.	

To	Do this	Button
Schedule a task	Drag the task onto the Calendar icon on the Outlook Bar, and then enter start and end dates in the appointment form.	
Schedule a task from the TaskPad	In the appointment area in the Calendar folder, select the appropriate time slots for the appointment you want to schedule. Drag the task from the TaskPad into the selected time period.	
Create a recurring task	Create or select a task. On the Standard toolbar, click the Recurrence button. Select a recurrence pattern and range, and then click OK.	

For online information about	On the Help menu, click Contents And Index, click the Index tab, and then type
Creating tasks	**Tasks, creating** *or* **creating, tasks**
Editing tasks	**Tasks, editing**
Working with categories	**Categories**
Organizing tasks	**Groups, creating** *or* **sorting**
Scheduling tasks	**Appointments**
Setting recurring tasks	**Recurrence pattern** *or* **recurring tasks**

Coordinating Schedules with Other Users

Estimated time
25 min.

In this lesson you will learn how to:

- View other users' schedules using the Meeting Planner.
- Send meeting requests.
- Assign tasks to others.

The Calendar in Microsoft Outlook helps you organize your schedule. In addition, you can use Calendar over a network to coordinate meetings with the other people in your office. You can use the *Meeting Planner* feature to review your schedule along with the schedules of your co-workers, and to schedule meetings at mutually available times. You can also use *AutoPick* to quickly determine an acceptable meeting time and location. You can send out meeting requests via e-mail and receive responses in your Outlook Inbox. You can also change meeting dates and times, and easily inform attendees of the changes without creating and addressing a new meeting request.

Everyone involved with Margo Tea Company's new product line is hard at work on his or her piece of the project. As the Operations Coordinator, you need to schedule meetings with the entire team so that everyone can be kept informed on the products and the advertising campaign as they develop. In this lesson, you'll learn how to view your co-workers' schedules using the Meeting Planner. You'll also learn how to request meetings in the Calendar folder, and add meetings to your schedule. Finally, you'll learn how to assign particular tasks to other people and track their progress on those tasks.

IMPORTANT Because this lesson explores the interactive aspects of the Calendar and Tasks folders in Outlook, you'll use your own profile and work with your own schedule. You will not be able to complete the exercises as written if you are not using Outlook in a networked environment with a global address list, such as an organization. You'll need to recruit some help from one or two other people on your network to complete the exercises. Find at least one person on your network who will cooperate with your practice meeting and task requests.

Start Outlook

In this exercise, you start Outlook and switch to the Calendar folder.

If you receive a reminder for an appointment or a task during this lesson, click the Dismiss This Reminder option button.

1   Start Outlook using your own profile name.

    You should use your own profile for this lesson so that you can work with other people on your network.

2   On the Outlook Bar, click the Calendar icon.

    The contents of your Calendar folder appear in the Information viewer; your schedule for the current date appears.

Scheduling a Meeting

In the Calendar folder, you can see all your appointments in some detail and display them a day, a week, or a month at a time. But what if you want a more graphical representation of your schedule, where you can see your free and busy times at a glance? You can use the Meeting Planner to view your schedule, and others' schedules, in a timeline format. With the Meeting Planner, you can easily see the times that are blocked off on your schedule for existing appointments and the times that are available for new meetings or appointments.

View your own schedule

In this exercise, you display the Meeting Planner to look over your entire schedule, and then check specific details for an appointment.

IMPORTANT This lesson will be the most useful and interesting if you and your co-workers have appointments scheduled. If you don't have any appointments on the current date, you can add some, or move to a date in the future when you and your co-workers have appointments. You can switch to any future date by using the Date Navigator or the Go To Date command on the Edit menu.

Plan A Meeting

For consistency, the illustrations in this lesson will continue to use the Shawn Davis profile that was used in the previous lessons.

1 On the Standard toolbar, click the Plan A Meeting button.

The Plan A Meeting dialog box appears. The current date appears in the Meeting Planner grid, and the time periods during which you have an appointment or a meeting scheduled are marked with a solid line, but no details are shown. Your screen should look similar to the following illustration.

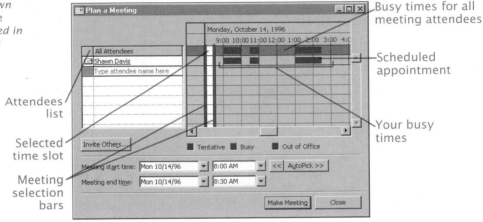

You cannot use the right mouse button to click busy bars in the darker "All Attendees" line at the top of the grid.

2 Use the right mouse button to click a busy time slot.

The appointment time and description appear. Your screen should look similar to the following illustration.

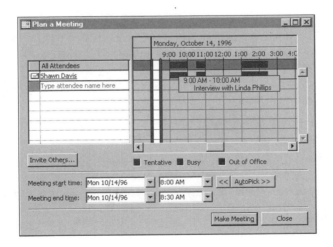

157

Viewing Other People's Free and Busy Times

In the Plan A Meeting dialog box, you can see at a glance when your schedule is open for new appointments. But how can you find out when other people are available so you can set the time and date for a meeting? Using Outlook and with access to your network, you can easily view your co-workers' schedules and determine the best time for a meeting.

You will learn more about access permissions in Lesson 11, "Granting Others Access to Your Outlook Files."

By default, although your co-workers can view your free and busy times, they cannot read the details of your appointments and tasks. If you want certain people to be able to see more details about your schedule, you can grant them different levels of access permissions, as long as they are using Outlook with a Microsoft Exchange Server.

Your name always appears in the Attendees box located next to the Meeting Planner grid. To add names to the Attendees box and display their schedules, you can type in their names or choose them from your organization's global address list.

 NOTE Most Microsoft Schedule+ files are compatible with Outlook files, so if some of your co-workers have not yet upgraded to Outlook, you will still be able to exchange scheduling information with them. If you do not have a global address list, skip this exercise.

Display another person's schedule

In this exercise, you display your co-workers' schedules in the Meeting Planner grid.

1   In the Plan A Meeting dialog box, click Invite Others.

The Select Attendees And Resources dialog box appears. Names from your organization's global address list are shown, in addition to your own name.

2   Select the names of the people working with you on this lesson, and then click Required.

The names appear in the list of required attendees.

3   Click OK.

The names of your co-workers appear in the All Attendees list, and each attendee's busy times are marked in the Meeting Planner grid. Busy times appear in blue, tentative appointments in gray, and out-of-office appointments in dark blue.

TIP If you want to coordinate a meeting with a colleague in another time zone, you can display an additional time zone in your Calendar. This is useful if members of your organization are working in satellite offices nationwide, for example, and you occasionally need to schedule meetings or conference calls. To display a second time zone, on the Tools menu, click Options, and then click the Calendar tab. Click Time Zone. Select the Show An Additional Time Zone check box. In the Label box, type a description, such as Northwest District. Click the Time Zone down arrow, select the zone you want to use, and click OK. You can quickly switch to the second time zone in Day view by using the right mouse button to click the blank space above the appointment area, and then clicking Change Time Zone.

Requesting a Meeting

The AutoPick function is the easiest way to schedule a meeting with several of your co-workers. When you use AutoPick, you do not need to look at each person's individual schedule to determine free and busy times. You select your attendees, the location, and any equipment you need, and specify a duration for the meeting. Then, you use AutoPick to search the schedules of attendees for the first available time that meets all your requirements.

When you select attendees for a meeting, you can decide to make them required attendees or optional attendees. Optional attendees are informed of the meeting but are not required to attend. The meeting request they receive is similar to a carbon copy. If you name any optional attendees, you can check their schedules for available times using AutoPick. But even if you don't, all optional attendees receive a carbon copy of the meeting request message, so they can choose to attend if they wish.

If schedules for locations and other resources are maintained on your network, you can also select a meeting location and request specific equipment using the Meeting Planner. A *resource* can be a conference room, an overhead projector, a VCR, or any other equipment you might need at a meeting. If you select a resource, this information will also appear on the meeting request form.

After you select a meeting time with AutoPick, you can send a message to each of the attendees, asking whether he or she is available. Although you could switch to the Inbox and send out messages inviting people to the meeting, you create and send a meeting request form without leaving the Calendar folder using AutoPick.

For a demonstration of how to schedule a meeting, double-click the Camcorder Files On The Internet shortcut on your Desktop or connect to the Internet address listed on p. xxx.

You can also drag the meeting selection handles to change the meeting duration.

The button to the left of the AutoPick button, with the left-pointing arrows, searches for available times earlier than the selected date.

Schedule a meeting using AutoPick

In this exercise, you use the AutoPick function to quickly find a convenient time and schedule a meeting with required attendees. For the purposes of this exercise, you will not select any optional attendees, locations, or resources.

1   Be sure that the Plan A Meeting dialog box is active and that the names of the people working with you on this lesson appear in the All Attendees list.

The date and time selected in the Meeting Planner grid correspond to the current date and time on your computer.

2   Click the Meeting End Time down arrow.

A list of times and durations appears.

3   Select the time that corresponds to a two-hour duration.

The time you choose will vary depending on the current time on your computer. In the Meeting Planner grid, the meeting selection bars move to enclose a two-hour time period.

4   Click AutoPick.

The meeting selection bars appear around the first two-hour time period available for all attendees. Your screen should look similar to the following illustration.

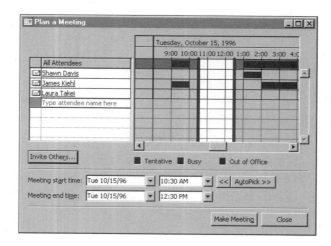

5 Click Make Meeting.

A blank meeting request form, which is very similar to the appointment form, appears. The names of your co-workers appear in the To box, and a note appears in the Comment area at the top of the form, informing you that invitations to this meeting have not yet been sent. Your screen should look similar to the following illustration.

This note appears until you send the meeting request.

The time and date selected by AutoPick appear here automatically.

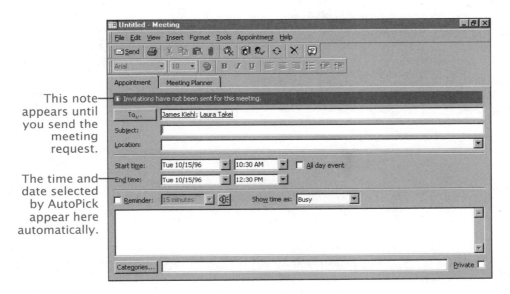

6 In the Subject box, type **Ad campaign update**

7 In the Notes area at the bottom of the form, type **Now that we have some feedback from Debbie Abdul, let's meet and review our project schedule.**

8 Select the Reminder check box.

You want each attendee to receive a reminder for the meeting when it comes up in his or her schedule.

9 On the Standard toolbar, click the Send button.

The meeting request is sent, and the meeting is added to your schedule in the appropriate time slots. Your screen should look similar to the following illustration.

If the first available meeting time you found using AutoPick is on a different date, click that date in the Date Navigator to see the meeting.

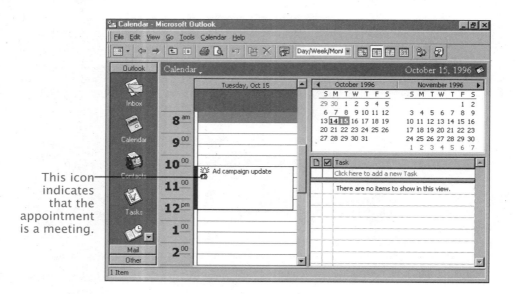

This icon indicates that the appointment is a meeting.

TIP Suppose you need to plan a meeting with a group of individuals, each of whom has a very tight schedule. You could use AutoPick, but what if the next available date it finds is three months away? In situations like this, it is often easier to organize a meeting by selecting a specific time in the Meeting Planner. If other users of your network have given you access to their schedules, you can view the details of their appointments and ask them to reschedule items if your meeting takes precedence.

Viewing Responses to Meeting Requests

After recipients respond to the meeting requests you've sent out, you can view the responses without leaving the Calendar folder. The Meeting Request tab in the appointment form displays the list of meeting attendees and their responses to your request. You can also view other users' schedules on the Meeting Planner tab and invite additional meeting attendees, if you wish.

When you send a meeting request, the invitees can respond in three ways: Accept, Decline, or Tentatively Accept. When they receive a meeting request, they click one of these option buttons to send their decision back to you. They can also choose to add a text message to their response. You can view these messages in your Inbox in Outlook, or track the responses on the Meeting Planner tab for the meeting appointment in your Calendar. When your co-workers accept or tentatively accept a meeting request, the meeting is automatically added to their schedules.

Verify attendee responses

In this exercise, you open the "Ad campaign update" meeting appointment and double-check the information on the Meeting Planner tab.

 IMPORTANT Be sure to ask your co-workers whom you've recruited for this lesson to send responses to your meeting request so that you can complete this exercise.

1 Double-click the "Ad campaign update" meeting appointment.

The appointment form opens. The number of responses you have received appears in the Comment area at the top of the form.

2 Click the Meeting Planner tab.

The Meeting Planner tab appears, and the Show Attendee Status option button is selected. The responses from your co-workers are listed in the table. Your screen should look similar to the following illustration.

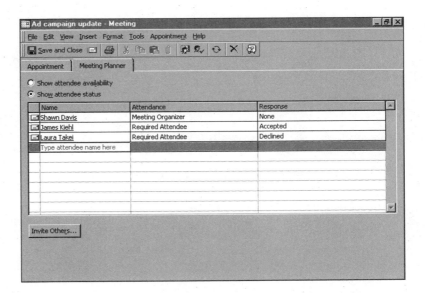

3 Click the Show Attendee Availability option button.

The Meeting Planner grid appears. A blue bar between the selected time slots for a name indicates that the meeting has been added to the schedule for that person. Your screen should look similar to the following illustration.

This person declined the meeting, so the meeting time does not appear busy in her schedule.

If you requested a meeting location, it also appears when you click the blue bar using the right mouse button.

4 Use the right mouse button to click the blue bar for a name in the meeting time slot.

The meeting time and the text "Ad campaign update" appear.

5 Click anywhere to cancel the selection, and then close the appointment form.

 TIP You can transform a regular appointment into a meeting by opening the appointment, and then inviting attendees using the Meeting Planner tab.

Changing Meeting Times and Locations

Sometimes you will find that, although the schedules look clear for a meeting time when you view them in the Meeting Planner, something might have come up or people you invited might have other appointments they haven't added in Outlook. When someone declines a meeting or asks if you could reschedule it, you can easily make changes.

Reschedule a meeting

In this exercise, you change the time for a meeting and notify attendees.

1 Position the mouse pointer over the left move handle on the "Ad campaign update" meeting.

The pointer changes to a four-headed arrow.

2 Drag the meeting to have it start two hours later.

A message appears, asking if you want to send an update to meeting attendees to inform them of the change.

3 Click Yes.

A new meeting request form, addressed to the co-workers who are helping you with this lesson, appears. The new meeting start and end times appear in the appropriate boxes, and the text of your original message is appended to the new form.

4 Select the text in the Notes area, and then type **Sorry, change in schedule!**

5 On the Standard toolbar, click the Save And Close button, and then click Yes to send the message.

The new meeting time is sent to your co-workers. They can accept or decline the request, but this is not necessary to complete this lesson.

TIP You can check attendees' free and busy times in the Meeting Planner grid before you reschedule a meeting.

Assigning Tasks to Others

In Lesson 6, you learned how to create and maintain a list of your own daily tasks. In addition to keeping a personal task list, you can *assign* tasks to other people on your network. For example, you can assign tasks to members of your project team or to an administrative assistant. If the recipient accepts your *task request*, you can then track his or her progress on the assignment.

As the Operations Coordinator for Margo Tea Company, you manage projects for your fellow employees, and assign tasks to others as needed so that everything runs smoothly. In the following exercises, you practice assigning tasks to your co-workers and maintain a record of their progress by requesting periodic status reports on the assigned tasks.

Sending a Task Request

When you create a task in your task list, you are the *owner* of the task. As owner, you are the only person who can edit the task; for example, you can make changes to the due date or the status of the task. However, when you send a task request to another user, you are effectively giving that person ownership of the task. If the recipient accepts the task, he or she becomes the task owner and the only one who can make changes. As the creator of the task, you can keep a copy of the assigned task in your task list, and you can request status reports from the recipient so that your copy stays up to date.

If a recipient declines a task, it is returned to you. You can reclaim ownership of the task by returning it to your own task list, or you can assign it to someone else. In addition, task recipients can in turn send a task assignment on to another person instead of accepting or declining the task. If a recipient sends your task on to another person, you are updated as to the new task owner, and both you and the person who reassigned the task are kept informed on the task progress. You can select an existing task in your task list and send it to a recipient, or create a new task request with a menu command.

 NOTE   You can also assign tasks to contacts outside of your enterprise, if the contact is also using Outlook and if that person's e-mail address is listed in your Outlook Address Book.

Send a new task request

In this exercise, you assign a new task to one of your co-workers, and then send that person a task request.

 IMPORTANT   If you assign a task to more than one person, you will not be able to keep an updated copy of the task in your own task list. For the purposes of this exercise, you will assign a task to just one of the people who are helping you with this lesson. If you want to send a task request to more than one person, you must first make a copy of the task in your own task list, and then send it to the second recipient.

1   On the Outlook Bar, click the Tasks icon.

Your task list appears in the Information viewer.

2   On the File menu, point to New, and then click Task Request.

A blank task request form, which is very similar to both the task form and the Mail Form, appears. A note in the Comment area at the top of the form indicates that the task request has not been sent yet. Your screen should look similar to the following illustration.

Comment area
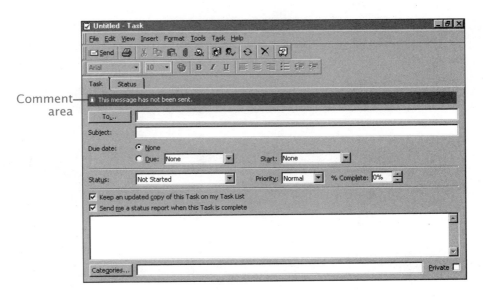

3 Click To.

The Select Task Recipient dialog box appears.

4 Select the name of one of the people helping you with this exercise, click To, and then click OK.

5 In the Subject box, type **Prepare logo design for printer**

6 In the Due Date area, click the Due option button.

The current date appears in the Due Date box, and a note appears in the Comment area, indicating that the task is due today.

7 Be sure that the Keep An Updated Copy Of This Task On My Task List check box is selected.

When the task recipient makes changes to the task, the updates will appear in the copy of the task in your task list.

8 Be sure that the Send Me A Status Report When This Task Is Complete check box is selected.

When the task recipient marks the task as complete, you will receive a message.

9 In the notes area at the bottom of the form, type **Can you have this ready to go by this afternoon?**

10 On the Standard toolbar, click the Send button.

The task request is sent to your partner, and a copy of the assigned task appears in your task list. Your screen should look similar to the following illustration.

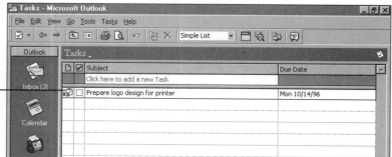

This icon indicates that the task has been assigned to someone else.

 IMPORTANT To complete the following exercises, you must make sure that your co-worker accepts your task request. Tell your partner to open and accept the task request message in his or her Inbox, without editing it or adding any text. If you are or your partner is waiting for mail delivery, on the Tools menu, click Check For New Mail to speed up the process.

Tracking Task Status

When you send a task request, it appears as a message in the recipient's Inbox. When the recipient opens the task request message, it looks very similar to a meeting request; the recipient can accept or decline the task assignment by clicking the appropriate toolbar button. He or she can also choose to add a text message to the response. If a recipient accepts the task request, the task is added to his or her task list, and the request message is deleted from his or her Inbox automatically. If the recipient declines the task request, it is not added to his or her task list, and the request message is deleted from his or her Inbox automatically.

To learn more about Inbox views, refer to Lesson 3.

You can view the responses to your task requests in your Inbox. If you have requested task updates and status reports with your task request, you can keep track of the task status in your task list. Whenever a task recipient modifies a task—for example, by changing the task status to In Progress—a task update message is automatically sent to you. The message appears in your Inbox. If you are viewing your incoming messages with AutoPreview, the task subject, due date, and status appear below the message header in your Inbox. You can open the task update message for more details about the task in progress. After you have opened the message, the task status is updated in the copy of the assigned task that appears in your task list.

View a response to your task request

In this exercise, you read your partner's response to your task request.

1 On the Outlook Bar, click the Inbox icon.

The contents of your inbox folder appear in the Information viewer. Your screen should look similar to the following illustration.

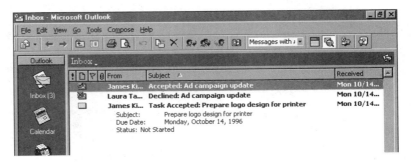

If the acceptance message does not appear in your Inbox, on the Tools menu, click Check For New Mail.

2 Double-click the "Task Accepted: Prepare logo design for printer" message from your partner.

A read-only accepted task request form appears, containing information such as when and by whom the task was accepted. Your screen should look similar to the following illustration.

The task was accepted at this time.

The task recipient is now the owner of this task.

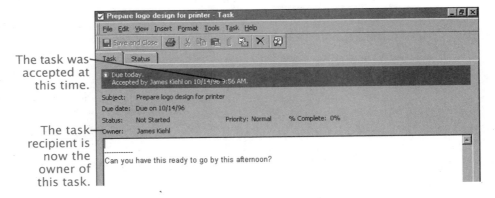

3 Close the message.

The task acceptance message is automatically deleted from your Inbox.

View a task update

In this exercise, you open and read a task update message from your partner, and then check the updated copy of the task in your task list.

 IMPORTANT To complete this exercise, ask your partner to open the "Prepare logo design for printer" task form in his or her task list, change the percentage in the % Complete box to 50%, and then save and close the task form.

If the accep-
tance message
does not appear
in your Inbox,
on the Tools
menu, click
Check For New
Mail.

1 Double-click the "Updated: Prepare logo design for printer" message from your partner.

A read-only task update form appears. A note in the Comment area informs you when the task is due and when the update was sent. The task status is In Progress and is 50% complete. Your screen should look similar to the following illustration.

Your partner made this status change.

Status has changed to reflect the percent complete.

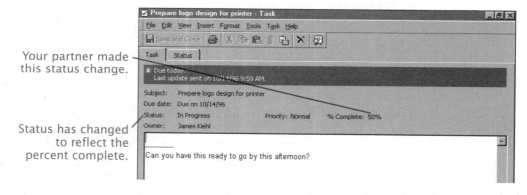

2 Close the update message.

3 On the Outlook Bar, click the Tasks icon.

Your task list appears in the Information viewer.

4 On the Standard toolbar, click the Current View down arrow, and then select Detailed List.

Your tasks appear in Detailed List view. The status of the "Prepare logo design for printer" task has changed to In Progress and the % Complete column shows 50%. Your screen should look similar to the following illustration.

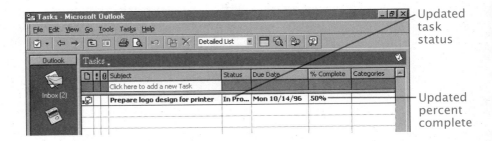

Updated task status

Updated percent complete

5 On the Outlook Bar, click the Inbox icon.

The contents of your Inbox appear in the Information viewer.

Creating a Task from an E-mail Message

Occasionally, you receive an e-mail message that requires some follow-up action on your part. For example, your manager might send you a message reminding you to call an important client later this afternoon. The message is an ordinary e-mail message, not a formal task request, but you still want to make sure you remember to make the call. You can easily turn a regular e-mail message into a task and add it to your task list in Outlook, and then cross it off once you have completed the phone call.

Set up the Inbox

For the purposes of the following exercises, you must drag a message from the Outlook SBS Practice folder into the Inbox to simulate receiving mail. Normally, sent messages appear automatically in the Inbox.

IMPORTANT To complete this exercise, you must move a practice message from the practice disk into your Outlook Inbox. If you have not yet set up the practice files, work through the "Installing and Using the Practice Files" section, earlier in this book.

---

1 Click the Start button, point to Programs, and then click Windows Explorer.

2 On the left side of the window, titled All Folders, click Drive C.

3 On the right side of the window, titled Contents Of, double-click the Outlook SBS Practice folder, and then double-click the Lesson 7 folder.

4 Click an open area on the taskbar with the right mouse button, and then click Tile Horizontally to tile the Exploring–Lesson 7 window and the Inbox–Microsoft Outlook window.

Your screen should look similar to the following illustration.

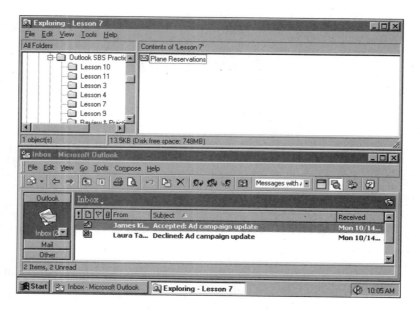

5   With the Exploring–Lesson 7 window active, select the Plane Reservations message.

6   Drag the selected message into the Information viewer in the Inbox–Microsoft Outlook window.

The practice file is copied, and you are ready to start the exercise. The Information viewer should look similar to the following illustration.

7   Close the Exploring–Lesson 7 window, and then maximize the Inbox–Microsoft Outlook window.

Create a task from a message

The messages in your Inbox should appear in Messages With AutoPreview view by default. In this view, you can read the entire Plane Reservations message from Margo Wilson and quickly find out that she wants you to confirm your upcoming flight. In this exercise, you add the message to your task list so that you remember to confirm the reservations.

1   In the Information viewer, click the Plane Reservations message from Margo Wilson.

The message is selected.

2   Drag the message onto the Tasks icon on the Outlook Bar.

A task form appears. "Plane Reservations" appears automatically in the Subject box, and the text of Margo Wilson's message appears in the Notes box at the bottom of the form. Your screen should look similar to the following illustration.

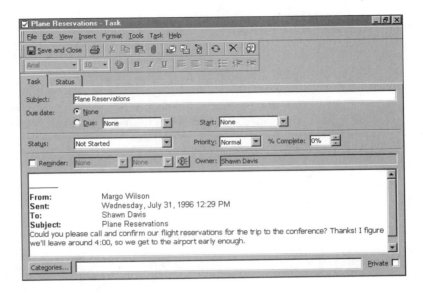

3 In the Due Date area, click the Due option button.

The current date appears in the Due box and a note appears in the Comment area, informing you that the task is due today.

4 On the Standard toolbar, click the Save And Close button.

The task form closes.

View the task list

In this exercise, you view your task list to make sure that the "Plane Reservations" task was added.

➤ On the Outlook Bar, click the Tasks icon.

Your task list appears and the "Plane Reservations" task appears in the list. Your screen should look similar to the following illustration.

The due date varies based on the current date on your computer.

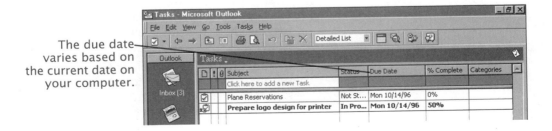

Finish the lesson

Follow these steps to delete the practice items you created in this lesson.

> **IMPORTANT**   Because you are logged on to Outlook with your own profile, be sure you delete only the practice tasks, appointments, and messages you added or created during this lesson.

Delete

1   In the task list, select the tasks that you created in this lesson.

2   On the Standard toolbar, click the Delete button.

    If a Delete Incomplete Task message appears, click OK.

3   In the Calendar folder, delete the meeting you scheduled in this lesson. Do not notify meeting attendees of the change.

4   In your Inbox, delete messages you created in this lesson.

5   To continue to the next lesson, on the Outlook Bar, click the Calendar icon.

6   If you are finished using Outlook for now, on the File menu, click Exit And Log Off.

Lesson Summary

To	Do this	Button
View your schedule in the Meeting Planner	Switch to the Calendar folder. On the Standard toolbar, click the Plan A Meeting button.	
View other user's schedules	In the Plan A Meeting dialog box, click Invite Others. Select names from one of the address lists.	
Select a meeting time during which each required attendee is available	In the Plan A Meeting dialog box, be sure that the names of all attendees appear in the All Attendees list and then click AutoPick.	
Request a meeting	In the Plan A Meeting dialog box, be sure that the time you want is selected, and then click Make Meeting. Type a subject and any other necessary information in the meeting request form, and then send the message.	

To	Do this
Track meeting request responses	Double-click the meeting appointment in your schedule. Click the Meeting Planner tab, and then click the Show Attendee Status option button.
Reschedule a meeting	In your schedule, position the pointer over the move handle for the meeting appointment. Drag the meeting to a new location. Click Yes to notify attendees of the change. Type any additional information in the meeting request form, and then send the message.
Send a task request	On the File menu, point to New, and then click Task Request. Click To to select a recipient name. Enter a subject for the task, add a due date if necessary, and then send the message.
View a task update	Double-click the Updated message in your Inbox folder.
Create a task from an e-mail message	In the Inbox, select the message and drag it onto the Tasks icon on the Outlook Bar. Add any necessary information to the task form, and then save and close the form.

For online information about	On the Help menu, click **Contents And Index**, click the **Index** tab, and then type
Scheduling meetings	**Meeting requests, scheduling** *or* **scheduling meetings**
Responding to meeting requests	**Meeting requests, responding to** *or* **responding**
Assigning tasks to others	**Tasks, assigning** *or* **assigning tasks**

Part

2

Review & Practice

You will review and practice how to:

Estimated time
25 min.

- Schedule appointments in Calendar.
- Edit appointments.
- Create and organize a task list.
- Schedule meetings with co-workers on your network.
- Assign tasks to others and track their progress.

Before you move on to Part 3, which covers tracking your work in Journal and managing all of your Microsoft Office 97 files using Microsoft Outlook, you can practice the skills you learned in Part 2 by working through this Review & Practice section. You will add several appointments to your schedule in Calendar, as well as edit your appointments to reflect new information. You will also create several new tasks for your task list. Finally, you'll use the Meeting Planner to schedule a meeting with one of your co-workers, and then assign your co-worker a related task and track its progress.

Scenario

You are continuing your preparations for the quarterly budget meeting. You want to schedule an appointment with the caterer, without having to cancel or reschedule any of your current commitments. To prepare for your own presentation at the meeting, you decide to add some relevant tasks to your task list and prioritize them. Then, you formally invite the other Margo Tea

177

Company employees to the meeting, and send a task request to one of your co-workers asking for help in setting up the meeting.

 IMPORTANT To complete this Review & Practice, you'll need to recruit some help from one or two co-workers on your network.

Step 1: Schedule Appointments in Calendar

You have selected a caterer for the quarterly budget meeting and you want to schedule an appointment with her to discuss the possible brunch menu. You also need to schedule an interview with a summer internship candidate whose resume was forwarded to you. In this step, you schedule both appointments.

 IMPORTANT For the purposes of this Review & Practice, you will use your own Outlook profile so that you can send meeting and task requests to actual co-workers on your network.

1 Start Outlook using your own profile, and then switch to the Calendar folder.

2 Go to the date Monday, February 22, 1999.

The dates in these exercises are set to 1999 to avoid any confusion with your real appointments.

3 Schedule an appointment from 10:00 A.M. to 11:00 A.M. Call the appointment **Review brunch menu with Jo-lynn Stone**.

4 Schedule an appointment from 3:30 P.M. to 4:30 P.M. Call the appointment **Interview with Jordan Davis**.

For more information about	See
Changing dates	Lesson 5
Creating appointments	Lesson 5

Step 2: Edit Appointments

Your doctor's office calls to remind you of your yearly check-up appointment which conflicts with the Jordan Davis interview. In this step, you reschedule the interview and add the doctor's appointment to your schedule.

1 Move your appointment with Jordan Davis to 1:00 P.M.

2 Schedule an appointment from 3:00 P.M. to 4:00 P.M. and call it Yearly Checkup.

3 Add the "Lakeview Medical Center" location to the "Yearly Checkup" appointment.

4 Show the "Yearly Checkup" appointment time as Out Of Office time in your schedule.

5 Make the "Yearly Checkup" appointment private. Save and close the appointment.

For more information about	See
Editing appointments	Lesson 5
Changing how appointments appear	Lesson 5
Making appointments private	Lesson 5

Step 3: *Create and Organize a Task List*

As a speaker at the budget meeting, you must perform several tasks to ensure that your presentation is professional and up-to-date. In this step, you add these tasks to your task list so that you can approach them in an orderly way.

1 Switch to the Tasks folder.

2 Add three tasks to the task list: Draft presentation outline, Rehearse slide show, and Call John about lunch.

3 Add a due date of 2/24/99 to the "Draft presentation outline" task, and then give the task a high priority.

4 Assign the "Draft presentation outline" task and the "Rehearse slide show" task to the Goals/Objectives category.

5 Apply the Detailed List view to the Tasks folder.

6 Group the tasks by category. (Hint: Use the Group By toolbar button.)

7 Remove the grouped categories.

For more information about	See
Creating and editing tasks	Lesson 6
Setting priorities	Lesson 6
Assigning items to categories	Lesson 6
Grouping tasks	Lesson 6

Step 4: *Schedule Meetings with Co-workers on Your Network*

Now that your meeting preparations are complete, it's time to invite everyone. In this step, you invite the appropriate people and track their responses.

1 Switch to the Calendar folder. Open the Plan A Meeting dialog box, and display your co-workers' schedules in the Meeting Planner grid. (Hint: Click the Invite Others button, and then use the Required option.)

2   Find the next available time and date for a two-hour meeting. Request a meeting with your co-workers.

3   In the Subject box, type **Quarterly Budget**. In the Location box, type **Main Conference Room**. In the Notes box, type **It's time once again to discuss the quarterly financial picture. Please join us!** Send the meeting request.

4   After your co-workers respond to your meeting request, view the responses using the Meeting Planner tab.

For more information about	See
Viewing other people's schedules	Lesson 7
Requesting a meeting	Lesson 7
Viewing responses to meeting requests	Lesson 7

Step 5: Assign Tasks to Others and Track Their Progress

You're going to need some help setting up the conference room for your presentation. In this step, you ask for a co-worker's assistance by sending a task request.

 NOTE   Ask your co-worker to accept the task request you send, and then check off the task as complete so that you receive a task update.

1   Switch to the Tasks folder, and then create a new task request.

2   Address the task request to your co-worker. In the Subject box, type **Set up overhead projector**. In the Notes box, type **Do you think you could help me with this before the meeting?**

3   Set the due date for the task request as the meeting date you selected in the previous exercise. Send the task request.

4   After your co-worker has accepted and completed the task, review the Task Update message in your Inbox.

For more information about	See
Creating a task request	Lesson 7
Tracking assigned tasks	Lesson 7

Finish the Review & Practice

Follow these steps to delete the practice messages you created in this Review & Practice, and then quit Outlook.

1   Delete the appointments you created during this Review & Practice. Delete the meeting without sending a cancellation message.

2   In the Tasks folder, reapply the Simple List view to your task list, and discard the current view settings. Delete the tasks you created during this Review & Practice.

3   In the Inbox, delete any messages you received during this Review & Practice.

4   If you are finished using Outlook for now, on the File menu, click Exit And Log Off.

Part
3

Managing Your Work with Microsoft Outlook

Tracking Your Work in Journal

Estimated time
35 min.

In this lesson you will learn how to:

- Create new journal entries.

- Add existing items to Journal.

- Record journal entries automatically.

- Change views in Journal.

If you want a precise record of everything you do during a day's work, you can record all of your daily activities in *Journal*. Your Journal acts as a catch-all area where you can record all your other Microsoft Outlook items, including e-mail messages that you send or receive, appointments, and tasks. Items in the Journal folder are displayed in a timeline format so you can keep track of the amount of time you spent working on each recorded item. Just as you use your schedule and task list to remind you of upcoming activities, you use your journal entries to create a record of past activities that you can review at a later time.

In addition to recording Outlook items in the Journal folder, you can keep track of your interactions with important contacts. For example, you can create an entry to mark the time and duration of an important phone call to a client. You can also create entries for conversations you have with your colleagues or letters you receive in the mail.

You will learn more about using Outlook with other Microsoft Office programs in Lesson 9.

If you use other Microsoft Office programs, you can keep track of the time you spend working on files using those programs. For example, if you spend several hours composing a report in Microsoft Word, you can record that activity as a journal entry.

As the Operations Coordinator for Margo Tea Company, it's essential that you keep a close eye on your own schedule as well as everyone else's so you can provide accurate progress reports and cost records to your supervisor. Now that you are comfortable working with different types of Outlook items, you decide to start keeping a record of your daily activities in one place so that you can review your entire day at a glance.

Start the lesson

In this exercise, you start Outlook using the Shawn Davis profile, and switch to the Journal folder.

1 Start Outlook using the Shawn Davis profile.

2 On the Outlook Bar, click the Journal icon.

The contents of the Journal folder appear in the Information viewer. The current month appears above the timeline, and the current day is selected on the timeline.

Creating New Journal Entries

There are a number of different ways to create new entries in your Journal, depending on the type of entry you want to create, and whether or not the entry is based on an existing Outlook item. Certain items can be recorded automatically. For example, you can set options to record all e-mail messages that you send to or receive from a certain contact. You can also set options to automatically record any Microsoft Office 97 documents and the length of time you work on them.

Some journal entries, such as appointments and tasks, must be entered manually. You must first create the appointment or task, and then create a journal entry from the existing item. Any existing item, in addition to appointments and tasks, can also be added to Journal manually. Finally, you can also create new journal entries manually by opening a journal entry form and typing information into the form fields.

By default, you view the Journal folder in By Type view. Items appear on a timeline and are grouped automatically into categories based on item types. For example, all e-mail messages appear in one group while all phone calls appear in another. The different types of journal entries are also represented by different icons. Most journal entry icons resemble the icons used to represent other Outlook items; for example, the icon for a Note journal entry, like the Notes icon on the Outlook Bar, looks like a yellow sticky note. Each journal entry icon also includes a little clock face in the lower left corner of the icon.

Icon	Entry type	Icon	Entry type
	Appointment		Meeting request or meeting response
	Conversation		Document
	E-mail message		Fax
	Letter		Microsoft Access database
	Microsoft Excel workbook		Microsoft Office Binder document
	Microsoft PowerPoint presentation		Microsoft Word document
	Note		Phone call
	Task		Task request or task response
	Item with attachment		

Create a new journal entry

In today's mail delivery, you received a brochure advertising a series of training seminars for business professionals. You want to make a note of the brochure in your Journal in case you need to refer to it later. In this exercise, you manually create a new journal entry regarding the mailing.

New Journal

1   On the Standard toolbar, click the New Journal button.

A new journal entry form appears. The current date and current time set on your computer appear in the Start Time boxes.

2   Maximize the form.

3   In the Subject box, type **Seminar Brochure**

4   Click the Entry Type down arrow.

A list of the available journal entry types appears.

5   Select Letter.

This entry will appear in the Letter category.

6   Click the Duration down arrow.

A list of durations appears.

7   Scroll up, and then select 5 minutes.

Receiving and reading this letter did not take much time, so you only need to indicate a short duration for this journal entry.

187

8 In the Notes box, type **Some courses in this list looked interesting!**

9 On the Standard toolbar, click the Save And Close button.

The journal entry form closes. A group heading, "Entry Type: Letter," appears in the Information viewer.

> **NOTE** The journal entry form includes a timer that is used primarily for recording the length of conversations. For example, if you want to keep track of the amount of time you spend on a long-distance call to a customer, you can create a journal entry for the call and start timing when you place the call.

View a journal entry

In this exercise, you expand the group heading for the entry you just created to show all entries in that group, and then open the entry.

1 Click the plus sign (+) next to the "Entry Type: Letter" heading.

The category expands, and an icon for the Seminar Brochure letter appears in the timeline at the time the journal entry was created. Your screen should look similar to the following illustration.

The current date corresponds to the settings on your computer.

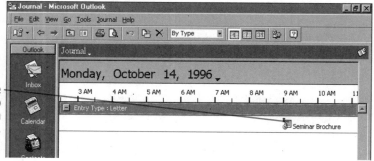

You can edit the entry by adding a note or changing the start and end times here.

2 Double-click the Seminar Brochure journal entry.

The journal entry form opens and the details of the item appear.

3 On the File menu, click Close.

The journal entry form closes.

Adding Appointments and Tasks

Appointments and tasks cannot be added to the Journal folder automatically. For example, if you want an appointment to appear in your Calendar and a record of that appointment to be logged in the Journal folder, you must first create the appointment in Calendar, and then create a journal entry for it. If you simply created a new journal entry for an appointment, that appointment would not automatically be added to your schedule in Calendar. Appointments appear in the Journal timeline at the time the appointment is scheduled, not at the time the journal entry was created. Tasks, on the other hand, appear in the Journal timeline at the time you created the journal entry, since tasks are not scheduled at a particular time by default. However, if a task has a specific due date, it will appear in the Journal timeline at 12:00 A.M. on the designated day.

Appointments and tasks must be added to the Journal folder manually, but you can create a journal entry from any other existing Outlook item. Once an item has been created, you can add it to your Journal folder.

Create an appointment

You need to schedule an interview with a prospective new employee. You want the appointment for the interview to appear in Calendar so that others will know you are busy at that time, and in Journal so that the daily timeline accurately reflects the time you spend in the interview. In this exercise, you create an appointment in your Calendar folder first so that you can add the appointment to your journal.

1 On the Outlook Bar, click the Calendar icon.

The contents of your Calendar folder appear and the current date appears in the Information viewer.

You can schedule overlapping appointments in the same time slots.

2 In the appointment area, select the time slots from 10:00 A.M. to 11:00 A.M.

3 Type **Interview with Harry Angstrom**, and then press ENTER.

The appointment is added to your schedule.

Add an appointment to Journal

In this exercise, you add the "Interview with Harry Angstrom" appointment to the timeline in your Journal folder so that it is included in your record of all activities for that day.

1 Be sure that the "Interview with Harry Angstrom" appointment is selected.

*You can also
press CTRL+J.*

2   On the Tools menu, click Record In Journal.

A journal entry form appears. The Start Time, Start Date, and Duration boxes have also been filled in, and a shortcut icon to the appointment appears in the Notes box. Your screen should look similar to the following illustration.

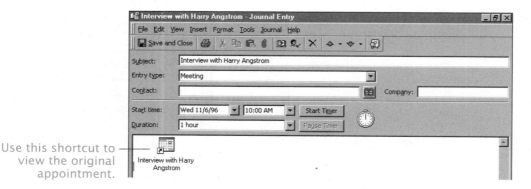

Use this shortcut to
view the original
appointment.

3   On the Standard toolbar, click the Save And Close button.

The journal entry is saved and your schedule reappears.

4   On the Outlook Bar, click the Journal icon.

The contents of the Journal folder appear in the Information viewer and a group heading, "Entry Type: Meeting," has been added.

5   Click the plus sign (+) next to the "Entry Type: Meeting" heading.

The group expands, and an icon appears. Your screen should look similar to the following illustration.

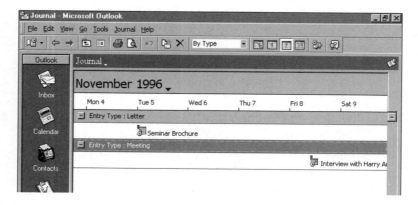

Use a shortcut in a journal entry

You want to add a note to the "Interview with Harry Angstrom" appointment to remind yourself of a topic you want to cover. Instead of switching folders and then locating and opening the appointment, in this exercise, you use a journal entry shortcut to view the original item.

1 In the Information viewer, double click the "Interview with Harry Angstrom" journal entry.

The journal entry form appears.

2 In the Notes box, double-click the "Interview with Harry Angstrom" shortcut icon.

The appointment form for the "Interview with Harry Angstrom" appointment appears.

3 In the Notes box on the appointment form, type **Be sure to ask about previous sales experience!**

4 On the Standard toolbar, click the Save And Close button.

The appointment form closes. The note is saved.

5 Close the journal entry form.

Add a task to the Journal folder

In this exercise, you create a task in your task list, and then add the task to your Journal folder.

1 On the Outlook Bar, click the Tasks icon.

The contents of your task list appear in the Information viewer.

2 In the Click Here To Add A New Task area, type **Review Harry Angstrom's resume**, and then press TAB.

The insertion point moves to the Due Date column.

You can also click the Due Date down arrow, and then click Today.

3 Type the current date, and then press ENTER.

The task is added to your task list.

4 Select the new task in your task list.

You must select a task before you can create a journal entry for it.

You can also press CTRL+J.

5 On the Tools menu, click Record In Journal.

A journal entry form for the task appears. The task information appears in the appropriate boxes and a shortcut icon for the original task appears in the Notes box. Your screen should look similar to the following illustration.

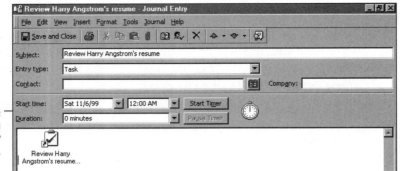

The start time and duration appear by default.

6   Click the second Start Time down arrow, and then select 8:30 A.M.

You can scroll down to see all the available times in the drop-down list.

7   Click the Duration down arrow, and then select 30 Minutes.

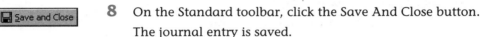

8   On the Standard toolbar, click the Save And Close button.

The journal entry is saved.

9   On the Outlook Bar, click the Journal icon.

The contents of the Journal folder appear in the Information viewer, and an "Entry Type: Task" group heading has been added.

Recording New Entries Automatically

It's not difficult to create journal entries from your existing Outlook items, but it can be time-consuming. To save yourself the effort of finding specific items and adding them to your Journal folder, you can set options to record certain types of items automatically. With the exception of appointments and tasks, most Outlook items can be recorded in your Journal folder automatically, if they are associated with a particular contact. In addition, you can automatically record the time you spend working on files using other Microsoft Office applications.

Recording All Activities for a Contact

For a demonstration of how to record all activities for a contact, double-click the Camcorder Files On The Internet shortcut on your Desktop or connect to the Internet address listed on p. xxx.

The Outlook items that you can record automatically in the Journal folder are all related to communicating with others. E-mail messages, including meeting requests, meeting responses, meeting cancellations, task requests, and task responses can be recorded automatically; faxes can also be recorded. Since all of these items convey information in some way, they all involve other individuals, either as senders or recipients.

Suppose you want to maintain a record of all your communication with an important Margo Tea Company customer. You can set Outlook options to automatically keep track of any e-mail messages you send to or receive from that customer, and store a list of those messages in the Journal folder. To record Outlook items automatically, you must first associate those items with a particular contact.

 IMPORTANT   Because this section involves setting Outlook options for the messages you receive, you'll need to recruit some help from another person on your network to complete the following exercises. Find at least one person on your network who will agree to read and respond to your practice messages.

Add a contact

In this exercise, you create a contact entry for the person helping you with this section. You will use this contact to help identify the messages you want to record automatically.

 NOTE   If the person helping you with this section already appears in your contact list, you can skip this exercise.

New Contact

1   On the Outlook Bar, click the Contacts icon.

Your contact list appears in the Information viewer.

2   On the Standard toolbar, click the New Contact button.

A blank contact form appears.

3   In the Full Name box, type the name of the person cooperating with you on these exercises.

Normally, you would also fill out the other fields on the contact form, but it is not necessary for this exercise.

4   On the Standard toolbar, click the Save And Close button.

Your partner's name appears in your contact list.

Set recording options

In this exercise, you set Outlook options so that all messages from or addressed to your partner will be recorded automatically in your Journal folder.

1   On the Tools menu, click Options.

The Options dialog box appears, and the General tab is selected.

2 In the Options dialog box, click the Journal tab.

The Journal options tab appears.

3 In the Automatically Record These Items box, select the E-mail Message check box.

4 In the For These Contacts box, select the check box corresponding to the name of the person helping you with this section.

5 Click OK.

Any messages you send to or receive from your partner will now be recorded in your Journal folder.

TIP When you create a new contact, you can click the Journal tab on the contact form, and then select the Automatically Record Journal Entries For This Contact check box to automatically record all items related to that contact in your Journal.

Send a message to test recording

In this exercise, you send a message to the person helping you with these exercises, and then check to see if the message was recorded in your Journal folder.

You can also switch to the Inbox, and then click the New Mail Message button.

1 On the File menu, point to New, and then click Mail Message.

A blank Mail form appears.

2 In the To box, type the name of the person helping you with this exercise.

3 In the Subject box, type **Automatic Recording Test**

4 In the message area, type **Please reply to this message.**

5 On the Standard toolbar, click the Send button.

The message is sent to your partner.

6 On the Outlook Bar, click the Journal icon.

The contents of the Journal folder appear in the Information viewer, and a group heading for "Entry Type: E-mail Message" has been added.

7 Click the plus sign (+) next to the "Entry Type: E-mail Message" heading.

The category expands, and an icon for the "Automatic Recording Test" message you sent to your partner appears in the current time slot.

Test automatic recording for received messages

Messages that you receive are not recorded automatically in the Journal folder until you open them. In this exercise, you read the response from your partner, and then make sure that it was also recorded automatically.

> **IMPORTANT** In order to complete this exercise, be sure that your partner has sent a reply to your "Automatic Recording Test" message.

1 On the Outlook bar, click the Inbox icon.

The contents of your Inbox appear in the Information viewer.

To make sure that your partner's message was delivered, on the Tools menu, click Check For New Mail.

2 Double-click the "RE: Automatic Recording Test" message from your partner.

The message opens in the Mail form.

3 Read, and then close the message.

4 On the Outlook Bar, click the Journal icon.

The contents of the Journal folder appear in the Information viewer. The "RE: Automatic Recording Test" message appears in the "Entry Type: E-mail Message" group on the timeline at the time you opened the message. Your screen should look similar to the following illustration.

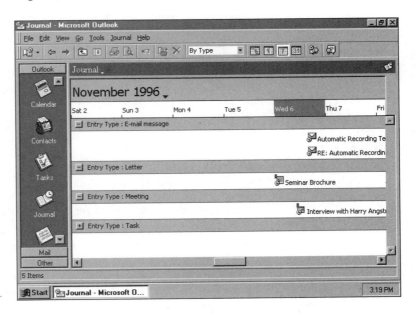

Viewing Items in Journal

If you have worked through the previous lessons in this book, you already have some understanding of how to apply and modify the standard views available in each Outlook folder. You can click the Current View down arrow, and then select a different standard view at any time. The following table describes the different views for the Journal folder.

View	Description
By Type	Journal entry icons appear grouped by type, and are arranged on a timeline.
By Contact	Journal entry icons appear grouped by the names of the contacts they are associated with, and are arranged on a timeline.
By Category	Journal entry icons appear grouped by assigned category names, and are arranged on a timeline.
Entry List	Journal entries appear in a table listing them by entry type, subject, start date, duration, and related contact or categories, if applicable.
Last Seven Days	Journal entries appear in a table listing them by entry type, subject, start date, duration, contact, and categories; only the entries that were made during the previous week appear.
Phone Calls	Journal entries that are phone calls appear in a table listing them by subject, start date, duration, contact, and categories; only the entries that are phone calls appear.

You can learn more about assigning items to categories in Lesson 6.

In addition to applying the different standard views, you can also change the time increments in any of the views that display journal entries in a timeline format. The default time increments are half-hour time slots, with one day at a time appearing in the Information viewer. However, you can change the timeline increments to view approximately a week's worth or a month's worth of journal entries at a time.

View entries by contact

In this exercise, you apply a different standard view so that you can see your entries appear based on the contacts associated with them.

1 On the Standard toolbar, click the Current View down arrow, select By Contact, and then discard the current view settings.

Two group headings appear in the Information viewer: a "Contact: None," heading, and a "Contact: *Your Partner's Name*" heading; the "Your Partner's Name" segment shows the name of the person who worked with you on the exercises in the previous section.

2 Click the plus sign (+) next to each group heading.

The categories expand, and the journal entries for the messages you sent to and received from your partner appear in the "Contact: *Your Partner's Name*" group. Your screen should look similar to the following illustration.

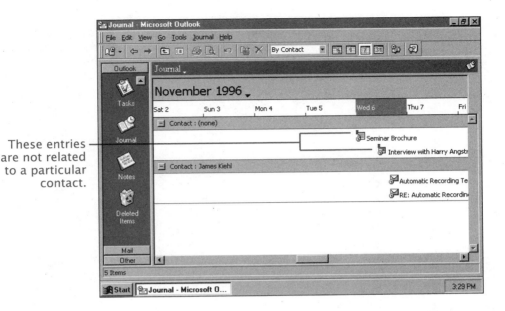

These entries are not related to a particular contact.

Change timeline increments

In this exercise, you display your journal entries for different time periods.

Month

1 On the Standard toolbar, click the Month button.

The Information viewer is not wide enough to show an entire month on the timeline; approximately half of the current month appears, depending on the current date. The Contact groupings are still expanded, and icons representing your journal entries are arranged on the current date.

2 Position the pointer over an icon in the Information viewer.

The subject appears as a ScreenTip.

Day

3 On the Standard toolbar, click the Day button.

A single day appears in the Information viewer, and your journal entries for the current date appear.

4 On the Standard toolbar, click the Current View down arrow, and then select By Type.

A message appears, asking if you want to save or discard the current view settings.

5 Click the Discard The Current View Settings option button.

The default Journal view, By Type, is restored.

6 Use the plus signs (+) next to the category headings to make sure that only the "Entry Type: Meeting" category is expanded.

TIP You can easily search for a specific journal entry by clicking Find Items on the Tools menu. In the Find dialog box, be sure that Journal Entries appears in the Look For box and that the Journal folder appears in the In box. Type the word or words you want to search for, select the field or fields you want to search, and then click Find Now.

Moving Existing Journal Entries

Schedules change rapidly in the business world, and you may need to re-organize your daily work as priorities change or as different activities take precedence over your scheduled tasks. You can move your journal entries to different times and dates to more accurately reflect the time you spend on a particular activity. You can also change the fields displayed in the Journal timeline so that your entries appear based on different criteria, such as the time you modified them, or the time you actually created the entry versus the time you performed the activity.

When you do modify start and end times in your journal entries, it's important to keep in mind the fact that changing a journal entry does not change the original item related to it. For example, if you change the start time of a journal entry based on an appointment, the appointment time in your Calendar will not change. You must go back to the Calendar folder to change the original item.

You have been on a business trip and away from your office for the past week. Since you're using the Journal folder to keep track of the way you spend your time during work, you decide to move the appointments and tasks you had planned on accomplishing during your business trip so that they match what actually took place during your week away from the office.

NOTE Because tasks are created with start dates, but not specific start times, you do not need to modify the original task entry in the Tasks folder to reflect the changed start time of the journal entry.

Move a journal entry

In this exercise, you change the start time for a journal entry because you were not able to work on the task at the time you'd originally planned to.

1 In the "Entry Type: Meeting" grouping, double-click the "Interview with Harry Angstrom" journal entry.

The journal entry form opens.

2   Click the second Start Time down arrow, and then select 2:00 P.M. from the drop-down list.

3   On the Standard toolbar, click the Save And Close button.

The journal entry moves to the 2:00 P.M. time slot on the timeline.

Finish the lesson

Follow these steps to delete the practice items you created in this lesson.

WARNING If your Journal folder contains entries in addition to the ones you created for this lesson, you should delete the practice journal entries individually to preserve your real entries.

1   In the Journal folder, expand the "Entry Type: E-mail Message" group heading, and then hold down SHIFT and click each of the other group headings.

The headings are selected.

2   On the Standard toolbar, click the Delete button.

A message appears, warning you that all items in the selected groups will be deleted.

Delete

3   Click OK.

Your journal entries are deleted.

4   In the Calendar folder, delete the "Interview with Harry Angstrom" appointment.

5   In the Tasks folder, delete the "Review Harry Angstrom's resume" task.

6   In the Contacts folder, delete the name of the person helping you.

7   In the Inbox folder, delete the "RE: Automatic Recording Test" message from your co-worker.

8   On the Tools menu, click Options, and then click the Journal tab. Clear the check boxes in the Automatically Record These Items list and in the For These Contacts list, and then click OK.

9   To continue to the next lesson, on the Outlook Bar, click the Other shortcut bar, and then click the My Computer Icon.

10   If you are finished using Outlook for now, on the File menu, click Exit And Log Off.

Lesson Summary

To	Do this	Button
Create a new journal entry	Switch to the Journal folder. On the Standard toolbar, click the New Journal button, and then type the information you want in the journal entry form.	
View a journal entry	Expand the Entry Type group, if necessary, and then double-click the journal entry.	
Create a journal entry from an existing item (for tasks and appointments)	In the appropriate item folder, select the item. On the Tools menu, click Record In Journal.	
Switch to an original Outlook item from a journal entry	Open the journal entry. In the Notes area, double-click the item shortcut icon.	
Record activities automatically for a contact	On the Tools menu, click Options, and then click the Journal tab. In the Automatically Record These Items box, select the appropriate check boxes. In the For These Contacts box, select the check box for the contact name. Click OK.	
Change standard views in Journal	On the Standard toolbar, click the Current View down arrow, and then select a view.	
Change timeline increments	On the Standard toolbar, click the Day, Week, or Month button.	
Move a journal entry	Open the journal entry. Change the start time, and then save and close the entry.	

For online information about	On the Help menu, click Contents And Index, click the Index tab, and then type
Creating journal entries	Journal, overview
Adding appointments and tasks to Journal	Appointments, recording in Journal or tasks, recording in Journal
Recording items automatically	Recording
Changing views	Journal, views

Integrating with Other Microsoft Office Programs

In this lesson you will learn how to:

Estimated time
40 min.

- Manage other program files using Outlook.
- Attach files to Outlook items.
- Record your work with files automatically in the Journal folder.
- Share files with others.

Now that you are familiar with the basics of Microsoft Outlook, you can begin to explore ways to combine its capabilities with those of other applications within the Microsoft Office 97 family. For example, you can use the My Computer folder in Outlook, in place of Windows Explorer, to view and arrange all of your files. You can create a document using Microsoft Word, and then send it to your co-workers as part of an e-mail message. In turn, your co-workers can make revisions to the document online, and then use Outlook to return the revised document to you. Finally, you can record the time you spend working on Microsoft Office 97 files in the Journal folder in Outlook.

Now that the new product line project is in full swing, you and your co-workers at the Margo Tea Company are developing a variety of materials such as reports and advertising brochures. To manage the project efficiently, you must organize your own files so that you can easily find documents and data when you need them. You must also be able to exchange files quickly and efficiently with your co-workers. In this lesson, you'll practice using Outlook to help you manage different files.

IMPORTANT   You must have Microsoft Word 97 installed on your computer to perform the exercises in this lesson. If you do not, skip this lesson.

Start the lesson

In this exercise, you start Outlook using the Shawn Davis profile and switch to the My Computer folder.

1   Start Outlook using the Shawn Davis profile.

2   On the Outlook bar, click the Other shortcut bar.

The icons in the Other folder group appear.

3   On the Outlook Bar, click the My Computer icon.

The contents of the My Computer folder appear in the Information viewer. The drives available on your computer are listed.

 IMPORTANT   If you haven't set up the Outlook SBS Practice folder yet, refer to "Installing and Using the Practice Files," earlier in this book.

Managing Your Files Using Outlook

Using the Other group, you can view and manage all of the available drives and folders on your computer, without ever leaving Outlook. You can open a folder and view its contents, including files and other folders; you can also move or copy items between folders or search through folders for specific items. If you have worked with Windows Explorer or My Computer in Microsoft Windows 95 or in Windows NT version 4.0, you will find that the My Computer folder in Outlook is very similar. In Windows 95 and Windows NT, you could use My Computer to open windows and folders one level at a time; in Outlook, the My Computer folder works more like Windows Explorer in Windows 95 and Windows NT, since it allows you to open folders in a hierarchical display.

Browsing Through Files Using My Computer

When you select the My Computer folder on the Outlook Bar, the available drives for your computer appear in the Information viewer. These typically include your local hard disk and a floppy disk drive, as well as any established connections to other computers on a network. You can also display the Folder List to see the hierarchy of all of your computer's folders and drives.

You can click any folder in the Information viewer to see its contents; you can also open individual files and items. If you open a file that was created in another Microsoft Office 97 program, and you have that program installed on your computer, the program starts automatically so that you can see and work with the file in the appropriate format.

Display the Folder List

In this exercise, you display the Folder List in the Information viewer so that you can see the relationship between the folders and files stored on your computer.

Folder List

1   On the Standard toolbar, click the Folder List button.

   The Folder List appears on the left side of the Information viewer.

2   Position the pointer over the right border of the Folder List.

   The pointer changes to a two-headed arrow.

3   Drag the border an inch or two to the right, until the Folder List is clearly visible.

   Your screen should look similar to the following illustration.

Plus sign (+) indicates hidden subfolders in these folders.

Browse through folder contents

In this exercise, you use My Computer to explore the folders and files on your computer.

1   In the Information viewer, double-click drive C.

   In the Information viewer, all of the top-level folders and files stored on the hard disk appear. In the Folder List, the My Computer category expands to show all the available drives. Your screen should look similar to the following illustration.

These drives previously appeared in the Information viewer.

2 In the Information viewer, double-click the Outlook SBS Practice folder.

The folders and files stored in the Outlook SBS Practice folder appear in the Information viewer, and the Folder List expands to show the folders on your hard disk. Your screen should look similar to the following illustration.

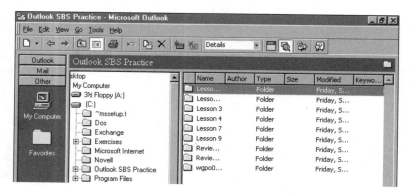

3 In the Information viewer, double-click the Lesson 9 folder.

The contents of the Lesson 9 folder appear in the Information viewer and the Outlook SBS Practice folder expands in the Folder List.

4 On the Standard toolbar, click the Folder List button.

The Folder List is hidden.

Folder List

Open a file

In this exercise, you start Microsoft Word and open a document from the Outlook SBS Practice folder.

1 In the Information viewer, double-click the History document.

Microsoft Word starts. If the User Name dialog box appears, type your name and initials. The History document, describing the history of the Margo Tea Company, opens.

2 Maximize the Word window.

Your screen should look similar to the following illustration.

Microsoft Word is the active program.

Close button

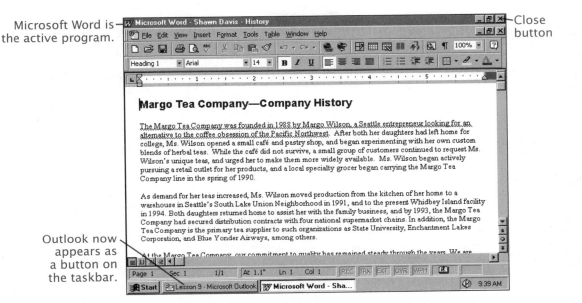

Outlook now appears as a button on the taskbar.

Margo Tea Company—Company History

The Margo Tea Company was founded in 1988 by Margo Wilson, a Seattle entrepreneur looking for an alternative to the coffee obsession of the Pacific Northwest. After both her daughters had left home for college, Ms. Wilson opened a small café and pastry shop, and began experimenting with her own custom blends of herbal teas. While the café did not survive, a small group of customers continued to request Ms. Wilson's unique teas, and urged her to make them more widely available. Ms. Wilson began actively pursuing a retail outlet for her products, and a local specialty grocer began carrying the Margo Tea Company line in the spring of 1990.

As demand for her teas increased, Ms. Wilson moved production from the kitchen of her home to a warehouse in Seattle's South Lake Union Neighborhood in 1991, and to the present Whidbey Island facility in 1994. Both daughters returned home to assist her with the family business, and by 1993, the Margo Tea Company had secured distribution contracts with four national supermarket chains. In addition, the Margo Tea Company is the primary tea supplier to such organizations as State University, Enchantment Lakes Corporation, and Blue Yonder Airways, among others.

If you are prompted to save changes, click No.

3 On the Microsoft Word program window, click the Close button.

The History document and Microsoft Word close. Outlook becomes the active program and the contents of the Lesson 9 folder appear in the Information viewer.

Previewing a Document Using Quick View

If you want to preview the contents of a file without actually starting the program and opening the document, you can look at it in Quick View, a feature that can be installed as a component of Windows 95 or Windows NT. In Quick View, you can look at a file in plain text without formatting, but you cannot edit or otherwise make changes to a file. If, after previewing a file, you decide you want to work with it, you can open the file from the Quick View window.

 TROUBLESHOOTING If the Quick View command is not available on the shortcut menu, you need to install Quick View on your computer. For more information, click Start, and then point to Help. On the Help menu, click the Index tab, and then type **installing, Windows components.**

Preview a document

In this exercise, you use Quick View to preview a logo.

1   In the Information viewer, use the right mouse button to click the Margo bitmap image.

A shortcut menu appears.

You can also click Quick View on the File menu.

2   Click Quick View.

The Products–Quick View window opens and the Margo Tea Company logo appears. Your screen should look similar to the following illustration.

You can click here to open the file.

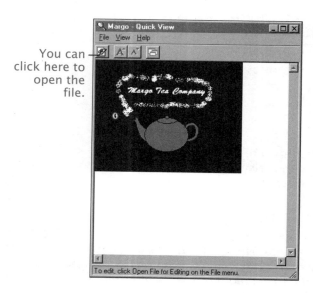

3   Close the Quick View window.

Creating Shortcuts to Folders

By default, shortcuts to the My Documents folder and Favorites folder appear in the Other group on the Outlook Bar. If there are other folders that you use frequently, you can also add shortcuts to these folders to the Outlook Bar. This way, you can quickly open the chosen folder and review its contents instead of searching through the hierarchy of all available drives and folders on your computer.

Add a shortcut to the Outlook Bar

In this exercise, you create a shortcut to the Lesson 9 folder on your Outlook Bar.

1   Be sure that the contents of the Lesson 9 folder appear in your Information viewer.

The name of the current folder appears on the Outlook title bar at the top of the screen.

2   On the Standard toolbar, click the Up One Level button.

The contents of the Outlook SBS Practice folder appear in the Information viewer.

3   Use the right mouse button to click the Lesson 9 folder.

A shortcut menu appears.

4   Click Add To Outlook Bar.

An icon for the Lesson 9 folder appears on the Outlook Bar in the Other group.

5   On the Outlook Bar, click the Lesson 9 icon.

The contents of the Lesson 9 folder appear in the Information viewer.

Up One Level

Associating Files with Outlook Items

Suppose you have information in a Microsoft Word document that you want to share with a colleague in another city. You could print the document and mail it, but this would take time and might be costly. With Outlook, you can send the file by inserting it into an e-mail message. Your colleague would then receive the file within minutes instead of days. In the same way, you can *attach* file shortcuts to other items in Outlook. For example, if you have scheduled several hours during the day to work on a particular budget worksheet, you can attach a shortcut to the worksheet to the appointment within your Calendar folder. Then, when the appointment comes up in your schedule, you can immediately use the shortcut to open the associated file and begin working on it. You can also set certain Outlook options so that the time you spend working on different files is automatically recorded in your Journal folder.

Sending a File Using an E-mail Message

To insert a file directly into a message, you can *embed* the file as an *object*. Objects can include files of any type or even parts of a file. You can insert one of several object types, depending on what programs you have installed on your computer. For example, you could insert a Microsoft Excel spreadsheet, a

Paint graphic, or a Microsoft Word document. When you embed an object in a message, the recipient can view the object without opening the program in which it was created. If the recipient of a message doesn't have the program used to create the object installed on his or her computer, he or she can still view the data in the message, but he or she won't be able to edit it.

Embedding files is helpful if you want the message recipients to be able to view an object without making changes to it (although they can modify an embedded object, if they have the appropriate program installed). However, if you want the recipients to be able to easily copy a file to their hard disk, you should *attach* the file to your message. If the recipients have the program that was used to create an attached file or if they have a program that recognizes the file type, they can open and edit the file on their computer.

To help you figure out whether to embed or attach objects in messages, refer to the following table.

When you want to	Do this in your message
Allow the recipient to view the information in a file without opening a program.	Embed the file as an object.
Allow the recipient to view the information in a file using a program, but you also want to condense the amount of space used by the object.	Embed the file as an icon.
Allow the recipient to view and edit all or part of the information in a file without affecting the original file.	Embed the file as an object.
Send a file to a recipient who used an e-mail system that doesn't support embedded objects.	Attach the file to the message.
Send an object to a recipient so that he or she can easily copy it to his or her hard disk.	Attach the file to the message.
Send a heavily formatted file to a recipient who isn't able to view the formatting.	Attach the file to the message as a text-only file.

In the following exercises, you'll learn how to embed objects in and attach files to your e-mail messages.

Create a new message

In this exercise, you start a new message about the Margo Tea Company's new logo design, and address it to a co-worker.

1   On the Outlook Bar, click the Outlook shortcut bar.

The icons in the Outlook group appear on the Outlook Bar.

2   On the Outlook Bar, click the Inbox icon.

The contents of the Inbox folder appear in the Information viewer.

New Mail Message

3   On the Standard toolbar, click the New Mail Message button.

A blank Mail Form appears.

4   In the To box, type **James**, and then press TAB twice.

The Address Book is automatically checked for matching names, and the underlined name "James Kiehl" appears in the To box.

5   In the Subject box, type **New Logo Design**

6   In the message area, type **Let me know what you think of this, so we can begin work on the new package labels.**

7   Press ENTER twice.

The insertion point moves to a new line.

Embed a graphic object

You want feedback from James on the new logo being considered for the Margo Tea Company. In this exercise, you embed the graphic in your message so that your co-worker can quickly view the graphic, and then return his comments on it.

1   On the Insert menu, click Object.

The Insert Object dialog box appears.

2   Click the Create From File option button.

You are creating an embedded object from an existing bitmap (.bmp) image file on your computer.

3   Click Browse.

The Browse dialog box appears.

4   Open the Outlook SBS Practice folder on your hard disk, and then open the Lesson 9 folder.

5   Select the Margo bitmap image, and then click OK.

The path to the Margo bitmap image appears in the File box in the Insert Object dialog box.

6   Click OK, and then maximize the message.

The embedded bitmap image appears in your message. Your screen should look similar to the following illustration.

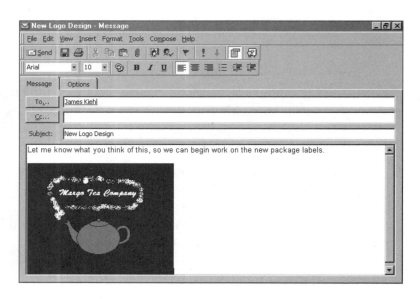

7 On the Standard toolbar, click the Send button.

The message with the embedded object is sent.

Attach a file

In this exercise, you attach a file to a message so that another one of your co-workers can open and read the file, and then save it to work with later.

1 On the Standard toolbar, click the New Mail Message button.

A blank Mail Form appears.

New Mail Message

2 Address the message to Tammy Wu.

3 In the Subject box, type **Corporate History**

4 In the message area, type **Here's the information your new client requested.**, and then press ENTER twice.

5 On the Standard toolbar, click the Insert File button.

The Insert File dialog box appears.

Insert File

6 Open the Outlook SBS Practice folder on your hard disk, and then open the Lesson 9 folder.

7 Select the Microsoft Word document named History.

8 In the Insert As area, be sure that the Attachment option button is selected, and then click OK.

The attached file appears as an icon, as shown in the following illustration.

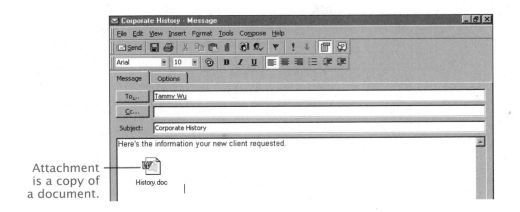

Attachment is a copy of a document.

9 On the Standard toolbar, click the Send button.

Your message, with the attached document, is sent.

Adding Files to Items in Your Schedule

When you add files to Outlook items, you can add them as attachments or create a shortcut to an original file within the item. The option you choose depends on your needs and on the item type to which you're adding the file. For example, if you are adding a document to an appointment so that you can work on it at a scheduled time, you might want to create a shortcut to the document in the appointment. That way, when the time comes for you to work on it, you can use the shortcut to open the original document stored on your computer and begin working immediately. On the other hand, if you are adding a file to a task request, for example, you might want to add it as an attachment. Then, the recipient of the task request can save the attached file to his or her hard disk and work on it there, while you retain the original file on your own computer.

Create an appointment containing a file shortcut

In this exercise, you schedule time to work on the product list document, and add a document shortcut to a new appointment in your Calendar folder.

1 On the Outlook Bar, click the Other shortcut bar, and then click the Lesson 9 icon.

The contents of the Lesson 9 folder appear in the Information viewer.

2 In the Information viewer, select the Microsoft Word document named Products.

The Information viewer still contains the Lesson 9 folder contents, because you have not selected a new folder yet.

3 On the Outlook Bar, click the Outlook shortcut bar.

Icons for the folders in the Outlook group appear on the Outlook Bar.

4 Drag the Products document onto the Calendar icon.

As you drag, the pointer changes to an arrow with a plus sign (+), indicating that the file is being copied. After a moment, a new appointment form appears with a shortcut icon to the Products document in the Notes area. Your screen should look similar to the following illustration.

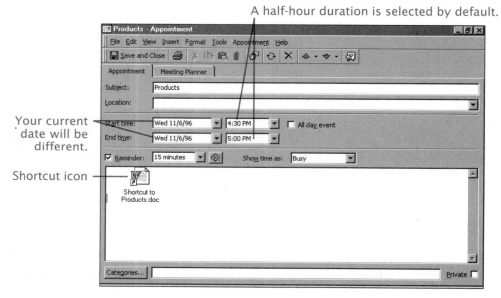

A half-hour duration is selected by default.

Your current date will be different.

Shortcut icon

5 In the Subject box, select the current text, and then type **Revise product list**

The text is replaced as you type.

6 In the Start Time box, change the date to 2/15/99.

7 On the Standard toolbar, click the Save And Close button.

The appointment, with its attached shortcut, is added to your schedule. You will test the shortcut in a later exercise.

> **TIP** If you use the right mouse button to drag a file onto an Outlook Bar icon, a shortcut menu appears. You can then choose to create an item with a shortcut or to create an item with an attachment by clicking the appropriate command on the shortcut menu.

Record File Activity Automatically

In Lesson 8, you learned how to record e-mail messages to and from specific contacts automatically in your Journal folder. You can also keep track of the amount of time you spend working on different Microsoft Office 97 files. You can create journal entries for Microsoft Office files manually or record your work on those files automatically by setting options in advance.

Use a file shortcut in an appointment

In this exercise, you view the appointment you created from the Products document, and then open the document using the shortcut in the appointment.

1 On the Outlook Bar, click the Calendar icon.

Your schedule for the current date appears in the Information viewer.

You can also press CTRL+G.

2 On the Go menu, click Go To Date.

The Go To Date dialog box appears.

3 In the Date box, type **2/15/99**, and then click OK.

The date changes to Monday, February 15, 1999, and the "Revise product list" appointment appears in your schedule. Your screen should look similar to the following illustration.

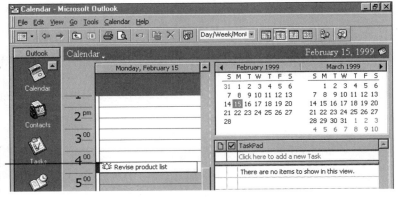

Your appointment time may be different.

4 Double-click the "Revise product list" appointment.

The appointment form opens, and the shortcut to the Products document appears in the Notes box.

5 Double-click the Products shortcut icon.

Microsoft Word starts and the Products document opens. Your screen should look similar to the following illustration.

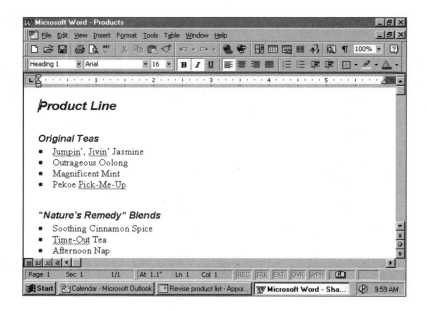

Edit the document

In this exercise, you make changes to the Product Line list. You will check your recorded activity in the Journal folder in the next exercise.

1   Click at the end of the "Pekoe Pick-Me-Up" line, and then press ENTER.

The insertion point moves to a new line and a new bullet appears.

2   Type **Groovy Green Tea**, and then press CTRL+END.

The insertion point moves to the end of the document.

3   Press ENTER, and then type **Wake-Up In a Cup**

4   On the Standard toolbar, click the Save button.

The changes to the file are saved.

Save

5   Close Microsoft Word.

6   Close the "Revise product list" form.

Check a recorded document in the Journal folder

In this exercise, you verify that the time you spent revising the Products document was recorded automatically in your Journal folder.

1   On the Outlook Bar, click the Journal icon.

The current date on the Journal timeline appears in the Information viewer.

Microsoft Word documents are automatically recorded in Journal.

2 Click the plus sign (+) next to the "Entry Type: Microsoft Word" heading.

The group expands, and an icon appears, indicating the path to the Products document and the time you spent working on it. Your screen should look similar to the following illustration.

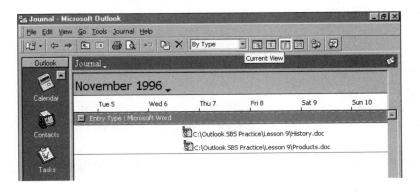

Open a file from a journal entry

In this exercise, you view the Products journal entry in detail, and then reopen the document.

1 In the Information viewer, double-click the Products journal entry.

The journal entry form opens, and the details of the entry appear. Because the appointment was recorded automatically, a shortcut to the "Products" document appears in the Notes box by default.

2 Double-click the Products shortcut icon.

Microsoft Word starts and the Products document opens.

3 On the taskbar, use the right mouse button to click the Products journal entry button.

A shortcut menu appears.

4 Click Close.

The journal entry closes.

Distributing Files to Others

You have already learned how to attach a file from another program to an Outlook message. But suppose that you are working on a file in another Microsoft Office program and want immediate feedback. Instead of switching to the Inbox, composing a new message, browsing for the file path, and then attaching the file, you can send a file to your co-worker without ever leaving the program you are in.

Send a document to a co-worker

In this exercise, you send the revised product list document to Tammy Wu so that she can show it to her new client.

 NOTE If you would like to use real names in this exercise, you can ask a co-worker to assist you. Instead of Tammy Wu, select your co-worker's name from the global address list.

1 On the File menu in Word, point to Send To, and then click Mail Recipient.

A new Mail Form appears, and an attachment icon for the "Products" document appears in the message area. Your screen should look similar to the following illustration.

Subject is taken from first line of document text.

Attachment icon

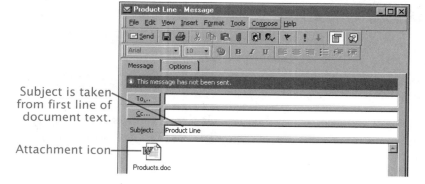

2 In the To box, type **Tammy Wu**

3 Click below the attachment icon, press ENTER, and then type **Here's the latest product list for your new client.**

 4 Click the Send button.

The message and the attachment are sent.

5 Close the Products document, but do not close Microsoft Word.

Routing Documents to Multiple Users

The company president wants to include the Company History document in this year's Annual Report. You'd like to distribute the document to several other people in the company so that they can review it and make any suggestions they might have. You could send them each a copy of the document using

Outlook, and then wait for them to submit their revisions to you, but you would be getting several documents back, and would need to consolidate the feedback into one document. Instead, you can attach a routing slip to your document. Each recipient can make his or her own revisions online, and when he or she is finished, send it; the document is automatically routed to the next person on the list.

If you want, you can set the options for the routing slip so that your document automatically opens in Revision mode. Any changes the recipient makes to the document are recorded as online revisions; the date, time, and name of the reviewer are also recorded. When the recipient has finished making revisions, he or she can either route the document to the next person on the list or return it to the sender.

After each recipient has seen the document, it is automatically returned to the sender. This way, you can be sure that everyone has seen the document and has entered his or her revisions online, and you can review all of their suggestions in one document.

For a demonstration of how to route a document, double-click the Camcorder Files On The Internet shortcut on your Desktop or connect to the Internet address listed on p. xxx.

Routing a document

In this exercise, you route the Company History document to Laura Takei in the Production department and to Margo Wilson, the company president, for their review and approval.

NOTE   If you would like to use real names in this exercise, you can ask two of your co-workers to assist you. Route the document to two team members. Ask them both to make a few simple revisions, and then send the document on to the next reviewer.

Open

1   On the Standard toolbar, click the Open button.

The Open dialog box appears.

2   From the Lesson 9 folder, select the History document, and then click Open.

The document opens.

3   On the File menu, point to Send To, and then click Routing Recipient.

The Routing Slip dialog box appears. Your profile name appears in the From area.

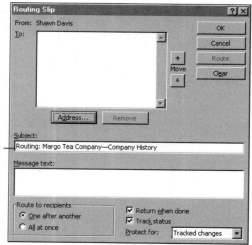

Subject is taken from the first line of text in the document.

4 Click Address.

The Address Book dialog box appears.

5 In the postoffice address list, select Laura Takei, and then click To.

Laura Takei is added to the To list.

6 Add Margo Wilson to the To list, and then click OK.

The Address Book dialog box closes. The recipient names appear, in numerical order, in the To box.

7 In the Message Text box, type **Could you please submit your revisions to me by Friday?**

8 In the Route To Recipients area, be sure that the One After Another option button is selected.

When the Track Status check box is selected, you receive update messages when each recipient routes the file to the next person.

9 Be sure that the Return When Done and Track Status check boxes are selected.

10 Be sure that "Tracked Changes" appears in the Protect For box.

Recipients will be able to make online changes to the document.

11 Click Route to send the document to the first recipient on your list.

12 Close Microsoft Word.

If you are prompted to save changes, click No.

TIP If you want to continue working on your document, you can close the Routing Slip dialog box without sending the document by clicking Add Slip. When you are ready to send the document, click Routing Recipient on the File menu. You can also make changes to the Routing Slip by clicking Edit Routing Slip on the File menu. However, you cannot change the routing for a document after it has been sent out; if you want to address it to different people, you must route the document a second time.

Set up the Inbox for this exercise

A practice document with simulated revisions by Laura Takei and Margo Wilson has been created for you on the Outlook SBS Practice disk. In this exercise, you add that file to your Inbox. If you used your co-workers' real names in the previous exercise, you need to open the message they returned to you for the next exercise.

1 On the Outlook Bar, click the Other shortcut bar, and then click the Lesson 9 icon.

   The contents of the Lesson 9 folder appear in the Information viewer.

The contents of the Information viewer do not change because you have not selected a new folder.

2 On the Outlook Bar, click the Outlook shortcut bar.

   The icons in the Outlook group appear on the Outlook Bar.

3 In the Information viewer, select the "Routed: Margo Tea Company" message, and then drag it onto the Inbox icon.

   The message is copied to the Inbox.

4 Click the Inbox icon.

   The "Routed Margo Tea Company" message appears in the Information viewer.

Open a revised document

After your co-workers have seen and revised a routed document, it is sent back to you if you have selected the Return When Done option. You can then open the document, and accept or reject any changes. In this exercise, you open the routed document returned to you by your co-workers.

1 Double-click the "Routed: Margo Tea Company" message from Margo Wilson.

   The message opens. A note informs you that the routing has been completed and the document is now available for your review. Your message should look similar to the following illustration.

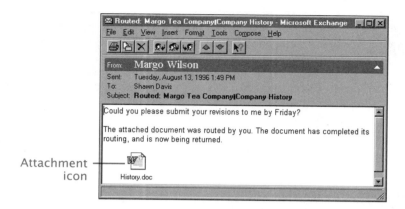

Attachment icon

2 Double-click the Microsoft Word attachment icon to view the document.

A copy of the document opens. A Route Document message appears, asking if you want to merge any revision marks into the original version of your document for your later review.

3 Click OK.

The Select File To Merge Into Current Document dialog box appears.

4 Open the Lesson 9 folder, and then select the History document.

5 Click Open.

The revisions are merged with the original document.

Set up the document for review

In this exercise, you prepare to accept or reject changes in the revised document.

▶ On the Tools menu, point to Track Changes, and then click Accept Or Reject Changes.

The Accept Or Reject Changes dialog box appears.

Review revisions

In this exercise, you review the changes Laura Takei and Margo Wilson made to the Margo Tea Company—Company History document, and decide whether or not you want to accept the changes.

You can move the Accept Or Reject Changes dialog box as needed to make the document visible by dragging its title bar.

1 In the Accept Or Reject Changes dialog box, click the Find button with the right arrow.

The first instance of revised text is selected.

2 Click Accept.

The change is made to the text. The next section of revised text is selected.

3 Click Accept.

The change is made and the next section of revised text is selected.

4 Click Reject.

The change is rejected and the original text is restored. The next section of revised text is selected.

5 Accept the rest of the revisions in the document by clicking Accept All, and then clicking Yes.

6 In the Accept Or Reject Changes dialog box, click Close.

7 On the Standard toolbar, click the Save button.

The revisions to the document are saved.

Save

If you are prompted to save changes, click No.

8 Close Microsoft Word, and then close the "Routed Margo Tea Company" message.

The contents of your Inbox appear in the Information viewer.

Embedding a Shortcut in a Message

If you and your co-workers are able to store files on a network, you can embed shortcuts to those files in your messages and send them to each other. For example, suppose you wanted one of your co-workers to update his or her department budget. The department budget worksheets are stored in a folder on your company network that the co-worker in question has access to. You can send a message to your co-worker, asking him or her to add this month's totals to the worksheet, and then include a shortcut to the worksheet in your message. When your co-worker receives the message, he or she can simply double-click the shortcut icon to immediately open the file on the network and start entering information.

NOTE You can embed a shortcut to a file on your own computer in a message instead of a shortcut to a file on a group network. However, the recipient will only be able to use the shortcut if you have given him or her shared access to the file on your own hard disk. You can refer to your Windows online help for more information about shared access.

In the following exercises, you'll practice embedding a shortcut to a file in a message, and then test the shortcut by sending a copy of the message to yourself.

IMPORTANT To complete the following exercises, you must have access to a file on your organization's network. If you are not sure if you have access to files on your network, ask your system administrator.

Embed a shortcut in a message

In this exercise, you select a file on your office network, and then create a new message containing a shortcut to that file.

1 On the Outlook Bar, click the Other shortcut bar, and then click the My Computer icon.

The available drives for your computer appear in the Information viewer. For the purposes of this book, the illustrations show the network drive "E." Your screen should look similar to the following illustration.

Your available drives will look slightly different.

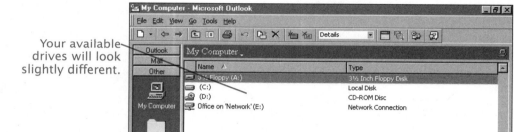

2 In the Information viewer, double-click your network drive.

The files and folders stored on your network appear in the Information viewer.

3 Double-click the folder where the file you want to use is stored.

The contents of the folder appear in the Information viewer.

4 On the Outlook Bar, click the Outlook shortcut bar.

The icons for the folders in the Outlook group appear on the Outlook Bar. The contents of the Information viewer do not change.

5 In the Information viewer, use the right mouse button to drag the file you have chosen onto the Inbox icon on the Outlook Bar.

A shortcut menu appears.

6 Click Send With Shortcut.

A new Mail Form appears. The name of the document appears in the Subject box and a shortcut icon to the file appears in the message area. Your screen should look similar to the following illustration.

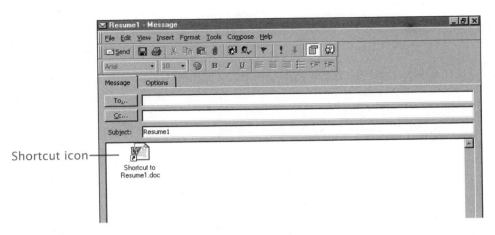

Shortcut icon

7 Address the message to yourself and one of your real co-workers, if you wish.

You can select the name of your co-worker from the global address list.

8 In the Subject box, select the current text, and then type **Shortcut Test**

9 On the Standard toolbar, click the Send button.

The message is sent.

Test the shortcut

In this exercise, you open the copy of the message in your Inbox, and then test the shortcut to the file on your network.

IMPORTANT You can ask your co-worker to test the shortcut by following these same steps. However, you and your co-worker might not be able to view the same file simultaneously; one of you will be able to open the original and the other will need to make a copy of the file to view it.

1 On the Outlook Bar, click the Inbox icon.

The contents of your Inbox appear in the Information viewer and your copy of the "Shortcut Test" message should appear. The path to the shortcut file is shown in Messages With AutoPreview view.

If the message has not yet arrived in your Inbox, on the Tools menu, click Check For New Mail.

2 Double-click the "Shortcut Test" message.

The message opens and the shortcut to the file on your network appears in the message area.

3 Double-click the shortcut icon.

The program used to create the file starts, and after a moment the file opens.

4 Close the program window, and then close the "Shortcut Test" message.

Finish the lesson

Follow these steps to delete the practice items you created in this lesson.

Delete

1 Select the practice messages in your Inbox folder and Sent Items folder, and then, on the Standard toolbar, click the Delete button.

2 In the Calendar folder, delete the "Revise product list" appointment you created on February 15, 1999.

3 In the Journal folder, select the "Entry Type: Microsoft Word" group heading, and then, on the Standard toolbar, click the Delete button. Click OK to delete the group and all the items in it.

4 On the Outlook Bar, switch to the Other group. Use the right mouse button to click the Lesson 9 icon, click Remove From Outlook Bar, and then click Yes when prompted to confirm the removal.

The shortcut is removed from the Outlook Bar.

5 To continue to the next lesson, on the Outlook Bar, click the Inbox icon in the Outlook group.

6 If you are finished using Outlook for now, on the File menu, click Exit And Log Off.

Lesson Summary

To	Do this	Button
Display the Folder List	On the Standard toolbar, click the Folder List button.	
Open a file	On the Outlook Bar, click the Other shortcut bar, and then click the My Computer icon. In the Information viewer, double-click the appropriate drive, and then double-click the folder where the file you want to open is stored. Double-click the file to start the program and open the file.	
Preview a file	In the Information viewer, use the right mouse button to click a file. On the shortcut menu, click Quick View.	

To	Do this	Button
Add a shortcut to the Outlook Bar	Be sure that the Other group appears on the Outlook bar. In the Information viewer, use the right mouse button to click a folder. On the shortcut menu, click Add To Outlook Bar.	
Embed an existing object into a message	Create or open a message. On the Insert menu, click Object. Click the Create From File option button, and then click Browse. Locate and click the file, and then click Open.	
Attach a file to a message	Create, reply to, or forward a message. On the Standard toolbar, click the Insert File button. Locate and click the file, and then click the An Attachment option button. Click OK.	
Add a file to an Outlook item	In the Information viewer, select the file you want. Drag the file onto the appropriate folder icon in the Outlook Bar.	
Record file activity automatically in the Journal folder	Switch to the Journal folder. On the Tools menu, click Options. On the Journal tab, select the Check boxes for the file types you want to record in the Also Record Files From box.	
Send a file	On the program File menu, point to Send To, and then click Mail Recipient. Type the name of the recipient and the subject of the message. Type the message text, and then click the Send button.	
Route a document to multiple users	On the File menu, point to Send To, and then click Routing Recipient. Click Address. In the Address Book, select recipients' names from the list, and then click To. Click OK. Type a subject and any message text. Select a routing order option, a return option, and a protection option, and then click Route.	

225

To	Do this
Review a revised document	Open the document in your Inbox. In the Revised Document message, click OK. In the Select File To Merge Into Current Document dialog box, be sure that the original document is selected, and then click Open. On the Tools menu, point to Track Changes, and then click Accept Or Reject Changes. Use the Find buttons to review the changes.
Embed a shortcut in a message	On the Outlook Bar, click the Other shortcut bar, and then click the My Computer icon. In the Information viewer, click your network drive, and then select the file you want to create a shortcut to. On the Outlook Bar, click the Outlook shortcut bar. Use the right mouse button to drag the file onto the Inbox icon. Click Send With Shortcut on the shortcut menu, and then address and send the message.

For online information about	On the Help menu, click Contents And Index, click the Index tab, and then type
Opening files with Outlook	**Opening, files**
Embedding objects and attaching files	**Embedded objects** *or* **Files, inserting**
Adding shortcuts to items	**Shortcuts, creating**
Recording file activity in the Journal folder	**Recording**
Creating file shortcuts	**Files, creating shortcuts to** *or* **shortcuts, creating**

Keeping Your Outlook Files Up to Date

Estimated time
25 min.

In this lesson you will learn how to:

- Archive outdated items.
- Export items to a different folder.
- Retrieve archived items.

During a typical business week, a number of memos, reports, and other paper documents probably accumulate on your desk. Periodically, you probably clean up your work space by sorting through these documents, filing the important but not vital documents in a drawer or file cabinet, and recycling the items that are out of date and no longer necessary.

Just as papers can pile up on your desk, old messages, appointments, and other items can clutter up your Microsoft Outlook folders, making it more difficult and time-consuming to find exactly the items you need. To help streamline your folders and prevent this overcrowding, you can periodically transfer outdated items to a storage folder, and only retrieve them if you need to. You can also delete items that you know you will no longer need.

As Operations Coordinator for Margo Tea Company, you are constantly adding new information to your Outlook folders—everything from team meetings to task updates from your fellow employees and e-mail messages from the executive in charge of your advertising campaign. In order to work more efficiently with all of these items, you want to explore the different ways of storing and deleting older items, both manually and automatically.

Start Outlook and set up the Inbox for this lesson

For the purposes of this lesson and to be able to complete the following exercises, you must drag messages from the Outlook SBS Practice folder into the Inbox to simulate receiving e-mail. Normally, messages you receive appear automatically in the Inbox.

 IMPORTANT   If you have not yet set up the practice files, work through the "Installing and Using the Practice Files" section, earlier in this book.

For detailed steps on copying the practice files, see "Set Up Your Inbox for This Lesson" in Lesson 3.

1   Start Outlook using the Shawn Davis profile.

The contents of your Inbox folder appear in the Information viewer by default.

2   Copy the practice files from the Outlook SBS Practice\Lesson 10 folder to your inbox.

Archiving Outdated Items

You can learn more about attaching files in Lesson 9.

When you *archive* particular Outlook items, those items are removed from their current Outlook folders and stored separately in a *personal folder file* created on your hard disk. The default storage folder for archived items is the My Documents folder; archive files are saved with a .pst extension. However, you can save, copy, and move a personal folder file, just as you can with any other file. You can also retrieve items archived in a personal folder file, if you need them again. For example, if you need to refer to your first communication with a client, you can review your earliest e-mail messages to that person in an archive file. You can archive items manually with a menu command, or you can set them to be archived automatically according to dates that you define. Any Outlook item, such as an appointment, a contact, or an e-mail message, can be archived. You can also archive files, such as documents or spreadsheets, but only if they are stored in a mail folder as attachments to an item.

Manually archive a folder

Among the messages in your Inbox is one from your boss, Margo Wilson, thanking everyone for their contributions to the company's quarterly profits. The message is dated 5/3/96, and is therefore out of date. However, because it contains important profit information, you want to save it so that you can refer to it later if you need to. In this exercise, you archive the message to a storage folder.

1   Be sure that the contents of the Inbox appear in the Information viewer.

You can archive messages without opening them because the entire folder will be searched for any messages that meet the archiving conditions you set.

2   On the File menu, click Archive.

The Archive dialog box appears. In the list of folders to archive, the Inbox is selected and the path to the default archive folder, My Documents, appears in the Archive File box. Your screen should look similar to the following illustration.

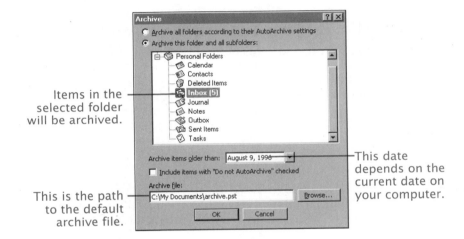

Items in the selected folder will be archived.

This date depends on the current date on your computer.

This is the path to the default archive file.

3   Be sure that the Archive This Folder And All Subfolders option button is selected and that the Inbox folder is selected in the folder list.

The default setting archives items older than 3 months.

4   Select the text in the Archive Items Older Than box, and then type **6/1/96**

Items dated prior to June 1, 1996 will be archived.

5   Click OK.

Three messages, including the "Congratulations" message from Margo Wilson, are removed from your Inbox because they were sent on 5/3/96. Although you cannot see them, they have been moved to the archive folder. You will view the contents of the archive folder in the next exercise.

View an archive file

In this exercise, you open the My Documents folder to make sure that the archived item is stored there.

1   On the Outlook Bar, click the Other shortcut bar.

The folders in the Other group appear on the Outlook Bar.

2   On the Outlook Bar, click the My Documents icon.

The contents of the My Documents folder appear in the Information viewer. A file named archive.pst appears.

3   Switch back to the Inbox folder in the Outlook group.

 TROUBLESHOOTING   You cannot double-click an archive file in the My Documents folder to open it. However, you can import the file to a personal folder to see the archived item again. You will learn how to import archived items later in this lesson.

Archiving Items Automatically

Although you can easily archive items manually whenever you choose, it can be time-consuming to sort through all the different items in your Outlook folders and decide which ones you want to archive. To simplify the process, you can use *AutoArchive* to transfer older items to storage automatically or to delete those outdated items that you no longer need. With AutoArchive, you can set properties for each of your Outlook folders to determine when items are considered old and where they should be moved to once they reach the specified archiving date.

When you install Outlook, several of the Outlook folders already have AutoArchive enabled by default, with different default aging periods already set. You can change the aging periods for any of these folders or turn off AutoArchiving entirely, if you wish. The following table lists the Outlook folders and the default aging periods for each.

Folder	AutoArchiving enabled at setup	Default aging period
Inbox	Yes	None
Calendar	Yes	6 months
Contacts	No	None
Tasks	No	6 months
Journal	Yes	6 months
Notes	No	None
Sent Items	Yes	2 months
Deleted Items	Yes	2 months

Contacts cannot be archived.

After AutoArchive is enabled for a folder, the process runs automatically each time you start Outlook. The AutoArchive settings for each folder are checked by date—any items that have aged past the archiving date are moved to your archive file, or deleted, depending on your specifications.

Enable AutoArchiving

In this exercise, you enable AutoArchive capabilities for all Outlook folders, and then set the AutoArchive properties for individual folders.

1 On the Tools menu, click Options, and then click the AutoArchive tab.

The AutoArchive tab appears. You set general options here to activate AutoArchive.

2 Select the text in the AutoArchive Every ___ Days At Startup box, and then type **1**

The AutoArchive process will run daily when you start Outlook.

3 Be sure that the Prompt Before AutoArchive check box is selected.

You will be asked to confirm the transfer of items before any archiving is done.

You will learn more about deleting out-of-date e-mail messages later in this lesson.

4 Be sure that the Delete Expired Items When AutoArchiving check box is selected.

5 Be sure that the "C:\My Documents\archive.pst" path appears in the Default Archive File box.

Archived items will be sent to the default archive file.

6 Click OK.

AutoArchive has been enabled to archive all your Outlook folders on a daily basis. If you are prompted to AutoArchive folders now, click No. You will test AutoArchive later in this lesson.

IMPORTANT Although you have set AutoArchive to run daily when you start Outlook, it will only run the first time you start Outlook for a given date. That's why you will be asked to change the system date on your computer several times during this lesson in order to perform certain exercises.

Set AutoArchive properties for a folder

For a demonstration of how to set AutoArchive properties for a folder, double-click the Camcorder Files On The Internet shortcut on your Desktop or connect to the Internet address listed on p. xxx.

Although you have activated AutoArchive to run daily for all your Outlook folders, you have not yet set the archiving conditions for individual folders. In this exercise, you set the aging period for AutoArchiving items in the Calendar folder, and then direct archived Calendar items to a new archive file, mysched.pst. By archiving different item types in different files, you can find specific items more easily later.

1 On the Outlook Bar, use the right mouse button to click the Calendar icon.

A shortcut menu appears.

2 Click Properties.

The Calendar Properties dialog box appears.

3 Click the AutoArchive tab.

The default AutoArchive settings for the Calendar folder appear. Your screen should look similar to the following illustration.

4 Select the text in the Clean Out Items Older Than number box, and then type **1**

5 Click the Increment down arrow, and then select Weeks.

Appointments older than 1 week will be archived automatically.

6 Be sure that the Move Old Items To option button is selected.

7 Click OK.

Archived appointments older than 1 week will be moved to the "C:\My Documents\mysched.pst" file.

Test AutoArchive in the Calendar folder

In this exercise, you deliberately create an outdated appointment in your schedule file, and then test to see if it gets archived automatically.

1 On the Outlook Bar, click the Calendar icon.

Your schedule for the current date appears in the Information viewer.

2 In the Date Navigator, click a date older than one week ago.

The Monday of the previous week appears in the schedule area.

3 In the 8:00 A.M. to 8:30 A.M. time slot, type **Test AutoArchiving**, and then press ENTER.

4 On the File menu, click Exit And Log Off.

You must restart Outlook for the AutoArchive settings to take effect.

You can also double-click the Date/Time icon in Control Panel.

5 On the taskbar, double-click the clock.

Because AutoArchive is set to run once a day when you start Outlook, you must change your computer's system date to make it take effect in this practice session. The Date/Time Properties dialog box appears.

You will reset the correct date later in this lesson.

6 In the calendar, click tomorrow's date, and then click OK.

The date on your computer is changed to tomorrow's date.

7 Restart Outlook using the Shawn Davis profile.

After a few moments, a message appears, asking if you want to run AutoArchive now.

8 Click Yes.

AutoArchive runs. The outdated appointment is archived to the "C:\My Documents\archive.pst" file. The appointment is not deleted; only items in Mail folders are deleted after archiving.

9 Switch back to the Inbox folder in the Outlook group.

Deleting Expired Messages

Suppose you want to send a time-sensitive message—for example, an invitation to a brown-bag lunch to discuss the company credit union. Since the lunch is scheduled for a specific time and date, your message is no longer relevant when that date has passed. If you wish, you can set an *expiration date* for the message before you send it. When the message expires, its appearance in the recipient's Inbox changes. If the expired message has not been read yet, it appears dimmed, although it can still be opened; if the message has been opened, a line appears through it to indicate that it has expired. In addition to setting expiration dates on the messages you send, you can set expiration dates for the messages that you receive to remind you when they become out of date.

Although items like appointments, events, and tasks have specific end dates, only messages can have expiration dates.

Because time-sensitive messages are of little use after they have expired, you can set AutoArchive options to delete them automatically. Each time AutoArchive runs, any expired messages in your mail folders will be deleted. E-mail messages deleted by AutoArchive are removed permanently instead of being moved to the Deleted Items folder.

Set AutoArchiving options for the Inbox folder

In this exercise, you turn on AutoArchiving in the Inbox folder.

1 On the Outlook Bar, use the right mouse button to click the Inbox icon, and then click Properties.

The Inbox Properties dialog box appears.

2 Click the AutoArchive tab.

3 Select the Clean Out Items Older Than check box.

The aging option boxes become available.

4 Be sure that the aging option is set to 3 months.

5 Be sure that the Move Old Items To option is selected and that the "C:\My Documents\archive.pst" path appears in the box.

6 Click OK.

Send a message with an expiration date

In this exercise, you create a message with an expiration date, and then send it to yourself to test the date.

New Mail Message

1 On the Standard toolbar, click the New Mail Message button.

A blank Mail form appears.

2 In the To box, type **Shawn Davis**

3 In the Subject box, type **Expiration Test**

4 Click the Options tab, and then, in the Delivery Options area, select the Expires After check box.

Tomorrow's date and the time of 5:00 P.M. appear in the Expires After box by default.

5 Click the Expires After down arrow.

A calendar for the current month appears.

6 In the calendar, click the Monday of the previous week.

Because you are testing AutoArchive's message-deletion capabilities, you are sending yourself a practice message that is already expired. The selected date appears in the Expires After box.

7 On the Standard toolbar, click the Send button.

A message appears, asking you if you want to send a message that has already expired.

8 Click Yes.

The message is sent. After a moment, it appears, dimmed, in your Inbox. Your screen should look similar to the following illustration.

The expired message appears dimmed.

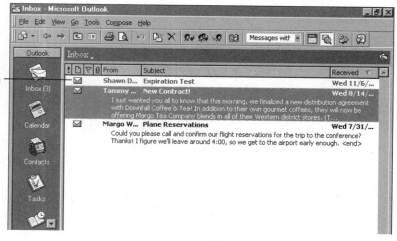

Open an expired message

In this exercise, you open the expired message to see how it appears in your Inbox after it has been read.

1 Double-click the "Expiration Test" message from Shawn Davis.

The message opens. A note informing you that it has expired appears in the Comment area at the top of the message header.

2 Close the message.

A line appears through the message in your Inbox, indicating that the message is expired.

Test automatic deletion of expired messages

In this exercise, you change the current date again, and then check to see that AutoArchive automatically deletes the expired message.

1 On the File menu, click Exit And Log Off.

2 On the taskbar, double-click the clock.

The Date/Time Properties dialog box appears.

3 In the calendar, click the tomorrow's date, and then click OK.

The date on your computer is changed.

4 Restart Outlook using the Shawn Davis profile.

After a few moments, a message appears, asking if you would like to run AutoArchive now.

5 Click Yes.

AutoArchive runs. The expired "Expiration Test" message is deleted from your Inbox and the copy of the message is deleted from your Sent Items folder. The other practice messages are more than three months old and are moved to the archive.pst file in your My Documents folder.

6 On the Outlook Bar, click the Mail shortcut bar, and then click the Sent Items icon.

No copy of the "Expiration Test" message appears in the Information viewer.

7 On the Outlook Bar, click the Deleted Items icon.

The "Expiration Test" message does not appear. It has been permanently deleted.

 NOTE The appointments that you archived in an earlier exercise will appear in the Deleted Items folder. The original items were deleted from your Calendar folder and copies were stored in an archive file.

Reset your computer's system date

In this exercise, you restore the current date on your computer.

1 On the taskbar, double-click the clock.

The Date/Time Properties dialog box appears.

2 In the calendar, select the current date, and then click OK.

3 On the Outlook Bar, click the Inbox icon.

The contents of the Inbox folder appear in the Information viewer.

Exporting Items to Another Folder

When you archive items, the original items are removed from your Outlook folders and stored in an archive file. However, if you want to keep the items in their original folders and create an archive file as a backup, you can *export* items to a personal folder file instead of archiving them. When you export items, the originals remain in their respective folders and a copy is stored in your archive file.

If you export items to a personal folder file, you can retrieve them and view them in Outlook at a later date if you need to, just as you can with archived items. You can also export items into other file types. For example, if an e-mail message contains information you want to use in a Microsoft Word document, you can export it to a text (.txt) file, and then open and work with the file in Microsoft Word. The following table suggests some instances where you might want to use each method.

If you want to	Do this
Move items out of your Outlook Outlook folders and into storage	Archive to a personal folder file
Copy items and leave the originals in your Outlook folders	Export to a personal folder file
Use information from items in other programs	Export to a file

Add a message to the Inbox

In this exercise, you send yourself another test message so that you have an item in your Inbox to export during the next exercise.

New Mail Message

1 On the Standard toolbar, click the New Mail Message button.

2 Type **Shawn Davis** in the To box, and then type **Exporting Test** in the Subject box.

3 On the Standard toolbar, click the Send button.

The message is sent. After a moment, it appears in your Inbox.

Export items to a personal folder file

In this exercise, you create a backup copy of the message in your Inbox by exporting the folder contents to a personal folder file.

If the "Exporting Test" message does not appear yet, on the Tools menu, click Check For New Mail.

1 Be sure that the contents of the Inbox folder appear in the Information viewer.

2 On the File menu, click Import And Export.

The Import And Export wizard appears.

3 In the Choose An Action To Perform box, select Export To A Personal Folder File (.pst).

You will be exporting items to a new personal folder file. A description of exporting to a personal folders file appears in the Description area.

4 Click Next.

Select the Include Sub-folder check box to include any subfolders you might have.

5 Be sure that the Inbox folder is selected in the Select The Folder To Export From box, and then click Next.

The location and duplication options appear.

6 Be sure that the "C:\My Documents\backup.pst" path appears in the Save Exported File As box.

The name "backup" is given to the file by default when you export to a personal folder file.

7 In the Options area, be sure that the Replace Duplicates With Items Exported option button is selected.

You should not have any duplicates because this is the first time you have exported this file.

8 Click Finish.

Copies of the contents of the Inbox are exported to the "backup.pst" file in the My Documents folder. The Exporting Test message remains in the Inbox.

View the exported file

In this exercise, you open the My Documents folder to confirm that the backup.pst file was created.

➤ On the Outlook Bar, click the Other shortcut bar, and then click the My Documents icon.

The contents of the My Documents folder appear in the Information viewer. The backup.pst file appears.

Retrieving Items from Archive Files

You archive or export items to a personal folder file so that you can get them back if you need to refer to them again. When you want to retrieve these items, you can do so in two ways: by *importing* the archive file back into your Outlook folders or by adding the archive file to your profile as a separate, self-contained folder. You can learn more about profiles in the "Installing and Using the Practice Files" section, earlier in this book.

Importing an Archive File

To import an archive file, you use the same Import And Export wizard that you use to export Outlook items. When you import an archive file, all the archived items in the file are restored and reappear in your Outlook folders. You can then work with the items just as you would any other item—you can move, copy, or delete items.

Import an archive file

In this exercise, you import the archive file containing the appointment you archived in a previous section.

1   On the Outlook Bar, click the Outlook shortcut bar, and then click the Inbox icon.

2   On the File menu, click Import And Export.

The Import And Export wizard appears.

You can import any .pst archive file that you have access to, not just files that you have exported.

3   In the Choose An Action To Perform box, select Import From A Personal Folder File (.pst), and then click Next.

The file selection and duplication options appear.

4   Click Browse.

The Connect To Personal Folders dialog box appears.

5   Be sure that My Documents appears in the Look In box, select "archive.pst," and then click Open.

6   Be sure that the Replace Duplicates With Items Imported option button is selected, and then click Next.

The location options appear.

7   Be sure that the Import Items Into The Same Folder In option is selected and that "Personal Folders" appears in the drop-down list, and then click Finish.

After a moment, the archived messages appear in your Inbox. Your screen should look similar to the following illustration.

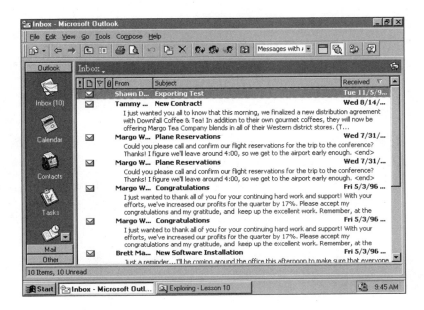

Adding an Archive File to Your User Profile

You can learn more about user profiles in the "Installing and Using the Practice Files" section earlier in this book.

If you want to have access to items in an archive file, without moving all the items back into your Outlook folders, you can add the archive file to your user profile as an *information service*. You use information services, such as Microsoft Mail or Microsoft Exchange, primarily to send and receive messages, but they are also used to store addresses, items, and other information. For example, the personal address book is an information service attached to your user profile. You can have multiple information services attached to your user profile.

When you attach an archive file to your profile, it remains a separate file that contains all the archived items. This way, you can view the items you need, without adding them to the more current information in your Inbox, Calendar, and other folders. Archived folders are given a structure identical to the folder structure in your mailbox; an archive file contains an *information store*, or parent folder, named Personal Folders, as well as a folder for each type of item you archive—an Inbox folder, a Calendar folder, and so on. When you attach an archive file to your profile, you can display the archive folders and view their contents in the Information viewer, just as you can view the contents of your current Outlook folders.

Add an information service to your profile

In this exercise, you add the backup.pst archive file to your profile as an information service so that you can view the items in the file.

1   On the Tools menu, click Services.

The Services dialog box appears.

239

2 Click Add.

The Add Service To Profile dialog box appears.

3 Select Personal Folders, and then click OK.

The service you are adding is based on a personal folder file. The Create/Open Personal Folders File dialog box appears.

4 Click the Look In down arrow, and then select Drive C.

The contents of drive C appear in the contents box.

5 Double-click the My Documents folder.

Archive files are stored in the My Documents folder by default.

Personal folders have a .pst extension.

6 Select "backup.pst" in the contents box, and then click Open.

The Personal Folders dialog box appears.

7 Click OK twice.

View the attached archive file

In this exercise, you view the contents of the backup.pst file you just attached to your profile.

Folder List

1 On the Standard toolbar, click the Folder List button, and then resize the Folder List so that you can see the Folder names.

The Folder List appears to the left of the Information viewer. Your screen should look similar to the following illustration.

2 Click the plus sign (+) next to the second set of personal folders.

The archived Inbox file appears.

3 In the expanded Personal Folders group, select the Inbox icon.

The archived messages, including the Exporting Test, appears in the Information viewer.

These personal folders are your archived personal folders.

This is your exported, archived message.

These personal folders are your current Outlook folders.

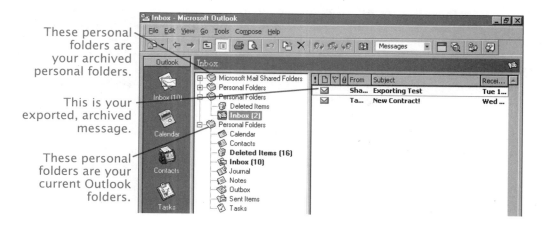

4   On the Standard toolbar, click the Folder List button again.

The Folder List is hidden.

Remove an information service

If you have reviewed the archived items you wanted to see and no longer need access to them, you can remove the information service. In this exercise, you detach the archive file from your mailbox by removing the Personal Folders information service you just added.

1   On the Tools menu, click Services.

The Services dialog box appears. Two sets of Personal Folders are listed; one of them contains your default mailbox folders while the other is the attached archive file.

2   In the list, select the second Personal Folders entry, and then click Properties.

The Personal Folders dialog box appears. The "C:\My Documents\ backup.pst" path should appear in the Path box. This ensures that you are removing the correct set of personal folders. Your screen should look similar to the following illustration.

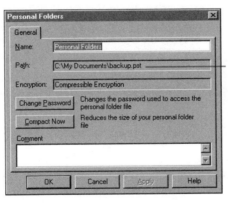

Be sure you have selected the set of personal folders containing the path to the backup.pst file.

3   Click OK to close the Personal Folders dialog box.

4   Click Remove.

A message appears, asking if you want to remove this information service from the profile.

5   Click Yes, and then click OK to close the Services dialog box.

The dialog box closes. The Personal Folders group is still selected, but the contents can no longer appear in the Information viewer.

6   On the Outlook bar, click the Inbox icon.

The contents of your Inbox appear in the Information viewer.

TIP To prevent your Outlook folders from becoming too large over time, you can compact them so that they take up less room. To do this, view the properties of your Personal Folders information service, and then click Compact Now.

Finish the lesson

Follow these steps to delete the practice files you used in this lesson.

Delete

1 Select the practice messages in your Inbox folder. On the Standard toolbar, click the Delete button.

2 On the Tools menu, click Options, and then click the AutoArchive tab.

3 Clear the AutoArchive Every ___ Days At Startup check box, and then click OK.

4 On the Outlook Bar, use the right mouse button to click the Calendar icon. Choose Properties, and then click the AutoArchive tab.

5 In the Clean Out Items Older Than box, change the aging period to 6 months, and then click OK. If you are prompted to set global AutoArchive options, click OK.

You have already disabled the global AutoArchive feature.

6 To continue to the next Review & Practice, on the Outlook Bar, click the Inbox icon.

7 If you are finished using Outlook for now, on the File menu, click Exit And Log Off.

Lesson Summary

To	Do this	Button
Manually archive items	On the File menu, click Archive. Select the folder you want to archive from the list. In the Archive Items Older Than box, set an archiving date. In the Archive File box, check the path, and then click OK.	
Enable automatic archiving of outdated items	On the Tools menu, click Options, and click the AutoArchive tab. Select the AutoArchive Every ___ Days At Startup check box, and then set a frequency. Set the options and the file path that you want, and then click OK.	

To	Do this	Button
Set AutoArchive properties for a folder	Use the right mouse button to click the folder icon, and then click Properties. Click the AutoArchive tab. Set an archiving age, choose an archiving option, and then click OK.	
Send a message with an expiration date	Create and address a new message. On the Options tab, select the Expires After check box, and then enter a date in the Expires After box. Click the Send button.	
Export items to a personal folder file	On the File menu, click Import And Export. Select Export To A Personal Folders File from the list, and then click Next. Select the folder to export from, and then click Next. Enter a path for the exported file, set duplication options, and then click Finish.	
Import an archive file	On the File menu, click Import And Export. Select Import From A Personal Folders File, and then click Next. Select the file to import and the duplication options, and then click Next. Select a destination folder for the imported items, and then click Finish.	
Add an archive file to your user profile	On the Tools menu, click Services. Click Add. Select Personal Folders, and then click OK. Locate the personal folder file you want to add to your profile, and then click Open. Click OK to close each dialog box.	
View an attached archive file	On the Standard toolbar, click the Folder List button. In the Folder List, expand the attached group of personal folders, and then select the folder whose contents you want to view.	

To	Do this
Remove an information service	On the Tools menu, click Services. Select the information service you want to remove, and then click Remove. Click Yes to confirm the removal, and then click OK.

For online information about	On the Help menu, click Contents And Index, click the Index tab, and then type
Archiving items	**Archiving**
Exporting items	**Backing up** *or* **exporting**
Importing items	**Retrieving, archived items** *or* **importing**
Attaching archive files to your user profile	**Retrieving, archived items**

Review &
Practice

Estimated time
20 min.

You will review and practice how to:

- Track your work using the Journal folder.
- Open files using the My Computer shortcut.
- Send files to others.
- Archive Outlook items.
- Import a personal folder file to retrieve archived items.

Before you move on to Part 4, which covers using Microsoft Outlook features that are only available in connection with Microsoft Exchange Server, you can practice the skills you learned in Part 3 by working through this Review & Practice section. You will record an appointment in Journal. You will also open a worksheet file using My Computer, and then send that file to another user as an e-mail message. Finally, you'll archive the items in your Inbox, and then import the archive file to restore the items.

Scenario

The quarterly budget meeting was a success, and you are now working on some follow-up activities with other Margo Tea Company employees. You need to meet with the company's Finance Director to discuss the budget figures proposed at the meeting, and you want to add this appointment to both your Calendar and Journal folders. You have a Microsoft Excel worksheet with the current budget information stored on your computer, and you decide to send it to the Finance Director to help him prepare for your appointment. Finally, you practice archiving the out-of-date items in your Inbox, and then import the archive file in order to view them again.

Step 1: *Track Your Work in the Journal Folder*

You schedule an appointment with Manuel Diaz, the Finance Director, to discuss the findings from the quarterly budget meeting. You want a record of this appointment to also appear in the Journal timeline. In this step, you manually add the appointment to the Journal folder.

1 Start Outlook using the Shawn Davis profile, and then switch to the Calendar folder.

2 Display the date 2/22/99. (Hint: On the Go menu, click Go To Date.)

3 Enter the "Discuss budget with Manuel Diaz" appointment in the 10:00 A.M. to 10:30 A.M. time slot.

4 Record the appointment in your Journal. (Hint: Use a command on the Tools menu to create a journal entry from the appointment.)

5 Save and close the appointment form.

For more information about	See
Tracking your work in Journal	Lesson 8

Step 2: *Open Files Using the My Computer Shortcut*

You've entered the budget findings from the meeting into a Microsoft Excel spreadsheet that is currently stored on your hard disk. In this step, you open the file and make sure that everything is in place.

1 Switch to the My Computer folder.

2 Open the Microsoft Excel document named Budget in the Review & Practice 3 folder, which is a subfolder of the Outlook SBS Practice folder.

3 In cell C6, change the number to 17850. Save the changes.

For more information about	See
Opening files using My Computer	Lesson 9

Step 3: *Send Files to Others*

You want to send the updated budget document to Manuel Diaz before your meeting so that he has time to review the changes. In this step, you send it to him as an attachment in an e-mail message, without leaving Microsoft Excel.

1 From Microsoft Excel, send the workbook to Manuel Diaz. Address a carbon copy of the message to your profile name, Shawn Davis. (Hint: On the File menu, click Send To.)

2   Change the message subject to **For our discussion**. In the message area, add the text **I thought you'd like to review this before we met.**

3   Send the message. Close Microsoft Excel.

For more information about	See
Sending files to e-mail recipients	Lesson 9

Step 4:   *Archive Outlook Items*

Because the message regarding your upcoming meeting is time-sensitive, you decide to remove it from your Inbox after the meeting. In this step, you remove the message and store it in an archive file.

1   Switch to the Inbox folder.

2   Turn on AutoArchiving. Set your folders to AutoArchive every day at startup, and change the default archive filename to "budget.pst." (Hint: On the Tools menu, click Options, and then click the AutoArchive tab.)

3   Change the AutoArchive settings for the Inbox so that items older than one day are archived, and change the default archive filename to "budget.pst."

4   Exit and log off Outlook. Change the system date on your computer to tomorrow's date. (Hint: Double-click the clock on the taskbar to change the system date.)

5   Restart Outlook and accept the AutoArchive prompt when it appears.

For more information about	See
Turning on AutoArchiving	Lesson 10
Setting AutoArchive properties for Outlook folders	Lesson 10

Step 5:   *Import a Personal Folders File to Retrieve Archived Items*

You need to retrieve the archived "For our discussion" message and forward it to Margo Wilson. In this step, you restore the message to your Inbox by importing the "budget.pst" archive file.

1   Start the Import And Export wizard.

2   Import the personal folders file, "budget.pst," without allowing duplicates to be imported.

For more information about	See
Importing files	Lesson 10

Finish the Review & Practice

Follow these steps to delete the practice messages you created in this Review & Practice, and then quit Outlook.

1 In the Inbox, delete any messages you used during these exercises.

2 In the Calendar folder, delete the "Discuss budget with Manuel Diaz" appointment you created on February 22, 1999.

3 In the Journal folder, delete the "Discuss budget with Manuel Diaz" entry on February 22, 1999.

4 On the Tools menu, click Options, and then click the AutoArchive tab. Clear the AutoArchive Every ___ Days At Startup check box, and then click OK.

5 If you want to continue to the next lesson, on the Outlook Bar, click the Inbox icon.

6 If you are finished using Outlook for now, on the File menu, click Exit And Log Off.

Using Outlook with the Microsoft Exchange Server

Granting Others Access to Your Outlook Files

Estimated time
30 min.

In this lesson you will learn how to:

- Share access to folder contents with a co-worker.
- Name a delegate to help you manage your Outlook folders.
- Choose a delegate's access permissions for each of your Outlook folders.
- Send messages and accept requests on someone else's behalf.
- Set up advanced security.

Your workload might require you to get extra help. For example, you might hire an Administrative Assistant to help you coordinate your schedule and manage your incoming paper mail; or you might ask a colleague to take over some of your daily tasks while you are out of the office on a business trip. Just as you can give someone access to your desk or your file cabinets, you can give others access to your Microsoft Outlook folders so that they can help you manage your e-mail messages and your schedule electronically.

IMPORTANT To perform the exercises in this lesson, your computer must be able to access a Microsoft Exchange Server computer on a networked environment. In addition, your practice profile must contain the Microsoft Exhange Server information service, as outlined in "Installing and Using the Practice Files." If your setup does not meet these requirements, skip this lesson. If you need help setting up your practice profile, contact your system administrator.

For detailed steps on copying the practice files, see "Set Up Your Inbox for This Lesson" in Lesson 3.

Start Outlook and set up the Inbox for this lesson

For the purposes of this lesson, you must copy messages from the Outlook SBS Practice disk into your Inbox. Normally, sent messages are delivered to your Inbox automatically.

1 Start Outlook using the Shawn Davis profile.

2 Copy the practice files from the Outlook SBS Practice\Lesson 11 folder to your Inbox.

3 On the Standard toolbar, click the Folder List button.

The Folder List appears on the left side of the Information viewer.

Folder List

Sharing Folder Access with Others

Suppose you are going on a week-long business trip. You'd like one of your colleagues to periodically check all the messages in your Inbox, and notify you by phone if any messages arrive that require your immediate attention. In order for your co-worker to open your Inbox and view its contents, you must give him or her *permission* to access the Inbox folder.

There are two ways to allow other people to use your Outlook folders. You can *share* a private folder with someone else by granting that person permission to access the folder and, in some cases, work with its contents. Depending on the permissions you choose, you can allow someone to read, modify, create, and/or delete information in a particular folder.

You can also assign someone a more advanced level of permission by granting him or her *delegate access* to one of your Outlook folders. Delegates can not only perform actions attributed to specific permissions, but also send messages and respond to requests on your behalf. You will learn more about delegate access later in this lesson.

After you have granted someone shared access to one or more of your Outlook folders, you must also grant that person access to your mailbox so that he or she can see and open the individual folders. When you are using Outlook with the Microsoft Exchange Server, your mailbox appears as an *information store*, or container for folders, at the top of your Folder List. You can create many folders inside an information store, but you cannot create a new information store. However, if you add different types of mail delivery services to your Outlook profile, information stores might be added to your mailbox automatically as part of a service package. If you grant someone access to your mailbox, for example, that person can display your mailbox folders within his or her own information store.

Choosing Levels of Permission

You control who has access to your personal folders. If you want to share a folder with one of your co-workers, you can define exactly what actions that person will be able to perform in the folder. For example, you can grant someone permission to view the appointments in your Calendar, but not allow that person to add any new appointments to it.

Outlook comes with several combinations of predefined permissions, called *roles*. If you assign one of your co-workers a role in a specific folder, the associated permissions are automatically given to that person. You can also pick and choose individual permissions to create a custom role for any individual. The following table lists the roles and associated permissions that you can assign to another user.

Granting another user the authorization to read items in your mailbox is the minimum permission required to allow that person to open one of your folders.

Role	User privileges
None	No access to folder contents.
Contributor	Can create new items in the folder.
Reviewer	Can read existing items in the folder.
Author	Can read existing items, create new items, and edit or delete items he or she created.
Publishing Author	Can read existing items, create new items, create subfolders, and edit or delete items he or she created.
Editor	Can read existing items, create new items, and edit or delete all items.
Publishing Editor	Can read existing items, create new items, create subfolders, and edit or delete all items.
Owner	Can read existing items, create new items, create subfolders, edit or delete all items, and change other users' access permissions in the folder.

 IMPORTANT   Because this lesson explores the interactive aspects of Outlook, you'll need to recruit some help from a co-worker on your network in order to complete the following exercises.

Grant permission to another user

In this exercise, you grant a co-worker permission to read the messages in your Inbox so that he or she can notify you of any important e-mail while you are out of the office.

NOTE You can't assign permissions while working *offline*, where your computer is not connected to a Microsoft Exchange Server. You can learn more about working offline in Lesson 12, "Working When Away From the Office."

1 In the Folder List, click the Mailbox–Shawn Davis folder.

You select a folder to specify where to grant permissions; you must grant your co-worker access to your mailbox before he or she can access specific folders. The mailbox information store appears at the top of the Folder List.

2 Use the right mouse button to click the mailbox folder.

A shortcut menu appears.

3 Click Properties for "Mailbox-Shawn Davis" and then click the Permissions tab.

The Permissions tab should look similar to the following illustration.

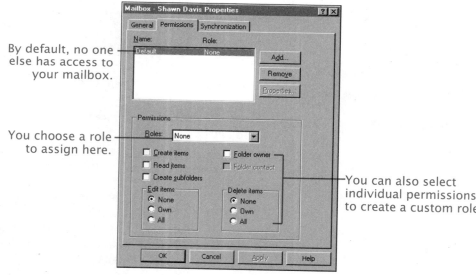

By default, no one else has access to your mailbox.

You choose a role to assign here.

You can also select individual permissions to create a custom role here.

4 Click Add.

The Add Users dialog box appears. The names from your organization's global address list appear by default.

5 Select your co-worker's name, and then click Add.

The selected name appears in the Add Users box on the right.

6 Click OK.

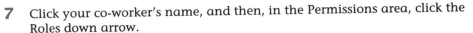

7 Click your co-worker's name, and then, in the Permissions area, click the Roles down arrow.

The list of available roles appears.

8 Select Reviewer.

Your co-worker will be able to read items in your mailbox after you give him or her access to individual folders.

9 Click OK.

The permission is granted to your co-worker.

10 In the Folder List, select your Inbox, and then repeat steps 2 through 9 to assign your co-worker Reviewer permission in your Inbox.

You must also grant permission to your Inbox so that your co-worker can access the individual folder.

 IMPORTANT When you grant someone access permission to your mailbox, it is effective immediately. If at any time during this lesson you do not want your co-worker to be able to work in your mailbox or read your messages, select your mailbox, click Properties on the File menu, click the Permissions tab, click your co-worker's name, and then click Remove.

Have your co-worker open your mailbox

Now that your co-worker has permission to open your mailbox and view the contents of your Inbox, that person must add your mailbox to his or her information store.

 IMPORTANT Have your co-worker perform the following exercise on his or her computer.

1 Start Outlook.

2 On the Tools menu, click Services, and be sure that the Services tab is active.

The Services dialog box appears.

3 Be sure that Microsoft Exchange Server is selected, and then click Properties.

The Microsoft Exchange Server dialog box appears.

4 Click the Advanced tab.

Options for the Microsoft Exchange Server information service appear.

255

5 In the Mailboxes area, click Add.

The Add Mailbox dialog box appears.

To check the mailbox name, on the Tools menu, click Services, click Microsoft Exchange Server, and then click Properties.

6 Type the name of the mailbox to which you've been given access, and then click OK.

The name of the mailbox you've been granted permission to access appears in the Open These Additional Mailboxes list.

7 Click OK to close the Microsoft Exchange Server dialog box, and then click OK to close the Services dialog box.

8 On the Standard toolbar, click the Folder List button.

Folder List

Your co-worker's mailbox now appears under the information store in your folder list. Your screen should look similar to the following illustration.

Information store

Mailboxes will appear in alphabetical order by mailbox name.

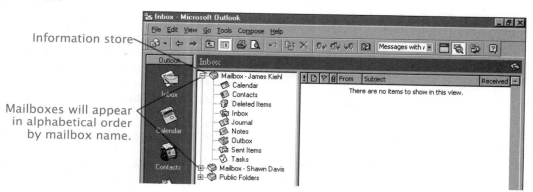

9 Click the plus sign (+) next to your co-worker's mailbox.

The mailbox is expanded; the folders it contains appear in the Folder List.

10 In the Folder List, click your co-worker's Inbox.

The contents of your co-worker's Inbox appear in the Information viewer.

Have your co-worker test the access you have assigned

In this exercise, your co-worker tests the Reviewer role you have assigned by opening a message and attempting to make changes.

IMPORTANT   Have your co-worker perform the following exercise on his or her computer.

1   In the Information viewer, double-click the "Congratulations" message from Margo Wilson.

    The message opens in read-only format. Because you have been granted Reviewer access, you can read messages, but not modify them.

2   On the Standard toolbar, click the Delete button.

Delete

    A message appears, indicating that you do not have sufficient permission to perform this action. As a Reviewer, you cannot delete messages from this person's Inbox.

3   Click OK to close the permission message.

4   On the "Congratulations" message, click the Close button.

Have your co-worker close your mailbox

In this exercise, your co-worker removes your mailbox from his or her information store.

IMPORTANT   Have your co-worker perform the following exercise on his or her computer.

1   On the Tools menu, click Services, and be sure that the Services tab is active.

    The Services dialog box appears.

2   Be sure that Microsoft Exchange Server is selected, and then click Properties.

    The Microsoft Exchange Server dialog box appears.

3   Click the Advanced tab, be sure that the mailbox you added to your information store is selected in the Mailboxes area, and then click Remove.

    A message appears, asking you to confirm the deletion of the mailbox.

4   Click Yes, and then click OK twice to close each dialog box.

    The second mailbox is removed from your information store; it does not appear anymore in the Folder List.

Naming a Delegate to Your Outlook Folders

If you want to allow still greater control over the contents of your Outlook folders to someone else, you can make that person a delegate. Delegate access permissions are similar to the permissions roles used to share folders—depending on the degree of permission, delegates might be able to read, create, modify, and delete items on behalf of the folder *manager*, or owner. When you are naming a delegate, you can choose different access permissions for each of your Outlook folders from a single dialog box. The basic privileges that accompany different levels of delegate access are listed in the following table.

Delegates with this permission	Can perform these actions in a folder
None	None. Cannot open the folder.
Reviewer	Open the folder and read existing items.
Author	Read, create, modify, and delete their own items.
Editor	Read, create, modify, and delete any items, including those that the manager creates.

One important difference between regular access permissions and delegate access is that if you assign someone any level of delegate access permission, that person will be able to send messages on your behalf. Messages sent this way show both the delegate's name and the manager's name. Additionally, given the appropriate level of access to the correct folders, delegates can accept meeting or task requests on behalf of the manager.

 TIP If you want to hide personal items from a delegate, you can open any task, contact, journal entry, or appointment in any folder, and then select the Private check box in the lower-right corner of the form. For messages, on the Options tab, click the Sensitivity down arrow, and then select Private.

Delegate access can be useful if, for example, you have an assistant who helps you manage your correspondence and coordinate your schedule. As a delegate, your assistant can respond to many of your e-mail messages for you, and schedule meetings or tasks on your behalf, leaving you more time to work on other projects.

 NOTE While you can use Windows 95 or Windows NT to give others limited access permissions to share any private folder on your computer, you can only use the Delegate Access feature in Outlook to grant others specific delegate permissions, and only to Outlook folders.

Coordinating Permissions Between Outlook Folders

Depending on the activities you want your delegate to perform on your behalf, you might need to grant that person different degrees of access to different Outlook folders. For example, if you grant a delegate Reviewer permission in your Inbox, he or she can read your messages, including meeting requests. But if you want your delegate to accept a meeting request on your behalf, you must also grant that person Editor permission in your Calendar. Then, your delegate can create a meeting appointment for you by accepting the request. If your delegate is Reviewer, he or she can only read the meeting request, not accept it.

When you first name a delegate to your Outlook folders, that person is granted Editor permission to your Calendar and Tasks folders by default. This way, he or she can accept meeting and task requests on your behalf. This is the most powerful delegate role; Editors can also delete items in the folders where they have Editor access. You can change these default settings using the Delegate Permissions dialog box.

Name a delegate to your Outlook folders

In this exercise, you grant a co-worker delegate access to your Outlook folders. You give that person the appropriate permissions to send either messages on your behalf or messages that appear to have been sent by you directly. You also make sure that this delegate can accept task requests on your behalf.

TROUBLESHOOTING   If the Delegates tab is not available in the Options dialog box, you need to install the Delegate Access add-in file. On the Tools menu, click Options, and then click the General tab. Click Add-In Manager, click Install, select Dlgsetp.ecf, and then click Open. If the Dlgsetp.ecf file does not appear in the Add-Ins dialog box, see your system administrator for help.

1   On the Tools menu, click Options, and then click the Delegates tab.

2   Click Add.

  The Add Users dialog box appears. The names from your organization's global address list appear by default.

3   Select your co-worker's name, click Add, and then click OK.

  The Delegate Permissions dialog box appears.

4   Click the Calendar down arrow.

  A list of available permissions for this folder appears.

5   Click None.

  You want this delegate to have access to your task list, but not to your appointments. The Delegate Receives Copies Of Meeting-Related Messages Sent To Me check box is dimmed and no longer available. Your delegate will not be able to accept meeting requests on your behalf.

6   In the Tasks box, be sure that Editor appears.

  You want this delegate to be able to accept task requests on your behalf. He or she will accept a task request for you in a later exercise.

7   Click the Inbox down arrow, and then click Author.

  You want this person to be able to read your messages, as well as send messages on your behalf.

259

8 Select the Automatically Send A Message To Delegate Summarizing These Permissions check box.

Your co-worker will be automatically notified of his or her delegate access permissions.

9 Click OK twice to close each dialog box.

You can change permissions at any time by selecting a delegate's name on the Delegates tab, and then clicking Permissions.

 TIP Suppose you have an assistant who handles all of your scheduling needs. If you want meeting requests and responses to be sent directly to your delegate, to keep your Inbox free for other messages, on the Tools menu, click Options. On the Delegates tab, select the "Send Meeting Requests And Responses Only To My Delegates, Not To Me" check box, and then click OK. If you have these messages sent directly to a delegate, you do not need to grant the delegate Reviewer permission in your Inbox.

Acting on Behalf of Others

 IMPORTANT Several exercises in this section must be completed by the co-worker that you designated as a delegate for your Outlook folders. If you would like to practice these skills yourself, you must ask a co-worker to copy the Lesson 11 practice message to his or her Inbox, and grant you delegate access to his or her folders according to the steps in the previous exercise.

Once you have been given delegate access to a manager's Outlook folders, you can perform various actions on that person's behalf. You should receive a notification message from the folder manager, informing you that you have been designated as a delegate and explaining your privileges in the manager's different Outlook folders.

Have your delegate review the delegate access privileges

In this exercise, your delegate opens the automatically-sent message informing him or her that you have given him or her delegate access privileges in your Outlook folders.

 IMPORTANT Have your co-worker perform the following exercise on his or her computer.

1   In your Inbox, double-click the "You have been designated as a delegate for Shawn Davis" message from your co-worker.

The message opens. Your message should look similar to the following illustration.

Your permissions for each folder are listed here.

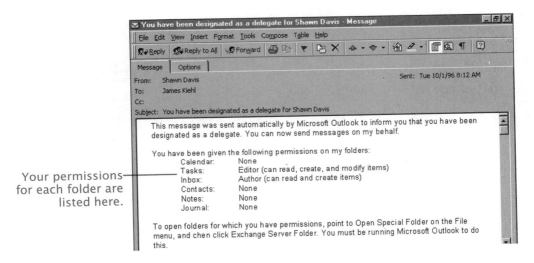

2   Read, and then close the message.

Sending Messages as a Delegate

If someone has given you any level of access permission to his or her Inbox, you are able to send messages on that person's behalf. For security reasons, you should keep this privilege in mind when you are deciding whether or not to make someone a delegate.

Have your delegate open your Inbox

In this exercise, your delegate opens your Inbox folder on the Microsoft Exchange Server.

 IMPORTANT   Have your co-worker perform the following exercise on his or her computer.

1   On the File menu, point to Open Special Folder, and then click Exchange Server Folder.

The Open Exchange Server Folder dialog box appears.

You can click Name to select a name from the Address Book.

2   In the Name box, type the name of the person who granted you delegate access permission.

261

3 Be sure that Inbox appears in the Folder box, and then click OK.

After a moment, the delegate window opens. The contents of the folder manager's Inbox appear. Your screen should look similar to the following illustration.

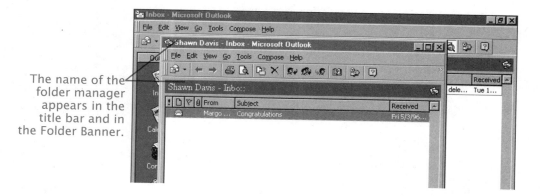

The name of the folder manager appears in the title bar and in the Folder Banner.

Have your delegate send a message on your behalf

In this exercise, your delegate sends a message on your behalf to test the delegate access permissions.

 IMPORTANT Have your co-worker perform the following exercise on his or her computer.

New Mail Message

1 On the Standard toolbar, click the New Mail Message button.

A blank Mail form appears.

2 On the View menu, click From Field.

The From box is added to the message header.

3 In both the From box and the To box, type the folder manager's (your co-worker's) name.

By entering a name in the From box, the message header will indicate that the message was sent by you as a delegate, on the manager's behalf.

4 In the Subject box, type **Delegate Test** and then type **Just testing** in the message area.

5 On the Standard toolbar, click the Send button.

The message is sent to the manager's mailbox.

6 Close the delegate window for your co-worker.

View the test message

Now that your delegate has sent you a test message, you return to your computer to view it. In this exercise, you open and read the message.

1 On your computer, double-click the "Delegate Test" message in your Inbox.

The message header indicates that the message was sent by your co-worker on your behalf. Your message should look similar to the following illustration.

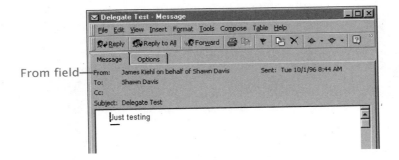

2 Read and then close the message.

Accepting Requests on Behalf of a Manager

Delegates who have at least Reviewer access to a manager's Inbox and Editor access to that manager's Calendar or Tasks folder can accept certain requests on behalf of the manager. With Editor access to the Calendar folder, delegates can accept meeting requests to add appointments to the manager's schedule; with Editor access to the Tasks folder, delegates can accept task requests to add tasks to the manager's task list. If you want your delegates to be able to accept requests on your behalf, it's important to coordinate their access privileges between the Inbox, Calendar, and Tasks folders, as you did earlier in this lesson.

Have your delegate send you a new task request

In this exercise, your delegate sends you a new task request so that he or she can work with that task request in your Inbox in the next exercise.

IMPORTANT Have your co-worker perform the following steps on his or her computer.

1 On the File menu, point to New, and then click Task Request.

A new task request form appears.

2   In the To box, type your co-worker's name.

3   In the Subject box, type **Distribute Production Schedules**

4   On the Standard toolbar, click the Send button.

The task request is sent.

Have your delegate accept the task request on your behalf

In this exercise, your delegate opens your Inbox folder and tests his or her delegate access permissions by accepting the "Distribute Production Schedules" task request for you.

 IMPORTANT   Have your co-worker perform the following exercise on his or her computer.

1   On the File menu, point to Open Special Folder, and then click Exchange Server Folder.

The Open Exchange Server Folder dialog box appears.

2   In the Name box, type the folder manager's (your co-worker's) name.

3   Be sure that Inbox appears in the Folder box, and then click OK.

The delegate window opens. The "Task Request: Distribute Production Schedules" message that you sent appears at the top of the list of messages. Your screen should look similar to the following illustration.

You sent this task request to the folder manager in the previous exercise.

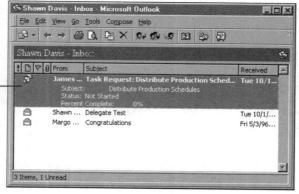

4 Double-click the "Task Request: Distribute Production Schedules" message at the top of the list.

The message opens. Your name appears in the Comment area.

5 On the Standard toolbar, click the Accept button.

A message appears, asking if you want to edit the task response or send it immediately.

6 Be sure that the Send The Response Now option button is selected.

The response is sent, and the task is added to the folder manager's task list.

7 Close the delegate window.

The contents of your own Inbox appear in the Information viewer. At the top of the list is a "Task Accepted: Distribute Production Schedules" message that has been sent to you automatically. You are notified of the acceptance because you sent the original task request.

8 Double-click the "Task Accepted: Distribute Production Schedules" message.

The message opens. Acceptance information appears in the Comment area above the message header.

9 Read, and then close the message.

The notification message is deleted automatically.

Have your delegate view the accepted task in your task list

In this exercise, your delegate opens your Tasks folder on the server to make sure that the accepted task has been added to your task list.

IMPORTANT Have your co-worker perform the following exercise on his or her computer.

1 On the Outlook File menu, point to Open Special Folder, and then click Exchange Server Folder.

2 Type your co-worker's name in the Name box.

3 Click the Folder down arrow, select Tasks, and then click OK.

The delegate window opens, and the folder manager's task list appears. The "Distribute Production Schedules" task appears at the top of the list. Your screen should look similar to the following illustration.

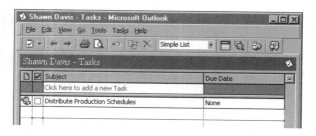

4 Close the delegate window.

Setting Up Advanced Security

If you want to ensure that the recipients of your messages can verify that the messages actually did come from you, you can *sign* them. Signing your messages also shows that they were not tampered with after you sent them. When you sign a message, it is sent with a digital signature. You cannot see a digital signature, but the recipient can confirm that a message has been signed by viewing the message properties. To sign a message, you need to have an advanced security password. You can sign each message you send individually, or you can sign all your outgoing messages automatically.

You can also *seal* a message, which ensures that only the recipients to whom you addressed your message can open it. A sealed message is *encrypted*, or scrambled, and in order to open sealed messages, the recipient must provide his or her own password. In order to be able to open sealed or signed messages, the recipients must be registered in a Microsoft Exchange security enterprise. Typically, an enterprise consists only of people who are part of your organization, and whose computers are connected to your organization's network.

Before you can sign or seal messages, your Microsoft Exchange Server administrator must configure your mailbox for advanced security and give you a *keyword*. The keyword is created by the security software on the Microsoft Exchange Server and is similar to a password except that it is used only during the setup procedure. After advanced security has been set up for your mailbox, you must establish your security password. The icons used to identify advanced security messages in the Information viewer are listed in the following table.

Icon	Description
	Sealed encrypted e-mail
	Digitally signed e-mail

IMPORTANT To perform the following exercises, you must first obtain the advanced security keyword from your system administrator.

Set up advanced security

In this exercise, you set up your advanced security password so that you are able to sign your messages.

TROUBLESHOOTING If your Options dialog box does not have a Security tab, you must install the Etexch.ecf file. On the Tools menu, click Options. Click Add-In Manager, click Install, select Etexch.ecf, and then click OK to close each dialog box.

1 On the Tools menu, click Options, and then click the Security tab.

2 Click Setup Advanced Security.

The Setup Advanced Security dialog box appears.

It is a good idea to make your advanced security password different from any of your other passwords.

3 In the Token box, type the keyword that your system administrator gave you.

4 In the Password box, type your advanced security password, press TAB, and then type your advanced security password again.

5 Click OK to close the Setup Advanced Security dialog box.

A message appears, indicating that your request for advanced security has been sent to the server. When your request is processed, you will receive a message from the system administrator. This may take several minutes, depending on how your network is configured.

6 Click OK to close the message, and then click OK to close the Options dialog box.

The contents of your Inbox appear in the Information viewer.

7 When the "Reply from Security Authority" message appears, double-click it.

A message appears, prompting you to enter your advanced security password.

8 Type your advanced security password, and then click OK.

A message appears, informing you that advanced security has successfully been enabled.

9 Click OK to close the message.

The "Reply from Security Authority" message is deleted automatically from your Inbox. Your mailbox is set up for advanced security, and you can now send and receive signed and sealed messages.

NOTE If you want to change your advanced security password, on the Tools menu, click Options, and then click the Security tab. Click Change Password, and then type your old and new passwords.

Sign a message

In this exercise, you sign a message as proof that you created the message, and then send it to a co-worker.

 IMPORTANT To complete the exercises in this section, you must recruit some help from another person on your network who also has advanced security enabled on his or her computer. You will send signed and sealed messages to this co-worker, and then view the results on his or her computer.

1 Create a new message, and then address it to a co-worker.
2 In the Subject box, type **Sign Test**
3 In the message area, type **This is an encrypted message.**
4 On the Standard toolbar, click the Digitally Sign Message button.
5 On the Standard toolbar, click the Send button.

Digitally Sign Message

The Microsoft Exchange Security Logon dialog box appears.

6 Type your advanced security password, and then click OK.

Your message is sent as an encrypted message.

TROUBLESHOOTING If you have enabled advanced security, but the Seal Message With Encryption and Digitally Sign Message buttons are dimmed, you might not have the Digital Security add-in file installed. To install it, on the Tools menu, click Options, and then click the General tab. Click Add-In Manager. Click Install, select the Etexch.ecf file from the Addins folder, and then click Open. Click OK to close each dialog box.

Seal a message

In this exercise, you seal and send a message so that only the designated recipient can open it.

TROUBLESHOOTING If a person to whom you are sending a sealed message does not have advanced security enabled, he or she will not be able to open the message. If a recipient is not using advanced security, you will be prompted to either send an unencrypted message or cancel the send operation.

1 Create a new message, and then address it to your partner.
2 In the Subject box, type **Sealed Message Test**
3 In the message area, type **This is a sealed message**.
4 On the Standard toolbar, click the Seal Message With Encryption button.
5 On the Standard toolbar, click the Send button, type your password, and then click OK.

*Seal Message
With Encryption*

Your message is sent as a sealed message.

TIP If you want all of your outgoing messages to be signed, on the Tools menu, click Options, and then click the Security tab. Under Options, select the Add Digital Signature To Message check box. If you want all of your outgoing messages to be sealed, select the Encrypt Message Contents And Attachments check box.

Have your co-worker view the messages

In this exercise, your co-worker opens the encrypted messages you sent him or her.

IMPORTANT   Have your co-worker perform the following exercise on his or her computer.

1   In your Inbox, double-click the "Sign Test" message.

The message opens. A password is not necessary to open a message that has been digitally signed.

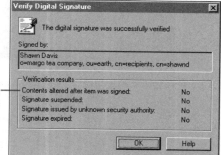

Read Digital Signature

2   On the Standard toolbar, click the Read Digital Signature button.

The Microsoft Exchange Security Logon dialog box appears.

3   Type your password, and then click OK.

The Verify Digital Signature dialog box appears. The digital signature is successfully verified.

No changes were made to the message after it was sent.

4   Click OK to close the Verify Digital Signature dialog box, and then close the message.

The first three lines of sealed messages do not appear in Messages With AutoPreview view.

5   Double-click the "Sealed Message Test" message.

A password is necessary to open a sealed message.

6   Type your password, and then click OK.

The message opens.

7   Close the message.

Finish the lesson

Follow these steps to delete the practice items and remove the access permissions you created in this lesson.

1   In the Folder List, use the right mouse button to click the Inbox folder, and then choose Properties.

The Inbox Properties dialog box appears.

2 On the Permissions tab, select the name of the co-worker who helped you with this lesson, click Remove, and then click OK.

3 Repeat steps 1 and 2 to remove your partner's access privileges to your mailbox.

Your co-worker no longer has access to your mailbox or Inbox.

4 On the Tools menu, click Options, and then click the Delegates tab.

5 In the Delegates box, select your co-worker's name, click Remove, and then click OK.

Your co-worker is no longer a delegate for your Outlook folders.

Delete

6 In the Inbox, select the practice messages you used in this lesson, and then click the Delete button. If you are prompted to delete the "Distribute Production Schedules" task, click Delete.

7 To continue to the next lesson, be sure that the contents of the Inbox appear in the Information viewer.

8 If you are finished using Outlook for now, on the File menu, click Exit And Log Off.

Lesson Summary

To	Do this
Grant another user permission to access a folder	In the Folder List, use the right mouse button to click a folder, and then click Properties. On the Permissions tab, click Add. Select a name, click Add, and then click OK. Select the name in the Names box. Click the Roles down arrow, select a role, and then click OK.
Add a mailbox to your information store	On the Tools menu, click Services, and then click Properties. On the Advanced tab, click Add, type the name of the mailbox you want to add, and then click OK to close each dialog box.
Name a delegate to your Outlook folders	On the Tools menu, click Options, and then click the Delegates tab. Click Add. Select a name, click Add, and then click OK. Select permissions for each Outlook folder, and then click OK to close each dialog box.

To	Do this	Button
Open a manager's folder	On the Outlook File menu, point to Open Special Folder, and then click Exchange Server Folder. Type the folder manager's name, select the folder you want to open, and then click OK.	
Send a message on a manager's behalf	In the manager's Inbox, click the New Mail Message button. On the View menu, click From Field. Type the manager's name in the From box, and then address and compose the message. On the Standard toolbar, click the Send button.	
Accept a request on a manager's behalf	In the manager's Inbox, open the request message. On the Standard toolbar, click the Accept button. Edit the reply, and then click the Send button.	
Set up advanced security	On the Tools menu, click Options, and then click the Security tab. Click Set Up Advanced Security. In the Token box, type your keyword. In the Password box, type your password, press TAB, and then type your password again. Click OK to close each dialog box.	
Sign a message	Create and address a new message. On the Standard toolbar, click the Digitally Sign Message button, and then send the message. Type your password when prompted.	
Seal a message	Create and address a new message. On the Standard toolbar, click the Seal Message With Encryption button, and then send the message. Type your password when prompted.	

For online information about	On the Help menu, click Contents And Index, click the Index tab, and then type
Sharing folders	**Folders, sharing** *or* **sharing folders**
Setting access permissions	**Permissions, delegate**
Using advanced security	**Security**

Working When Away From the Office

Estimated time
40 min.

In this lesson you will learn how to:

- Process your e-mail messages automatically using AutoAssistants.
- Set up remote access.
- Create and manage Outlook folders offline.

So far, you have learned how to use Microsoft Outlook in a networked environment, such as your office, where your computer is directly connected to the network. But if you need to send and receive messages from home or from an offsite computer outside of your organization's enterprise, you can work remotely using Outlook.

Imagine that you are on a business trip and want to keep up to date with your office communications. You can use Outlook and your laptop computer to work *offline*.

IMPORTANT   To perform the exercises in this lesson, your computer must be able to access a Microsoft Exchange Server computer on a networked environment and have Dial-up networking installed. In addition, your practice profile must contain the Microsoft Exchange Server information service, as outlined in "Installing and Using the Practice Files." If your setup does not meet these requirements, skip this lesson. If you need help setting up your practice profile, contact your system administrator.

Start Outlook and set up the Inbox for this lesson

In this exercise, you start Outlook using the Shawn Davis profile, and then copy the practice messages to your Inbox folder.

1 Start Outlook using the Shawn Davis profile.

For detailed steps on copying the practice files, see "Set Up Your Inbox for This Lesson" in Lesson 3.

2 Copy the practice files from the Outlook SBS Practice\Lesson 12 folder to your Inbox.

The messages are copied to your Inbox.

3 On the Outlook Bar, click the Inbox icon.

The contents of your Inbox appear in the Information viewer.

Managing Mail Automatically Using AutoAssistants

Suppose that you always process certain messages, such as daily progress reports, in the same way. You can automate most of the routine tasks you perform while using your Inbox. For example, you can specify that all incoming messages with the subject "Progress Report" are moved to a specific folder. Or, if you plan to be out of the office for any length of time, you can set options that send an automatic reply to anyone in your enterprise who sends you e-mail while you are gone so they know you are unavailable. This set of conditions is called a *rule*. When you set up one of the *AutoAssistant* features in Outlook, you create rules to process incoming or outgoing e-mail messages. You can set rules that move, respond to, or delete incoming messages that meet specific conditions, such as messages from a certain client. Rules are applied automatically when you receive messages, even when you are not using your office computer.

Setting Up the Out Of Office Assistant

When you are away from your office for any period of time, you can process your messages automatically by using the *Out Of Office Assistant*, one of the AutoAssistants available in Outlook. With the Out Of Office Assistant, you can notify the people who send you messages that you are away by creating an automatic reply. An *AutoReply* is a text message that is sent to each person within your enterprise who sends you mail. The Out Of Office Assistant sends only one response to each person who has sent you mail—regardless of the number of times the person sends you messages. This avoids sending each person duplicate AutoReply messages. When you return to the office and start Outlook to resume replying to your own messages, you are reminded that the Out Of Office Assistant is activated so that you don't forget to turn it off.

IMPORTANT   For security reasons, the Out Of Office Assistant only sends AutoReply messages to those people who send you e-mail from within your organization's enterprise. People outside your organization are not notified of your absence.

Before leaving on your business trip, you set up an automatic reply to notify any colleagues who send you messages that you are away from the office.

Set up an automatic reply

In this exercise, you use the Out Of Office Assistant to create an automatic reply to inform others of your absence.

1   On the Tools menu, click Out Of Office Assistant.

   The Out Of Office Assistant dialog box appears.

2   Click the I Am Currently Out Of The Office option button, and then press TAB.

3   In the AutoReply Only Once To Each Sender With The Following Text box, type **I'm out of the office until Monday. Tammy Wu (ext. 3480) will be handling all schedule updates until then.**

4   Click OK.

   The AutoReply is set up for any incoming messages.

Test your AutoReply

In this exercise, you test the AutoReply you just created to see if you receive the automatic message.

New Mail Message

1   On the Standard toolbar, click the New Mail Message button.

   A blank Mail form appears.

2   In the To box, type your name.

   You are sending a message to yourself as a test.

3   In the Subject box, type **AutoReply Test**

4   On the Standard toolbar, click the Send button.

   After a moment, your message is sent and two messages are delivered to your Inbox: the Out Of Office AutoReply message and your AutoReply Test message. Your screen should look similar to the following illustration.

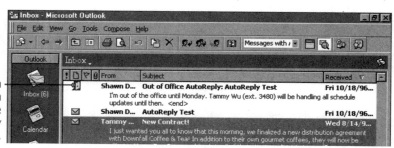

This icon indicates an Out Of Office AutoReply message.

5 Double-click the "Out Of Office AutoReply" message.

Your AutoReply message should look similar to the following illustration.

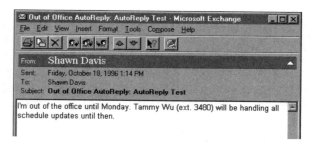

6 On the Out Of Office AutoReply window, click the Close button.

The message closes.

 IMPORTANT All senders of incoming messages will now receive your AutoReply message. If you want to disable the AutoReply message, click Out Of Office Assistant on the Tools menu, and then click the I Am Currently In The Office option button.

Creating Rules

In addition to using the Out Of Office Assistant to notify people of your absence, you can add rules that are used to process your messages while you are away from the office. You can use the Out Of Office Assistant to handle routine messages or deal with specific people who send you messages. For example, you can create a rule to forward the incoming messages from your project team to your assistant while you are away. However, you cannot use the Out Of Office Assistant to forward your messages to someone outside of your Outlook enterprise.

Outlook does not have to be open to use the Out Of Office Assistant. Rules are processed in your mailbox on the Microsoft Exchange Server. When you start

Outlook, you are reminded by a message that the Out Of Office Assistant is activated.

Set up a rule using the Out Of Office Assistant

 IMPORTANT To complete this exercise, you'll need to recruit help from two other people on your network. You'll create a rule that diverts messages from one of your co-workers to another, and then test the rule in a later exercise.

In this exercise, you create a rule to forward the messages that you receive from one of your co-workers to another who is acting as your assistant. This way, your assistant can respond to any urgent messages while you are traveling.

1 On the Tools menu, click Out Of Office Assistant.

2 Click Add Rule.

The Edit Rule dialog box appears.

3 In the When A Message Arrives That Meets The Following Conditions area, click From.

The Choose Sender dialog box appears. The names from your organization's global address list are listed.

4 Double-click the name of the first co-worker helping you with this lesson.

The name is added to the From box.

5 Click OK.

The Edit Rule dialog box appears again. Your co-worker's name appears in the From box.

6 In the Perform These Actions area, select the Forward check box, and then click To.

The Choose Recipient dialog box appears.

7 Double-click the name of the second co-worker helping you with this lesson.

Your co-worker will receive all messages from the person you specified in step 4 while you are out of the office.

8 Click OK to close the Choose Recipient dialog box, and then click OK to close the Edit Rule dialog box.

The Out Of Office Assistant dialog box reappears. The rule that you created is selected. Your screen should look similar to the following illustration.

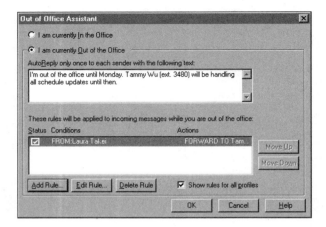

9 Click OK.

Incoming messages from your first co-worker will now be forwarded to your assistant.

IMPORTANT When you create a rule, it is applied immediately. If you do not want the rule to be applied now, you can cancel it by clearing the check box next to the rule in the Out Of Office Assistant dialog box.

Have your co-workers test the message

In this exercise, your first co-worker sends you a message, and your second co-worker checks to make sure that the message is forwarded to his or her Inbox.

NOTE A copy of the rule-forwarded message also remains in your Inbox so that you can view it if you choose when you return from your business trip.

1 Have your first co-worker create a new message and address it to you.

2 Have your first co-worker type **Forwarding Rule Test** in the Subject box.

3 Have your first co-worker type **This message was forwarded by a rule.** in the message area, and then send the message.

If the message has not been delivered yet, on the Tools menu, click Check For New Mail.

4 Have your second co-worker start Outlook, and then double-click the "FW: Forwarding Rule Test" message in his or her Inbox.

The message should look similar to the following illustration.

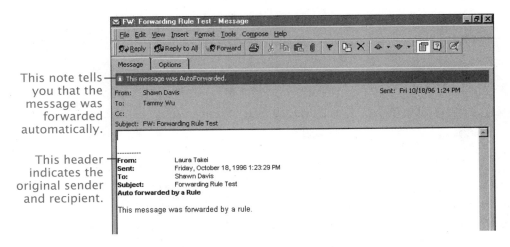

This note tells you that the message was forwarded automatically.

This header indicates the original sender and recipient.

5 Have your second co-worker close the message.

TIP You can also create rules to process your e-mail while you are in your office. On the Tools menu, click Inbox Assistant, and then select options in the Edit Rule dialog box to create a rule, just as you do when creating a rule with the Out Of Office Assistant.

Working Offsite with Outlook

Suppose you need to leave your office for a lengthy business trip. You're taking your laptop computer with you to work on reports and projects as you travel, but you'd also like to send e-mail to your co-workers to keep up to date with business in the office. Rather than let messages pile up in your Inbox while you are away, you can work *offline* to review your messages and compose new ones, and use a *dial-up connection* to periodically transfer information to and from the server in your office. When you work offline, your computer is not connected to the server. When you want to send and receive messages, you use a dial-up connection to quickly connect to your server, send and receive your messages, and then disconnect from the server.

If you wish, you can also establish a continuous dial-up connection. This provides continuous access to your office computer—as if you were working in the office. If you want to create offline folders for all your Outlook items, including tasks and appointments, you can use a continuous dial-up connection to keep your offline folders synchronized with the folders on your Microsoft Exchange Server. This method gives you easy access to your office, but it might be a less efficient use of telephone time and it might also be slower, depending on your modem and the speed of your connection. In addition, you can only create offline folders if your mail delivery service uses a Microsoft Exchange Server.

IMPORTANT The Exchange Server runs on a Windows NT server computer. To be able to work remotely with Outlook, your Windows NT server account must have dial-up access rights so that you can dial in to the Exchange Server. The system administrator is responsible for setting up your Windows NT server account; you can contact your system administrator if you need assistance.

Setting Up Offline Folders

When you are preparing to use *Dial-Up Networking*, you must make sure that your offsite computer is set up correctly so that you are able to connect to your server, and retrieve and send messages through the server. You also need a place to store the messages that you send and receive on your offsite computer, since your Outlook mailbox is physically located on the server at your company or organization. To store your messages, you must create an offline folder file on your offsite computer's hard disk. The offline folders that are included by default on your offsite computer are the same default folders that you use when you work online: Inbox, Outbox, Sent Items, Calendar, Contacts, and so on. You work with offline folders the same way you work with your regular mailbox folders or any other folders.

IMPORTANT To complete the exercises in the remainder of this lesson, your offsite computer must have a modem, a telephone line, and dial-up networking software so that you can establish a dial-up connection. In addition, you must have Outlook and Microsoft Exchange installed.

To work with offline folders, you must set up an offline folder file on your offsite computer. You can do this automatically when you create a user profile on your offsite computer.

TIP If you use the same computer to work remotely and in your office, you can create a separate profile that contains your remote configuration settings. For more information on creating user profiles, see "Installing and Using the Practice Files," earlier in this book.

Create the Shawn Davis profile on your offsite computer

In this exercise, you set up the Shawn Davis practice profile and an offline folder file on your offsite computer. Be sure to perform these steps on the computer you will be using while you are away from the office.

1 On your offsite computer, start Outlook, and then click New in the Choose Profile dialog box.

2 Select the Microsoft Exchange Server information service, clear all other check boxes, and then click Next.

If you don't know your server name, ask your system administrator for help.

3 Type **Shawn Davis offline**, and then click Next.

4 Type **your server name**, press TAB, type your mailbox name, and then click Next.

5 Under Do You Travel With This Computer, click the Yes option button.

You must select Yes to create a set of offline folders associated with this profile.

6 Click Next, enter the path to your personal address book, and then click Next.

7 Be sure that the Do Not Add Inbox To The StartUp Group option button is selected, click Next, and then click Finish.

The profile, with its set of offline folders, is created.

8 Click OK.

Outlook starts with the Shawn Davis offline profile.

 TROUBLESHOOTING If you did not select the Yes option button under Do You Travel With This Computer, you can create an offline folder file and add it to your user profile manually. To do so, first make sure that your Inbox is the current folder. On the Tools menu, click Services. Be sure that Microsoft Exchange Server is selected, and then click Properties. On the Advanced tab, click Offline Folder File Settings. In the File box, type the path to the file you want to use as the offline folder file. (The default filename is exchange.ost; if you rename the file, you may be prompted to create a separate file with the new name.)

Set up your dial-up networking connection

You want to download your Address Book to your offsite computer so that the e-mail addresses you use are available to you wherever you are working. To download the Address Book, your offsite computer must be connected to the server. In this exercise, you establish a dial-up network connection to use to connect to your server.

1 On the Tools menu, click Services.

The Services dialog box appears, with the Services tab active.

2 Be sure that Microsoft Exchange Server is selected, and then click Properties.

The Microsoft Exchange Server dialog box appears.

3 Click the Dial-Up Networking tab.

If you have already created a dial-up connection for your Microsoft Exchange Server, skip to step 9.

4 Be sure that the Dial Using The Following Connection option button is selected, and then click New.

The Make New Connection dialog box appears.

5 Be sure that My Connection is selected, and then type **Remote Outlook Connection**

This will be the name of your new connection.

6 Select your modem type, and then click Next.

7 Type the phone number for your Microsoft Exchange Server, and then click Next.

You might have to precede the phone number with a 9 and a comma (,) to establish an outside dial tone.

8 Click Finish.

Your dial-up connection, named Remote Outlook Connection, is complete.

If you are not sure of your Exchange Server name, ask your system administrator or click the General tab in the Services dialog box.

9 Click the Dial Using The Following Connection down arrow, and then select Remote Outlook Connection.

10 Type your username, password, and Microsoft Exchange Server domain name in the appropriate boxes.

The Dial-Up Networking tab should look similar to the following illustration.

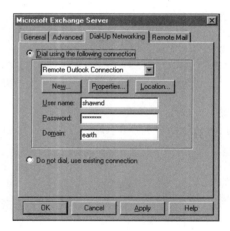

11 Click OK to close each dialog box.

TROUBLESHOOTING If, when you try to create a new connection, you receive an error message saying that Outlook cannot open the phone book file, you need to install dial-up networking. For additional help, see your system administrator.

Use a dial-up connection to download the Address Book

In this exercise, you use a temporary dial-up connection to download the Address Book for your Outlook enterprise so that you can address and send messages while working offline.

1 On the Tools menu, point to Synchronize, and then click Download Address Book.

 The Download Offline Address Book dialog box appears.

2 Be sure that the Download Offline Address Book option button is selected, and then click OK.

 A dial-up connection to your Microsoft Exchange Server is established, and your Address Book is downloaded to your offsite computer.

Set options for your start-up connection

You want to be prompted to choose a server connection type each time you start Outlook so that you can choose to connect to the Exchange Server or work offline.

1 Using your offsite computer, on the Tools menu, click Services.

 The Services dialog box appears.

2 Be sure that Microsoft Exchange Server is selected, and then click Properties.

 The Microsoft Exchange Server dialog box appears.

If the text of the server name and your mailbox are not underlined after clicking Check Names, contact your system administrator.

3 On the General tab, be sure that your Microsoft Exchange Server name and your mailbox appear, and that the text is underlined.

4 Select the Choose The Connection Type When Starting check box, and then click OK.

 The next time you start Outlook, you will be prompted to choose between connecting to the server or working offline.

5 Click OK to close the Services dialog box.

6 On the File menu, click Exit And Log Off.

 You must restart Outlook for the new settings to take effect. If a message appears, informing you that your offline folders will be synchronized with the server folders before you exit Outlook, click OK. You are logged off of Outlook and ready to work offline.

Working Offline

While you are working offline, your Exchange Server mailbox will still be receiving messages. Any messages you compose while you work offline are stored in your offline Outbox until they are sent; while in the Outbox folder, unsent messages are identified by italicized text in the message header. To transfer messages to and from the server, you need to establish a dial-up connection. During your Dial-Up Networking session, any new message you want to read will be transferred, or copied, to your offline folders. Similarly, any message that you want to send will be transferred from your offline folders to the server.

You are now on the road with your laptop computer, and you need to send a message. Because you don't have access to a phone line at the moment, you'll work offline and compose a message that will be stored in your Outbox. Later, you'll use Remote Mail to establish the dial-up connection to your server and transfer the message you've composed.

Create a message offline

In this exercise, you work offline in Outlook on your offsite computer. You send yourself a test message that will be stored in your Outbox mailbox until you can connect to the Exchange Server at Margo Tea Company.

 IMPORTANT Be sure to perform the following exercise on the computer you will use while out of your office.

1 On your offsite computer, start Outlook using the Shawn Davis offline profile.

   The Microsoft Exchange Server dialog box appears.

2 Click Work Offline.

   Outlook starts. No items appear in your offline Inbox, because you are viewing the Inbox folder on your offsite computer's hard disk, not your Inbox on the server.

3 On the Outlook Bar, click the Mail shortcut bar.

   The icons in the Mail group appear.

4 On the Outlook Bar, click the Sent Items icon.

   No items appear in the Information viewer; no messages are stored in the offline Sent Items folder because you have not sent any yet.

5 On the Outlook Bar, click the Outbox icon.

   No items are stored in the offline Outbox because you have not sent any messages offline yet.

6 On the Standard toolbar, click the New Mail Message button.

   A blank Mail form appears.

New Mail Message

7 In the To box, type your name.

8 In the Subject box, type **Offline Test**

9   In the message area, type **This message will be transferred using Dial-Up Networking.**

10   On the Standard toolbar, click the Send button.

A copy of your message is created in the offline Outbox folder. It is stored there until you connect to the Microsoft Exchange Server. The "Offline Test" message you sent appears in italicized text in the Outbox folder. Your screen should look similar to the following illustration.

Italic text indicates that this message has not yet been sent.

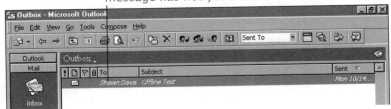

 WARNING   If you open an italicized message in the offline Outbox, and then close it without clicking the Send button, the message will not be sent when the offline folders are synchronized with the server folders.

Synchronizing Offline Folders with the Server

While you are working offline, you might want to periodically check your mailbox on the Microsoft Exchange Server for new messages. Or you might want to send the messages you composed that are stored in your offline Outbox. You can establish a temporary connection by using Dial-Up Networking, your modem, and a telephone line to dial in to the server.

Synchronize folders with a dial-up connection

In this exercise, you synchronize the contents of Outlook folders on your offsite computer with the Outlook folders in your Microsoft Exchange Server mailbox. You establish a temporary dial-up connection to send the Offline Test message you created offline and retrieve any new messages you've received.

 NOTE   When you synchronize your offline folders, a synchronization log file is recorded in your Deleted Items folder. This file shows the length of time you were connected, the names of the synchronized folders, and the numbers of items synchronized. You can double-click the file to view a record of the synchronization process.

Depending on the speed of your computer, your server, and your modem, synchronization may take several minutes.

1   On the Tools menu, point to Synchronize, and then click All Folders.

If you are prompted to continue dialing, click OK. The Synchronizing All Folders dialog box appears and a dial-up connection is established using the Remote Outlook Connection. After a moment, your outgoing mail is sent and messages from your mailbox on the server are transferred to your offline Inbox. When the transfer is complete, you are disconnected from the server automatically.

2   On the Outlook Bar, click the Inbox icon.

Your messages appear, including the new "Offline Test" message you composed and addressed to yourself offline. Your screen should look similar to the following illustration.

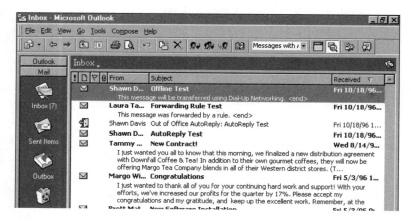

3   Minimize the Outlook window.

NOTE   Clicking All Folders on the Synchronize menu updates all of your offline Outlook folders so that, in addition to messages, any new appointments, tasks, or other items are transferred to your offline folders from the server. This can be useful if you have another person, such as a delegate, scheduling appointments for you back at the office. By synchronizing all folders, you can see the new appointments in your offline Calendar. You can choose to synchronize only the current folder by clicking This Folder on the Synchronize menu.

Using a Continuous Dial-Up Connection

When you work offsite, but still want to work with the Exchange Server as if you were using your office computer, you can dial in to your server to establish a continuous dial-up connection with Dial-Up Networking. Although the server might respond more slowly, you have the advantages of using features that you can only use while connected to an Exchange Server. For example, using a continuous dial-up connection allows you to work with folders on your organization's network so that you can save or retrieve documents and other files. In addition, you can send and retrieve messages instantly, instead of periodically making a connection to transfer items and working offline the rest of the time.

Since you know how to work offline and download your new messages, you now establish a connection and work with your Exchange Server just as you would if you were in your office. You must dial in to your server before starting Outlook from your offsite location.

Establish and use a dial-up connection

In this exercise, you establish a continuous dial-up connection, send yourself another test message, and then disconnect from the server.

1   On the Desktop, double-click the My Computer Icon.

The contents of My Computer appear.

2   Double-click the Dial-Up Networking folder.

The Dial-Up Networking window opens. The connection that you created earlier, named Remote Outlook Connection, is listed.

3   Double-click the Remote Outlook Connection icon.

The Connect To dialog box appears.

4   Type your password, if necessary, and then click Connect.

If you are prompted to continue dialing, click OK. After a few moments, the dial-up connection is established.

5   Maximize the Outlook window.

The contents of your Inbox appear in the Information viewer, allowing you to work directly with the server. If a message appears prompting you to turn off the Out Of Office Assistant, click No.

*New Mail
Message*

6   On the Standard toolbar, click the New Mail Message button, and then address the message to yourself.

You are sending the message to yourself as a test message to verify that using a continuous dial-up connection is similar to working at your computer in your office.

7   In the Subject box, type **Another Test**, and then click the Send button.

After a moment, your message appears in your Inbox because you are connected to the server.

8   On the File menu, click Exit And Log Off, and then click Disconnect to disconnect the Remote Outlook Connection dial-up.

If you are prompted to confirm the disconnection, click Yes.

What is Remote Mail?

If you use offline folders, you cannot use Remote Mail to download messages.

You can retrieve your e-mail messages while you are working offsite by using Remote Mail. Remote Mail is similar to using a dial-up connection: you connect to the server briefly to retrieve your message headers, work offline to decide which messages you want to see in detail, and then make another brief connection to retrieve or send specific messages. This method is usually the fastest and the most economical because it minimizes long-distance charges. Using Remote Mail is a good idea if you only want to download messages or if your organization uses a messaging system other than Exchange Server. To set up your offsite computer for Remote Mail, you must first:

Add a set of personal folders to your user profile. A personal folder file (.pst) contains duplicates of the same e-mail folders—Inbox, Outbox, Sent Items, and Deleted Items—that are in your mailbox on the server. The personal folder file on your offsite computer serves as the location where the messages you retrieve from the server are delivered.

Download the Address Book. You can download your Address Book to your offsite computer just as you do with Dial-Up Networking so that you can address and compose messages while working offline.

Set your mail delivery service options. Depending upon the mail delivery service you use, you might be able to set options for transferring messages with Remote Mail. For example, if you do use an Exchange Server, you can schedule Remote Mail sessions to occur at specific times.

Set new e-mail messages to be delivered to your personal folder file. The personal folder file you create on your offsite computer should be the location where your new messages will be received when you connect to your server.

You can use Remote Mail to view just the headers of messages in your mailbox; the header lists the sender, subject, and date. Viewing only the message header information in Remote Mail, rather than the preview text of every message, allows you to select only the messages you want to work with while offline. You can then retrieve only those messages, saving connection time as well as space in your offsite Inbox folder. If you previously have connected to your server, the headers will be updated in Remote Mail so that they represent what is currently in your server mailbox.

The Remote Mail window contains a Remote toolbar that includes buttons for frequently used tasks. For example, you can use the Connect button to quickly establish a connection with your server. When you start Remote Mail, a wizard guides you through the process so that you can transfer either message headers or entire messages to your offsite computer.

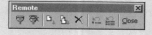

When you mark a message for deletion in the Remote Mail window, the message will be permanently deleted when you synchronize your folders. It won't be moved to the Deleted Items folder.

After you view your message headers, you are automatically disconnected from the server. Now you can *mark* individual message headers in the Remote Mail window to specify which ones you want to work with. When you mark a message for retrieval, the next time you connect with your server, the message will be *downloaded*, or moved, to your offsite computer. You can also retrieve a copy of a message, or delete a message from the server without downloading it. If you have not read a message, the header appears in bold. If you have chosen to download a message, it will appear in plain text. When you download a message, a copy is saved in your mailbox on the server.

Finish the lesson

Follow these steps to restore the default settings and delete the practice messages you created in this lesson.

1 Start Outlook on your office computer, using the Shawn Davis profile. If you are prompted to turn off the Out Of Office Assistant, click Yes.

2 Select the practice messages you used in this lesson in your Inbox folder and Sent Items folder, and then click the Delete button.

3 On the Tools menu, click Services, select Microsoft Exchange Server, and then click Properties.

4 Be sure that the Connect With The Network option button is selected in the When Starting area.

5 Clear the Choose The Connection Type When Starting check box, and then click OK to close each dialog box.

6 On the Tools menu, click Out Of Office Assistant. Select the I Am Currently In The Office option button.

7 Delete the rule you created in this lesson, and then click OK.

8 On the Outlook Bar, click the Inbox icon.

9 If you are finished using Outlook for now, on the File menu, click Exit And Log Off.

Lesson Summary

To	Do this
Set up an AutoReply	On the Tools menu, click Out Of Office Assistant. Click the I Am Currently Out Of The Office option button, and then type the message.

To	Do this
Set up an Out Of Office Assistant rule	On the Tools menu, click Out Of Office Assistant. Click Add Rule, and then select the settings.
Create a set of offline folders	On your offsite computer, double-click the Microsoft Outlook short-cut icon, and then click New. Follow the steps in the Inbox Setup wizard. When prompted to specify whether you travel with this computer, click the Yes option button.
Download the address book	On the Tools menu, point to Synchronize, and then click Download Address Book. Click the Download Address Book option button, and then click OK.
Work offline	After you have set up your computer to work offline, start Outlook, and then click Work Offline.
Synchronize your offline folders with folders on the network	On the Tools menu, point to Synchronize, and then click All Folders.
Establish a continuous dial-up connection	On the Desktop, click the My Computer icon. Double-click the Dial-Up Networking icon. Double-click the icon for the connection you want to use. Type your password, and then click Connect. Start Outlook, and then click Connect.

For online information about	On the Help menu, click Contents And Index, click the Index tab, and then type
Processing mail with AutoAssistants	**Inbox Assistant** *or* **Out Of Office Assistant**
Creating an AutoReply	**AutoReply**
Working offline	**Offline folders** *or* **offline setup**
Downloading messages	**Downloading**
Establishing a dial-up connection	**Dial-Up Networking** (in Windows Help)

Review & Practice

Estimated time
20 min.

- Create an AutoReply using the Out Of Office Assistant.
- Assign a delegate to help you manage your mail.
- Work with Outlook messages offline.
- Use a dial-up connection to send and retrieve messages.

Before you complete this book, you can practice the skills you learned in Part 4 by working through this Review & Practice section. You will use the Out Of Office Assistant to create an AutoReply and set rules to process your incoming e-mail messages. You'll also grant one of your co-workers delegate access to your Microsoft Outlook files so that person can help you manage your Outlook items. Finally, you'll practice working with Outlook offline and communicating remotely using the Microsoft Exchange Server.

Scenario

You have decided to try working from your home office two days a week instead of commuting. You also want your co-workers to know that you will be briefly unavailable while you configure your home office computer, so you set up an AutoReply to notify everyone. You assign one of your co-workers delegate access so that person can monitor your Inbox for important messages while you're setting up your computer. After setting up your home office, you work offline to check in for any new messages and you send a thank-you message to your co-worker.

IMPORTANT Because the exercises in this Review & Practice deal with some of the networking features of Outlook, you will need to recruit one of your co-workers to help you with these exercises.

Step 1: *Create an AutoReply with the Out Of Office Assistant*

You're setting up your offsite computer, and you want anyone who sends you a message to know that you are not available while you are making the transition to your home office. In this step, you create an AutoReply so that anyone who sends you a message will be informed that you are temporarily unavailable.

1 Enable the Out Of Office Assistant.

2 Create an AutoReply by typing the following text:

I am in the process of setting up my home office for telecommuting. My co-worker will be handling any urgent matters until then.

3 Use the Out Of Office Assistant to create a rule that forwards all your incoming messages to the co-worker who's assisting you with these exercises. (Hint: Click Add Rule, and then select an option in the Perform These Actions area.)

For more information about	See
Using Auto Assistants	Lesson 11
Creating an AutoReply	Lesson 11
Setting rules	Lesson 11

Step 2: *Assign a Delegate to Help You Manage Your Mail*

You've arranged for your incoming messages to be forwarded to your co-worker, but you also want that person to be able to accept requests and respond to people on your behalf. In this step, you give that person delegate access to your Outlook folders.

1 Name your co-worker as a delegate for your Outlook folders. (Hint: On the Tools menu, click Options, and then switch to the Delegates tab.)

2 Grant your co-worker Author permission to your Inbox, and Editor permission to your Calendar and Tasks folder.

For more information about	See
Granting delegate access	Lesson 11
Setting access permissions	Lesson 11

Step 3: *Work with Outlook Messages Offline*

You are now working at home and you want to compose and send a message. You have already set up Dial-Up Networking, downloaded the Address Book, and configured your modem, so you are ready to work offline. In this step, you work offline to create and send a new message.

1   Start Outlook and work offline on your offsite computer.

2   Create a new message titled "Thanks!" Type the following message to your co-worker: **Thanks for taking care of my messages while I'm getting settled!** Address a copy of the message to yourself.

3   Send the message.

For more information about	See
Setting up Dial-Up Networking	Lesson 12
Working offline	Lesson 12

Step 4: *Use a Dial-up Connection to Connect to Your Server*

Since you're working at home, you don't have direct access to your Microsoft Exchange Server. In this step, you use a dial-up connection to first send a message, and then download a copy of that message.

➤   From your offsite computer, connect to the network and synchronize all your Outlook folders.

For more information about	See
Connecting to the server from a remote location	Lesson 12
Retrieving messages with a dial-up connection	Lesson 12

Finish the Review & Practice

Follow these steps to restore the settings and delete the practice messages you used in this Review & Practice, and then quit Outlook.

1   Using your office computer, remove the permissions you assigned to your co-worker in Step 2.

2   Disable the Out Of Office Assistant and delete the rule that you created.

Delete

3   Select the practice messages you created in this exercise, and then click the Delete button.

4   If you are finished using Outlook for now, on the File menu, click Exit And Log Off.

293

Appendixes

If You Are New to Windows 95 or Windows NT and to Outlook

If you're new to Microsoft Windows 95 or Microsoft Windows NT version 4.0 and to Microsoft Outlook, this appendix will show you all the basics you need to get started. You'll get an overview of Windows 95 and Windows NT features, and you'll learn how to use online Help to answer your questions and find out more about using these operating systems. You'll also get an introduction to Outlook.

If You Are New to Windows 95 or Windows NT

Windows 95 and Windows NT are easy-to-use computer environments that help you handle the daily work that you perform with your computer. You can use either Windows 95 or Windows NT to run Outlook—the explanations in this appendix apply to both operating systems. The way you use Windows 95, Windows NT, and programs designed for these operating systems is similar. The programs have a common look, and you use the same kinds of controls to tell them what to do. In this section, you'll learn how to use the basic program controls. If you're already familiar with Windows 95 or Windows NT, skip to the "What is Microsoft Outlook?" section.

Start Windows 95 or Windows NT

Starting Windows 95 or Windows NT is as easy as turning on your computer.

1 If your computer isn't on, turn it on now.

In Windows 95, you will also be prompted for a username and password if your computer is configured for user profiles.

2 If you are using Windows NT, press CTRL+ALT+DEL to display a dialog box asking for your username and password. If you are using Windows 95, you will see this dialog box if your computer is connected to a network.

3 Type your username and password in the appropriate boxes, and then click OK.

If you don't know your username or password, contact your system administrator for assistance.

Close

4 If you see the Welcome dialog box, click the Close button.

Your screen should look similar to the following illustration.

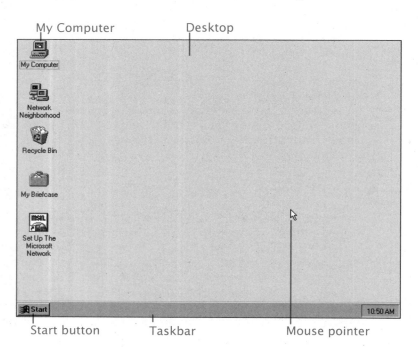

Using the Mouse

Although you can use the keyboard for most actions, it can be easier to use the mouse. The mouse controls a pointer on the screen, as shown in the previous illustration. You move the pointer by sliding the mouse over a flat surface in the direction you want the pointer to move. If you run out of room to move the mouse, lift it up, and then put it down in a more comfortable location.

You'll use five basic mouse actions throughout this book.

 NOTE   In this book, we assume that your mouse is set up so that the left button is the primary button and the right button is the secondary button. If your mouse is configured the opposite way, for left-handed use, use the right button when we tell you to use the left, and vice versa.

When you are directed to	Do this
Point to an item	Move the mouse to place the pointer on the item.
Click an item	Point to the item on your screen, and then quickly press and release the left mouse button.
Use the right mouse button to click an item	Point to the item on your screen, and then quickly press and release the right mouse button. Clicking the right mouse button displays a shortcut menu from which you can choose from a list of commands that apply to that item.
Double-click an item	Point to the item, and then quickly press and release the left mouse button twice.
Drag an item	Point to an item, and then hold down the left mouse button as you move the pointer.

Using Window Controls

All programs designed for use on computers that have Windows 95 or Windows NT installed have common controls that you use to scroll, size, move, and close a window.

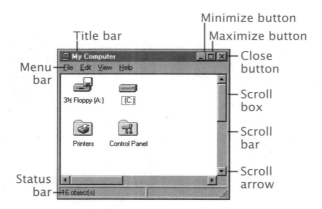

Title bar
Minimize button
Maximize button
Close button
Menu bar
Scroll box
Scroll bar
Scroll arrow
Status bar

To	Do this	Button
Move, or *scroll*, vertically or horizontally through the contents of a window that extends beyond the screen	Click a scroll bar or scroll arrow, or drag the scroll box. The illustration above identifies these controls.	
Enlarge a window to fill the screen	Click the Maximize button, or double-click the window's title bar.	
Restore a window to its previous size	Click the Restore button, or double-click the window title bar. When a window is maximized, the Maximize button changes to the Restore button.	
Reduce a window to a button on the taskbar	Click the Minimize button. To display a minimized window, click its button on the taskbar.	
Move a window	Drag the window title bar.	
Close a window	Click the Close button.	

Using Menus

Just like a restaurant menu, a program menu provides a list of options from which you can choose. On program menus, these options are called *commands*. To select a menu or a menu command, you click the item you want.

NOTE You can also use the keyboard to make menu selections. Press the ALT key to activate the menu bar. Press the key that corresponds to the highlighted or underlined letter of the menu name, and then press the key that corresponds to the highlighted or underlined letter of the command name.

Open and make selections from a menu

In this exercise, you open and make selections from a menu.

1 On the Desktop, double-click the My Computer icon.

The My Computer window opens.

You can also press ALT+E to open the Edit menu.

2 In the My Computer window, click Edit on the menu bar.

The Edit menu appears. Some commands are dimmed; this means that they aren't available.

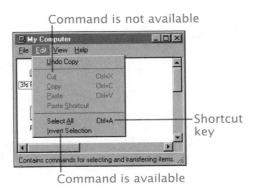

Command is not available

Shortcut key

Command is available

3 Click the Edit menu name to close the menu.

The menu closes.

4 Click View on the menu bar to open the View menu.

5 On the View menu, click Toolbar.

The View menu closes, and a toolbar appears below the menu bar.

On a menu, a check mark indicates that multiple items in this group of commands can be selected at one time. A bullet mark indicates that only one item in this group can be selected at one time.

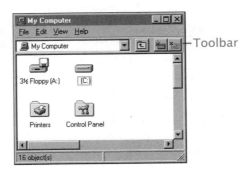

Toolbar

6 On the View menu, click List.

The items in the My Computer window now appear in a list, rather than as icons.

Large Icons

7 On the toolbar, click the Large Icons button.

Clicking a button on a toolbar is a quick way to select a command.

8 On the View menu, point to Arrange Icons.

A cascading menu appears listing additional menu choices. When a right-pointing arrow appears after a command name, it indicates that additional commands are available.

9 Click anywhere outside the menu to close it.

10 On the menu bar, click View, and then click Toolbar again.

The View menu closes, and the toolbar is now hidden.

11 Click the Close button in the upper-right corner of the My Computer window to close the window.

TIP If you do a lot of typing, you might want to learn the key combinations for commands you use frequently. Pressing the key combination is a quick way to perform a command by using the keyboard. If a key combination is available for a command, it will be listed to the right of the command name on the menu. For example, CTRL+C is listed on the Edit menu as the key combination for the Copy command.

Using Dialog Boxes

When you choose a command name that is followed by an ellipsis (...), a dialog box will appear so that you can provide more information about how the command should be carried out. Dialog boxes have standard features, as shown in the following illustration.

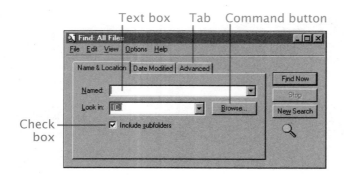

Text box   Tab   Command button

Check box

To move around in a dialog box, you click the item you want. You can also use the keyboard to select the item by holding down ALT as you press the underlined letter. Or you can press TAB to move between items.

Display the Taskbar Properties dialog box

Some dialog boxes provide several categories of options displayed on separate tabs. You click the top of an obscured tab to make it visible.

1 On the taskbar, click the Start button.

The Start menu appears.

2 On the Start menu, point to Settings, and then click Taskbar.

3 In the Taskbar Properties dialog box, click the Start Menu Programs tab.

Using this tab, you can customize the list of programs that appears on your Start menu.

4 Click the Taskbar Options tab, and then click to select the Show Small Icons In Start Menu check box.

When a check box is selected, it displays a check mark.

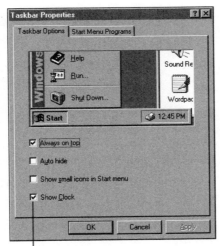

Click here. When you click a check box
that is selected, you turn the option off.

5 Click the check box a couple times, and watch how the display in the dialog box changes.

Clicking any check box or option button will turn the option off or on.

6 Click the Cancel button in the dialog box.

This closes the dialog box without changing any settings.

Getting Help with Windows 95 or Windows NT

When you're at work and you want to find more information about how to do a project, you might ask a co-worker or consult a reference book. To find out more about functions and features in Windows 95 or Windows NT, you can use the online Help system. For example, when you need information about how to print, the Help system is one of the most efficient ways to learn. The Windows 95 or Windows NT Help system is available from the Start menu. After the Help system opens, you can choose the type of help you want from the Help Topics dialog box.

To find instructions about broad categories, you can look on the Contents tab. Or you can search the Help index to find information about specific topics. The Help information is short and concise, so you can get the exact information you need quickly. You can use shortcut icons in many Help topics to directly perform the task you want.

Viewing Help Contents

The Contents tab is organized like a book's table of contents. As you choose top-level topics, called *chapters*, you see a list of more detailed subtopics from which to choose. Many of these chapters have Tips And Tricks sections to help you work more efficiently, and Troubleshooting sections to help you resolve problems.

Find Help about general categories

Suppose you want to learn more about using Calculator, a program that comes with Windows 95 and Windows NT. In this exercise, you'll look up information in the online Help system.

1   Click Start. On the Start menu, click Help.

    The "Help Topics: Windows Help" or "Help Topics: Windows NT Help" dialog box appears.

2   If necessary, click the Contents tab to make it active.

3 Double-click "Introducing Windows" or "Introducing Windows NT."

A set of subtopics appears.

4 Double-click "Using Windows Accessories."

5 Double-click "For General Use."

6 Double-click "Calculator: for making calculations."

A Help topic window opens.

7 Read the Help information, and then click the Close button to close the Help window.

Finding Help About Specific Topics

You can find specific Help topics by using the Index tab or the Find tab. The Index tab is organized like a book's index. Keywords for topics are organized alphabetically. You can either scroll through the list of keywords or type the keyword you want to find. You can then select from one or more topic choices.

With the Find tab, you can also enter a keyword. The main difference is that you get a list of all Help topics in which that keyword appears, not just the topics that begin with that word.

Find Help about specific topics by using the Help index

In this exercise, you use the Help index to learn how to change the background pattern of your Desktop.

1 Click Start, and then click Help.

The Help Topics dialog box appears.

2   Click the Index tab to make it active.

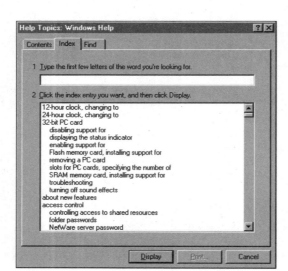

3   In the text box, type **display**

A list of display-related topics appears.

4   Click the topic named "background pictures or patterns, changing," and then click Display.

The Topics Found dialog box appears.

5   Be sure that the topic named "Changing the background of your desktop" is selected, and then click Display.

6   Read the Help topic.

7   Click the shortcut icon in step 1 of the Help topic.

Shortcut

The Display Properties dialog box appears. If you want, you can immediately perform the task you are looking up in Help.

8   Click the Close button on the Display Properties dialog box.

9   Click the Close button on the Windows Help window.

NOTE   You can print any Help topic if you have a printer installed on your computer. Click the Options button in the upper-left corner of any Help topic window, click Print Topic, and then click OK. To continue searching for additional topics, click the Help Topics button in any open Help topic window.

Find Help about specific topics by using the Find tab

In this exercise, you use the Find tab to learn how to change your printer's settings.

1   Click Start, and then click Help to display the Help Topics dialog box.

2   Click the Find tab to make it active.

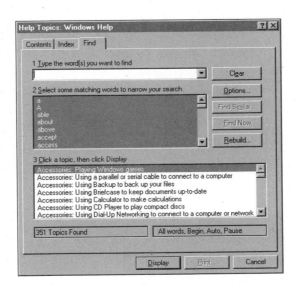

3   If you see a wizard, click Next, and then click Finish to complete the creation of the search index and close the wizard.

This might take a few minutes. The next time you use Find, you won't have to wait for the list to be created.

The Find tab appears.

4   In the text box, type **print**

All topics that have to do with printing appear in the list box at the bottom of the tab.

5   In step 3 of the Help dialog box, click the "Changing printer settings" topic, and then click Display.

The Help topic appears.

6   Read the Help topic, and then click the Close button on the Windows Help window.

Find Help in a dialog box

Almost every dialog box includes a question mark Help button in the upper-right corner of its window. When you click this button, and then click any dialog box control, a Help window appears that explains what the control is and how to use it. In this exercise, you get help on a dialog box control.

1   Click Start, and then click Run.

The Run dialog box appears.

Help

2   Click the Help button.

The mouse pointer changes to an arrow with a question mark.

3   Click the Open text box.

A Help window appears, providing information about how to use the Open text box.

4   Click anywhere on the Desktop or press ESC to close the Help window.

The mouse pointer returns to its previous shape and the Run dialog box appears again.

5   Click Cancel.

TIP   You can change the way the Help topics appear on your screen. Click the Options button in any Help topic window, point to Font, and then click the size you want the text to be.

What Is Microsoft Outlook?

Microsoft Outlook is a desktop information manager that you can use to perform many of your daily business activities with your computer. Using Outlook, it's easy to communicate with others by sending and receiving electronic mail, or *e-mail*. You can also record appointments and other events, such as conferences or birthdays, in an electronic Calendar, and schedule meetings with other people on your network. You can record important information about your business and personal colleagues in a contact list. To remind you of important duties you must perform during the day, you can create a task list. If you need to keep a detailed record of all your different daily activities, you can record them in an ongoing log in the Journal folder. Finally, you can view and organize other files and documents stored on your computer, and share them with or send them to other users, all without leaving the Outlook program window. In short, you can use Outlook to coordinate your entire business day.

More and more companies are efficiently communicating and gathering information online. Outlook is designed to keep you connected with other people, especially within your company. You can use Outlook, and its folder system, to organize and access all your e-mail messages, faxes, appointments, contacts, and tasks in one convenient location.

If you and your co-workers are all using Outlook to exchange information, your individual computers are all part of a Microsoft Outlook *enterprise*. An Outlook enterprise consists of any number of individual *client* computers (such as the computer you use at your desk), connected to one or more *server* computers. The servers act as central locations that receive information from, and distribute information to, the many different client computers.

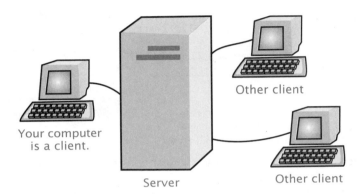

This client/server messaging system provides workgroups, such as an organization, with a method for accessing and exchanging information using programs such as Outlook. A system administrator installs and configures the server and adds new users.

What Is Electronic Mail?

Electronic mail, or *e-mail*, is your computer's version of the postal service or interoffice mail. Instead of hand-delivering printed documents, you send the information online, through the network, to other computer users. With e-mail, you can send messages to and receive messages from other people who have access to a mail delivery system and a modem.

The server acts as a postoffice, containing all user mailboxes and handling messages. Messages you receive are stored on the server and appear in your own electronic mailbox on the server. The following illustration shows how the server connects your mailbox to other mailboxes.

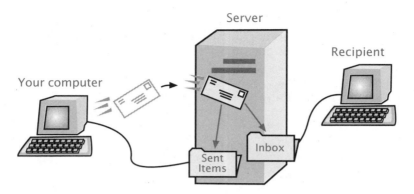

When you send a message, a copy of your message is stored on the server. A pointer to the message is placed in each recipient's Inbox and in your Sent Items folder.

Using Outlook, you are not limited to just text in your messages; documents, video, sound, and graphic images can be inserted in your messages and sent directly as separate files. You can send copies of your messages or forward them to other people. When you receive a message from another person, you can reply to it, forward it, or delete it; you can also have Outlook do this for you automatically.

Quit Windows 95 or Windows NT

1   If you are finished using Windows 95 or Windows NT, close any open windows by clicking the Close button in each window.

2   Click Start, and then click Shut Down.

   The Shut Down Windows dialog box appears.

3   Click Yes.

   A message indicates that it is now safe to turn off your computer.

 WARNING   To avoid loss of data or damage to your operating system, always quit Windows 95 or Windows NT by using the Shut Down command on the Start menu before you turn your computer off.

Matching the Exercises

Microsoft Outlook has many optional settings that can affect either the screen display or the operation of certain functions. Some exercise steps, therefore, might not produce exactly the same result on your screen as is shown in this book. If your screen does not look like an illustration at a certain point in a lesson, a note in the lesson might give you further instructions or direct you to this appendix for guidance. If you do not get the outcome described in the lesson, you can use this appendix to determine whether the options you selected are the same as the ones used in this book.

 NOTE Each computer system is configured with different hardware and software; therefore, your icons, folders, and menu options might not look exactly like the illustrations in this book. These system differences should not interfere with your ability to perform the exercises.

Matching the Screen Display to the Illustrations

Outlook makes it easy to set up the program window to suit your working style and preferences. If you share your computer with others, previous users might have changed the screen setup. You can easily change it back so that your screen matches the illustrations in the lessons. The following methods can help you control the screen display.

If you change the screen display as part of a lesson and leave Outlook, the next time you open Outlook, the screen will look the way you left it in the previous session.

If the filenames in the Open dialog box have extensions

A previous user might have changed a display option in Windows Explorer to see filename extensions, such as .doc for Microsoft Word files. To hide the extensions, you can change the setting in Windows Explorer, the file management program in Windows 95 and Windows NT version 4.0.

1   On the Start menu, point to Programs, and then click Windows Explorer.

2   On the View menu, click Options, and then click the View tab.

    Be sure you click the View menu in Windows Explorer, not in Outlook.

3   Select the Hide MS-DOS File Extensions For File Types That Are Registered check box.

4   Click OK, and then close Windows Explorer.

Display toolbars

If toolbars are missing at the top of the screen, previous users might have hidden them to make more room for text. You can display the toolbars that contain the buttons you need.

➤   On the View menu, point to Toolbars, and then click the name of the toolbar you need.

    Most of the lessons require that the Standard toolbar appears.

Hide extra toolbars

To use specific features in some of the lessons, additional toolbars appear in the program window. If, after completing a lesson, you no longer want these toolbars to appear, you can use a shortcut menu to hide toolbars you don't want to see. However, most of the lessons require that the Standard toolbar appears.

1   Use the right mouse button to click any toolbar.

    A shortcut menu appears.

2   On the shortcut menu, click the name of the toolbar you do not want to see.

If the Outlook program window does not fill the screen

A previous user might have made the Outlook program window smaller to allow quick access to another icon on the Desktop. You can easily enlarge the window by clicking a button.

➤ On the program window, click the Maximize button in the upper-right corner of the title bar.

If the right edge of the Outlook window is hidden so that you cannot see the Maximize button, point to "Microsoft Outlook" in the title bar at the top of the screen, and then drag the title bar to the left until you see the Maximize button. You can also double-click anywhere on the title bar to maximize the window.

If the Folder List appears

A previous user might have chosen to display the Folder List to view a hierarchy of all the folders on the computer. In the lessons in this book, you are prompted to display the Folder List only when it is necessary to complete an exercise. You can hide the Folder List using a toolbar button.

Folder List

➤ On the Standard toolbar, click the Folder List button.

The Folder List button is a toggle button; you can click it to hide or display the Folder List.

If the Date Navigator does not display two months

A previous user may have resized the appointment area in Calendar to make room for more appointment text. You can resize it by dragging the border of the appointment area.

1 In Calendar, position the pointer over the border between the Date Navigator and the appointment area.

The pointer changes to a two-headed arrow.

2 Drag the border to the left until it stops in the first third of the appointment area.

The Date Navigator displays two months.

If WordMail is installed as the e-mail editor

A previous user may have installed WordMail as the Outlook e-mail editor. This feature allows you to use Microsoft Word tools to edit and format your e-mail messages. If WordMail is being used, you may see additional toolbars and controls on the Mail form that you use to compose messages. You can turn off the WordMail option and use the default Mail message form instead.

1 On the Tools menu, click Options.

2 Click the E-mail tab.

3 Clear the Use Microsoft Word As The E-mail Editor check box, and then click OK.

313

Using the Default Views

Each of the Outlook folders on your computer—Inbox, Calendar, Contacts, Tasks, Journal, Notes, and so on—comes with a selection of predesigned views that you can apply to display information differently. For the lessons in this book, it is assumed that the default view is applied to each Outlook folder at the beginning of a lesson; during the exercises, you may be asked to switch or modify views. The following table lists the default views for each of the Outlook folders.

Folder	Default view	Other settings
Inbox	Messages With AutoPreview	
Calendar	Day/Week/Month	Single day displayed
Contacts	Address Cards	
Tasks	Simple List	
Journal	By Type	Single day displayed
Notes	Icons	
Deleted Items	Messages	
Sent Items	Sent To	
Outbox	Sent To	

NOTE   To apply a different view to a folder, on the Standard toolbar, click the Current View down arrow to display a list of the available views for that folder, and then click the view you want to use. In the Calendar folder and the Journal folder, you can display a single day at a time by clicking the Day button on the Standard toolbar.

Day

Using Outlook Forms to Organize Information

You have probably used paper forms on many occasions to apply for a job, or to fill out a time sheet or a tax return. Forms present information in an orderly structure that helps you view and enter information. With Microsoft Outlook, you can create and use electronic forms to keep track of the same information that is typically contained on paper. You can distribute electronic forms through e-mail to save time, paper, and storage space. You can also post electronic forms to your server so that the information is in a central location and can be accessible to everyone.

You have already worked extensively with some basic forms, such as the Mail form for addressing and composing e-mail messages and the contact form for adding relevant information to your contact list. In addition to these basic forms, Outlook comes with a variety of other forms that have been designed for specific uses. For example, you can use the Vacation Request form to keep track of employee requests for time off or use the While You Were Out form to take a message for another person and send it to that person via e-mail. You can also design your own forms by customizing any of these built-in forms to reflect any particular procedures followed in your organization.

Installing the Built-In Forms

In addition to the basic item forms that come with Outlook, you can add a set of supplementary forms to your user profile. These additional forms can be used to perform more complex messaging and scheduling tasks, or to post different types of information to public folders.

Outlook forms are based on three form types. E-mail forms are very similar to the Mail form and are used to send information from one user to another. Post forms resemble the Mail form, but instead of being sent to a specific person, post forms are sent to a public folder on the network where they can be viewed by multiple users. Microsoft Office 97 document forms are used to record and collect information in a table or spreadsheet format, such as a Microsoft Excel worksheet. The available Outlook supplementary forms are described in the following table.

Form	Type	Used to
Classified Ads	Database entry; response form	Enter classified ads into a standard database in a public folder or other folder on your network, and to respond to ads or purchase advertised items.
Sales Tracking	E-mail form	Record and process sales information; synchronized with the user's Calendar, Task, Journal, and Contact folders.
Training Management	E-mail form	Schedule and register for courses and seminars; synchronized with the user's Calendar.
Vacation Request	E-mail form	Report employee vacation time and sick leave; synchronized with the user's Calendar.
While You Were Out	E-mail form	Record an absent co-worker's messages; sent to the employee's Inbox

These sample forms (excluding While You Were Out) are not included automatically when you install Outlook; instead, they are available as part of the ValuPack on the Microsoft Office 97 CD-ROM. You must install the sample forms separately to make them available.

Install forms from the ValuPack

The supplementary Outlook forms are stored in the ValuPack folder on the Microsoft Office 97 CD-ROM. In this exercise, you install the personal folder file (.pst) containing the forms on your computer.

1   Insert the Microsoft Office 97 CD-ROM in your compact disc drive.

2   On the Outlook Bar, click the Other shortcut bar.

    The icons in the Other group appear on the Outlook Bar.

3   On the Outlook Bar, click the My Computer icon.

    The available drives for your computer appear in the Information viewer.

4   In the Information viewer, double-click the icon that corresponds to your compact disc drive.

The contents of the CD-ROM appear in the Information viewer.

5   In the Information viewer, double-click the ValuPack folder.

The contents of the folder appear in the Information viewer.

6   Double-click the Template folder, and then double-click the Outlook folder.

7   Double-click the Outlfrms icon.

The Outlook Sample Forms dialog box appears, containing the End-User License Agreement.

8   Read the agreement, and then click Yes if you accept the terms.

The destination, C:\Program Files\Microsoft Office\Office, for the Forms.pst file appears.

9   Click OK.

The destination, C:\Program Files\Microsoft Office\Templates, for the form template (.oft) files appears.

10   Click OK.

The files are installed on your computer. A message appears, telling you where the sample forms can now be found.

11   Click OK to close the message, and then close all open windows.

Add the set of sample forms to your Folder List

In this exercise, you add the set of folders containing sample Outlook forms to your Folder List, so that you can easily find a form when you want to use it.

1   Start Outlook. On the Outlook Bar, click the Outlook shortcut bar, and then click the Inbox icon.

The contents of your Inbox appear in the Information viewer.

Folder List

2   On the Standard toolbar, click the Folder List button.

The Folder List appears to the left of the Information viewer.

3   On the File menu, point to Open Special Folder, and then click Personal Folder.

The Connect To Personal Folders dialog box appears.

The path to the folder is C:\Program Files\Microsoft Office\Office.

4   Be sure that the Office folder appears in the Look In box.

5   Select the Forms.pst file, and then click OK.

The Sample Forms–Microsoft Outlook window appears.

6   Close the Sample Forms–Microsoft Outlook window.

The Sample Forms folder has been added to the bottom of your Folder List.

Each Sample Forms folder contains a Read Me message to help you learn about forms.

7 In the Folder List, click the plus sign (+) next to the Sample Forms icon.

The set of folders expands. Your screen should look similar to the following illustration.

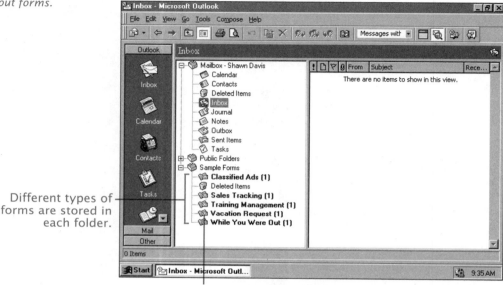

Different types of forms are stored in each folder.

Vacation Request folder

Use a sample form

In this exercise, you test the Vacation Request form by sending one to yourself.

When you select a folder, the available forms for that folder are added to the bottom of the Compose menu.

1 In the Folder List, click the Vacation Request folder.

You must select the folder that contains the form you want to work with.

2 On the Compose menu, click New Vacation Request.

A message appears, informing you that the form is being installed on your machine for the first time. After a moment, a blank Vacation Request form appears. Your screen should look similar to the following illustration.

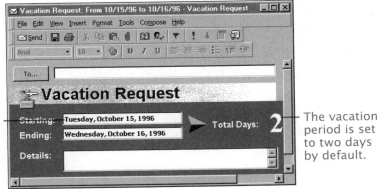

Tomorrow's date appears by default.

The vacation period is set to two days by default.

3 Select the text in the Ending box.

4 Using the mm/dd/yy format, type next Friday's date, and then press ENTER.

The end date and the vacation period change to reflect the new information. Your screen should look similar to the following illustration.

5 Click in the To box and address the message to yourself.

6 Click in the message box, and then type **I'm going to visit my mother-in-law!**

7 On the Standard toolbar, click the Send button.

The Vacation Request is sent.

You must install this form before you can approve the vacation request.

8 In the Folder List, click the Vacation Request folder.

9 On the Compose menu, click New Vacation Approved.

The form is installed, and a Vacation Approved form appears.

10 Close the Vacation Approved form.

Approve a Vacation Request

In this exercise, you view the received form in your Inbox, and then accept the request.

1 On the Outlook Bar, click the Inbox icon.

The contents of your Inbox appear in the Information viewer.

2 Double-click the Vacation Request message you sent to yourself.

The message opens. Your screen should look similar to the following illustration.

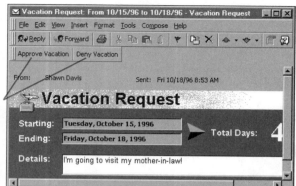

You use these buttons to grant or deny the request.

3 Click Approve Vacation.

A new "Approved: Vacation Request" form appears. Because you sent the original request to yourself, the message is addressed to you automatically.

4 In the message area, type **Have a good trip.**

5 On the Standard toolbar, click the Send button.

The "Approved: Vacation Request" form is sent. After a moment, it will appear in your Inbox.

6 Close the Vacation Request form.

Customizing an Existing Form

You can modify a built-in form by viewing it in design mode, and adding and removing controls, options, fields, and tabs. You can select fields to add to a form using the Field Chooser, which lists all the different fields available for a particular item type. For example, if you are modifying the Mail form, the Field Chooser lists those fields related to e-mail, such as To, From, Importance, and so on. You can also add your own fields to a form, if none in the Field Chooser meet your needs. For example, you can add a Project field to the message header in the Mail form to identify messages by project. You can also add your company name or a logo to a form to personalize it. After you have made your changes, you can save the form, and then *publish* it in a folder where it is ready to use. Depending on where you publish the form, it may be available for others to use or for your use alone. You will learn more about publishing forms later in this appendix.

In addition to your regular duties as Operations Coordinator, you perform other tasks related to the day-to-day operation of the corporate office. Recently, the Human Resources director asked you to help design a form to track employee donations to local charities. You decide to create a form that employees can use to send their donation requests to Human Resources as an e-mail message based on the Mail form.

Open a form in design mode

To be able to modify an existing form, you must first open the form you want to edit, and then switch to design mode so that the form design tools become available. In this exercise, you open the Mail form, and then view it in design mode.

1   Be sure that the contents of your Inbox appear in the Information viewer.

2   On the Standard toolbar, click the New Mail Message button.

A blank Mail form appears.

3   Maximize the form.

4   On the Tools menu, click Design Outlook Form.

*New Mail
Message*

The form appears in design mode. A grid to guide field placement appears on the gray areas of the Message tab, and the Field Chooser appears on the right side of the screen. Your screen should look similar to the following illustration.

You can currently enter the compose page of the form as it appears when you are addressing and composing a message.

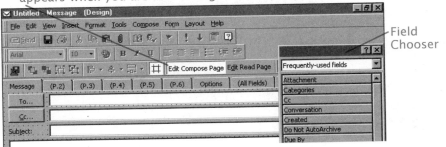

Field Chooser

Add a field to the message header

Some Margo Tea Company employees would like to keep their charitable donations anonymous, so you want to make sure that the donation request form you are creating has the appropriate security options. In this exercise, you add the Sensitivity field to the message header on the Mail form so that users can view or change the message sensitivity as they compose a donation request.

1   On the Field Chooser, scroll down, and then click the Sensitivity field.

The field is highlighted.

2 Drag the Sensitivity field onto the Message tab, place it below the Subject field in the message header, and then release the mouse button.

The header area expands to create room for the new field, and the Sensitivity field appears on the form, surrounded by selection handles. Your screen should look similar to the following illustration.

The Sensitivity field contains a drop-down list box where users can select a degree of sensitivity.

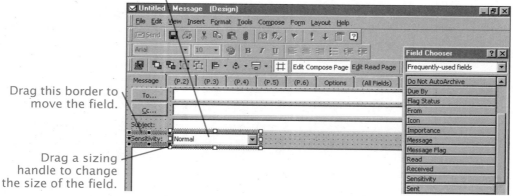

Drag this border to move the field.

Drag a sizing handle to change the size of the field.

Add a tab to a form

In design mode, several blank tabs appear along with the default tabs for a form. You can select and modify a blank tab to ensure that it will appear as part of the modified form. In this exercise, you select and rename a new tab to add to your customized form.

1 Click the (P.2) tab.

A blank tab appears. A grid appears on the tab to guide you in aligning new fields.

2 On the Form menu, click Display This Page.

The parentheses around the tab name disappear. This tab will appear when you use your modified form.

3 On the Form menu, click Rename Page.

The Rename Page dialog box appears.

4 In the Page Name box, type **Donation Details**, and then click OK.

The tab is renamed.

Label a field

When you add fields to a form, you should also label the fields, so users know what type of information to enter in a particular box—for example, on the Mail form, users know to type the subject of a message in the box labeled "Subject." In this exercise, you add a field label to the Donation Details tab. You will also add a drop-down list field next to the label in a later exercise.

Control Toolbox

You might need to move the Field Chooser down to see this button.

1 On the Standard toolbar, click the Control Toolbox button.

The Toolbox dialog box appears.

Label

2 Click the Label button.

The pointer changes to a crosshair with a Label icon.

3 Position the pointer in the upper-left corner of the Donation Details page, and then click.

A label is added to the form. The text "Label1" appears in the selected label by default.

4 Click inside the selected label area.

The selection border changes from gray dots to black diagonal lines. The label is now in text-edit mode.

5 Select the text "Label1," and then type **Charity**

The text is replaced as you type.

6 Click on a blank area of the form to cancel the selection.

Format a label

You might need to drag the Toolbox dialog box down to see the Properties button.

In this exercise, you format the text in the Charity label, and then resize the label area.

1 Click the Charity label to select it.

Sizing handles appear around the form.

2 On the toolbar, click the Properties button.

The Properties dialog box appears. The Display tab should be active.

Properties

You can align fields precisely
with these coordinates.

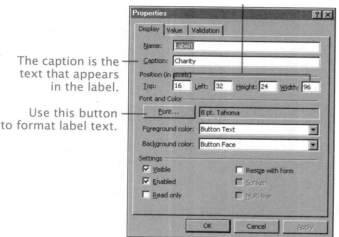

The caption is the
text that appears
in the label.

Use this button
to format label text.

3 Click Font.

The Font dialog box appears.

4 In the Font Style list, click Bold.

5 In the Size list, click 14.

6 Click the Color down arrow, select Navy, and then click OK.

The new label style appears in the Font field in the Properties dialog box.

7 Click OK to close the Properties dialog box.

The changes are applied to the label. Your screen should look similar to
the following illustration.

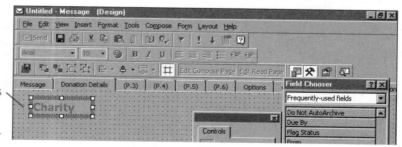

Use the sizing handles
to resize the label
border to fit the word
"Charity," if necessary.

Add a drop-down list to a form

In this exercise, you continue the customization of the form by adding a drop-down list field to the Donation Details tab.

ComboBox

1   In the Toolbox, click the ComboBox button.

The pointer changes to a crosshair with a ComboBox icon.

2   Position the pointer next to the Charity label, and then click.

A drop-down list box appears. Your screen should look similar to the following illustration.

The field is selected.

You can also drag the crosshair pointer to size a field as you add it to the form.

3   Drag the center sizing handle on the right border of the drop-down list box to the right until the drop-down list box is approximately twice its original width.

Set field values for a drop-down list

Typically, a drop-down list contains several items the user can choose from. In this exercise, you add several items, or values, to the drop-down list field properties.

1   Be sure that the drop-down list field is selected.

2   On the toolbar, click the Properties button.

The Properties dialog box appears.

Properties

3   Click the Value tab, and then click New.

You must name the new drop-down list field before you can change its properties. The New Field dialog box appears.

4   In the Name box, type **Charity List**

5   Verify that Text appears in the Type box and in the Format box, and then click OK.

The Value tab options become available.

6 Click in the Possible Values box, type **County Animal Shelter**, followed by a comma (,), and then press the SPACEBAR.

You must separate items in the list of possible values with commas.

7 Repeat step 6 to add the following values: **City School District, Community Food Bank, Senior Activity Center**

Be sure to type the commas and spaces as they appear above.

8 Click OK.

The values for the list are set.

9 Click the Close button on the Toolbox dialog box to close it.

Create a new field with the Field Chooser

You also want to add a field for the donation amount to the form, but none of the available fields meet your needs. In this exercise, you use the Field Chooser to create your own custom field.

1 At the bottom of the Field Chooser, click New.

The New Field dialog box appears.

2 In the Name box, type **Amount**

3 Click the Type down arrow, and then select Currency.

The text in the Format box changes to a monetary format, using a dollar sign and two decimal places.

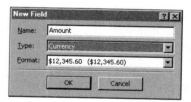

4 Click OK.

The list of User-Defined Fields In Inbox appear in the Field Chooser. The Charity List drop-down list field and the Donation field you just created appear in the Field Chooser.

You can drag the Amount field again to align it with the Charity field.

5 Drag the Donation field below the Charity field, and then release the mouse button.

6 Click anywhere to cancel the selection.

7 Close the Field Chooser.

Your screen should look similar to the following illustration.

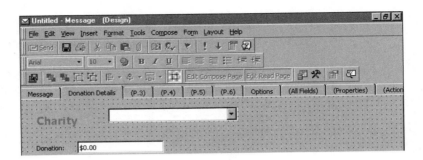

Protect the form

Now that you have designed your form, you want to protect it so that users cannot make changes without your permission.

1 Click the (Properties) tab.

The Properties tab becomes active.

2 On the right side of the tab, select the Protect Form Design check box.

The Password dialog box appears.

3 In the Password box, type **password**

This will be the password for the form. Only users who know the password will be able to modify the form once you have made it available.

4 Press TAB, and then type **password** in the Confirm box.

You must confirm the password you are setting.

5 Click OK.

The form is protected.

 NOTE To protect the information a user enters in a form field from tampering, you can edit the read version of the form. In design mode, select the field you want to protect and click the Edit Read Page button. Click the Properties button, and then click the Display tab. Select the Read Only check box and then click OK. If the Edit Page buttons are not available for the page you want to protect, on the Form menu, click Separate Read Layout.

Save the form

Save

➤ On the Standard toolbar, click the Save button.

The changes are saved; the new form is saved in your Inbox folder.

TIP If you want to see how your form will appear to users and test its function, you can switch quickly from design mode back to the standard run-time mode. To do this, on the Tools menu, click Design Outlook Form. The Design Outlook Form command acts as a toggle switch; you can use the same command to switch back and forth between the two modes.

Publishing a Form

Once a form has been created, it can be published to a special folder, or *library*, so it is accessible when you need it. When you publish a form, its characteristics are translated into programming code. The physical image of the form you've created is converted into a format that can be read by Outlook. You must publish a form before you, or anyone else, can use it.

You must have specific access permissions to publish a form to the organization forms library.

There are three types of libraries available in Outlook. An *organization forms* library is stored on the server; anyone with access to the server can use its forms. A *personal forms* library is stored where you send and receive your own mail; only you can use the forms there. A *folder forms* library is associated with a particular folder, either private or public; anyone with permission to use that folder can use its forms. If you are not sure if your network includes public folders, ask your system administrator.

Publish a form

In this exercise, you publish the Charity Donation form in your personal forms library because you want to test the form before making it available to other users.

Publish Form As

You can also click Publish Form As on the File menu.

1 On the Standard toolbar, click the Publish Form As button.

The Publish Form As dialog box appears.

2 In the Form Name box, type **Charity Donation**

3 Be sure that Personal Forms appears next to the Publish In button, and then click Publish.

After a moment, the form is published.

4 Click the Close button on the form.

If you are prompted to save changes, click Yes.

Test the form

In this exercise, you use the Charity Donation form you created to make a donation to a local charity, and then send the form to yourself to make sure that everything is working correctly.

1 On the Compose menu, click Choose Form.

The New Form dialog box appears.

2 Be sure that Personal Forms is selected, select the Charity Donation form, and then click OK.

A message appears, informing you that the form is being installed on your computer for the first time. After a moment, a blank Charity Donation form opens. Your screen should look similar to the following illustration.

You added this Donation Details tab.

You added this sensitivity field.

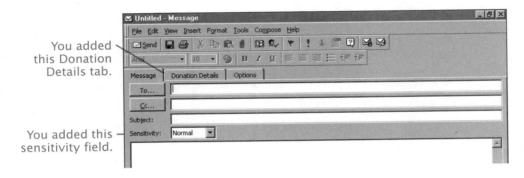

3 Address the form to yourself.

4 In the Subject box, type **Form Test**

5 Click the Sensitivity down arrow, and then select Private.

6 Click the Donation Details tab.

7 Click the Charity down arrow, select Senior Activity Center, and then press TAB.

The insertion point moves automatically to the Amount box, and the current text is selected.

8 Type **100**, and then press ENTER.

$100.00 appears in the Amount box.

9 On the Standard toolbar, click the Send button.

The form is sent. After a moment, it appears in your Inbox.

View the sent form

In this exercise, you open the test form you sent to yourself to make sure everything worked correctly.

1 In the Information viewer, double-click the Form Test message.

The message opens.

2 Click the Donation Details tab.

The information you entered appears.

3 Close the message.

Removing a Form

If you no longer want a form to be available to users, you can delete it, as long as you are the creator, or owner, of the form. You can only delete a form if you have ownership privileges for that form. As the creator of a form, you automatically have ownership privileges; you can also grant other people "Owner" permission if you want them to be able to modify or delete the form for you.

Remove a form

In this exercise, you remove the Charity Donation form from your personal forms library.

1   On the Tools menu, click Options, and then click the Manage Forms tab.

2   Click Manage Forms.

If Personal Forms is not selected, click Set, and then select Personal Forms from the Forms Library drop-down list.

The Forms Manager dialog box appears. The Personal Forms library should be listed in the Set box on the right.

3   Be sure that Charity Donation is selected in the list of forms, and then click Delete.

A message appears, asking you to confirm the deletion.

4   Click Yes, click Close, and then click OK to close the Options dialog box.

The form is removed from your personal folder forms library.

5   Delete all practice forms in your Inbox.

IMPORTANT—READ CAREFULLY BEFORE OPENING SOFTWARE PACKET(S). By opening the sealed packet(s) containing the software, you indicate your acceptance of the following Microsoft License Agreement.

MICROSOFT LICENSE AGREEMENT

(Book Companion Disks)

This is a legal agreement between you (either an individual or an entity) and Microsoft Corporation. By opening the sealed software packet(s) you are agreeing to be bound by the terms of this agreement. If you do not agree to the terms of this agreement, promptly return the un-opened software packet(s) and any accompanying written materials to the place you obtained them for a full refund.

MICROSOFT SOFTWARE LICENSE

1. GRANT OF LICENSE. Microsoft grants to you the right to use one copy of the Microsoft software program included with this book (the "SOFTWARE") on a single terminal connected to a single computer. The SOFTWARE is in "use" on a computer when it is loaded into the temporary memory (i.e., RAM) or installed into the permanent memory (e.g., hard disk, CD-ROM, or other storage device) of that computer. You may not network the SOFTWARE or otherwise use it on more than one computer or computer terminal at the same time.

2. COPYRIGHT. The SOFTWARE is owned by Microsoft or its suppliers and is protected by United States copyright laws and international treaty provisions. Therefore, you must treat the SOFTWARE like any other copyrighted material (e.g., a book or musical recording) except that you may either (a) make one copy of the SOFTWARE solely for backup or archival purposes, or (b) transfer the SOFTWARE to a single hard disk provided you keep the original solely for backup or archival purposes. You may not copy the written materials accompanying the SOFTWARE.

3. OTHER RESTRICTIONS. You may not rent or lease the SOFTWARE, but you may transfer the SOFTWARE and accompanying written materials on a permanent basis provided you retain no copies and the recipient agrees to the terms of this Agreement. You may not reverse engineer, decompile, or disassemble the SOFTWARE. If the SOFTWARE is an update or has been updated, any transfer must include the most recent update and all prior versions.

4. DUAL MEDIA SOFTWARE. If the SOFTWARE package contains both 3.5" and 5.25" disks, then you may use only the disks appropriate for your single-user computer. You may not use the other disks on another computer or loan, rent, lease, or transfer them to another user except as part of the permanent transfer (as provided above) of all SOFTWARE and written materials.

5. SAMPLE CODE. If the SOFTWARE includes Sample Code, then Microsoft grants you a royalty-free right to reproduce and distribute the sample code of the SOFTWARE provided that you: (a) distribute the sample code only in conjunction with and as a part of your software product; (b) do not use Microsoft's or its authors' names, logos, or trademarks to market your software product; (c) include the copyright notice that appears on the SOFTWARE on your product label and as a part of the sign-on message for your software product; and (d) agree to indemnify, hold harmless, and defend Microsoft and its authors from and against any claims or lawsuits, including attorneys' fees, that arise or result from the use or distribution of your software product.

DISCLAIMER OF WARRANTY

The SOFTWARE (including instructions for its use) is provided "AS IS" WITHOUT WARRANTY OF ANY KIND. MICROSOFT FURTHER DISCLAIMS ALL IMPLIED WARRANTIES INCLUDING WITHOUT LIMITATION ANY IMPLIED WARRANTIES OF MERCHANTABILITY OR OF FITNESS FOR A PARTICULAR PURPOSE. THE ENTIRE RISK ARISING OUT OF THE USE OR PERFORMANCE OF THE SOFTWARE AND DOCUMENTATION REMAINS WITH YOU.

IN NO EVENT SHALL MICROSOFT, ITS AUTHORS, OR ANYONE ELSE INVOLVED IN THE CREATION, PRODUCTION, OR DELIVERY OF THE SOFTWARE BE LIABLE FOR ANY DAMAGES WHATSOEVER (INCLUDING, WITHOUT LIMITATION, DAMAGES FOR LOSS OF BUSINESS PROFITS, BUSINESS INTERRUPTION, LOSS OF BUSINESS INFORMATION, OR OTHER PECUNIARY LOSS) ARISING OUT OF THE USE OF OR INABILITY TO USE THE SOFTWARE OR DOCUMENTATION, EVEN IF MICROSOFT HAS BEEN ADVISED OF THE POSSIBILITY OF SUCH DAMAGES. BECAUSE SOME STATES/COUNTRIES DO NOT ALLOW THE EXCLUSION OR LIMITATION OF LIABILITY FOR CONSEQUENTIAL OR INCIDENTAL DAMAGES, THE ABOVE LIMITATION MAY NOT APPLY TO YOU.

U.S. GOVERNMENT RESTRICTED RIGHTS

The SOFTWARE and documentation are provided with RESTRICTED RIGHTS. Use, duplication, or disclosure by the Government is subject to restrictions as set forth in subparagraph (c)(1)(ii) of The Rights in Technical Data and Computer Software clause at DFARS 252.227-7013 or subparagraphs (c)(1) and (2) of the Commercial Computer Software — Restricted Rights 48 CFR 52.227-19, as applicable. Manufacturer is Microsoft Corporation, One Microsoft Way, Redmond, WA 98052-6399.

If you acquired this product in the United States, this Agreement is governed by the laws of the State of Washington. Should you have any questions concerning this Agreement, or if you desire to contact Microsoft Press for any reason, please write: Microsoft Press, One Microsoft Way, Redmond, WA 98052-6399.

The
Step by Step
Practice Files Disk

The enclosed 3.5-inch disks contain timesaving, ready-to-use practice files that complement the lessons in this book. To use the practice files, you'll need Outlook 97 and either the Windows 95 operating system or version 3.51 Service Pack 5 or later of the Windows NT operating system.

The *Step by Step* lessons use practice files from the disk. Before you begin the *Step by Step* lessons, read the "Installing and Using the Practice Files" section of the book. There you'll find a description of each practice file and easy instructions telling how to install the files on your computer's hard disk.

Please take a few moments to read the license agreement on the previous page before using the enclosed disks.

Register your Microsoft Press® book today, and let us know what you think.

At Microsoft Press, we listen to our customers. We update our books as new releases of software are issued, and we'd like you to tell us the kinds of additional information you'd find most useful in these updates. Your feedback will be considered when we prepare a future edition; plus, when you become a registered owner, you will get Microsoft Press catalogs and exclusive offers on specially priced books.
Thanks!

I used this book as
- ● A way to learn the software
- ● A reference when I needed it
- ● A way to find out about advanced features
- ● Other_____

I consider myself
- ● A beginner or an occassional computer user
- ● An intermediate-level user with a pretty good grasp of the basics
- ● An advanced user who helps and provides solutions for others
- ● Other_____

I purchased this book from
- ● A bookstore
- ● A software store
- ● A direct mail offer
- ● Other_____

I will buy the next edition of the book when it's updated
- ● Definitely
- ● Probably
- ● I will not buy the next edition

The next edition of this book should include the following additional information:
1•_____
2•_____
3•_____
The most useful things about this book are_____
_____

This book would be more helpful if_____
_____

My general impressions of this book are_____
_____

May we contact you regarding your comments? ● Yes ● No
Would you like to receive Microsoft Press catalog regularly? ● Yes ● No

Name_____
Company (if applicable)_____
Address_____
City_____State_____Zip_____
Daytime phone number (optional) (_____)_____

Please mail back your feedback form___ postage free! Fold this form as described on the other side of this card, or fax this sheet to:
Microsoft Press, Attn: Marketing Department, fax 206-936-7329

NO POSTAGE
NECESSARY
IF MAILED
IN THE
UNITED STATES

BUSINESS REPLY MAIL
FIRST-CLASS MAIL   PERMIT NO. 53   BOTHELL, WA

POSTAGE WILL BE PAID BY ADDRESSEE

MICROSOFT PRESS
MICROSOFT® OUTLOOK™ 97 STEP BY STEP
PO BOX 3019
BOTHELL   WA   98041-9946

FOLD HERE